Bits and Atoms

OXFORD STUDIES IN DIGITAL POLITICS

Series Editor: Andrew Chadwick, Royal Holloway, University of London

Bits and Atoms

INFORMATION AND COMMUNICATION TECHNOLOGY
IN AREAS OF LIMITED STATEHOOD

EDITED BY STEVEN LIVINGSTON

and

GREGOR WALTER-DROP

OXFORD
UNIVERSITY PRESS

Oxford University Press is a department of the University of Oxford.
It furthers the University's objective of excellence in research, scholarship,
and education by publishing worldwide.

Oxford   New York
Auckland   Cape Town   Dar es Salaam   Hong Kong   Karachi
Kuala Lumpur   Madrid   Melbourne   Mexico City   Nairobi
New Delhi   Shanghai   Taipei   Toronto

With offices in
Argentina   Austria   Brazil   Chile   Czech Republic   France   Greece
Guatemala   Hungary   Italy   Japan   Poland   Portugal   Singapore
South Korea   Switzerland   Thailand   Turkey   Ukraine   Vietnam

Oxford is a registered trademark of Oxford University Press
in the UK and certain other countries.

Published in the United States of America by
Oxford University Press
198 Madison Avenue, New York, NY 10016

Cataloging-in-Publication Data on file with the Library of Congress.

ISBN 978-0-19-994161-2 (pbk.)
ISBN 978-0-19-994159-9 (hbk.)

9 8 7 6 5 4 3 2 1
Printed in the United States of America
on acid-free paper

Contents

Foreword

Statistics about the wild, tempestuous on-rush of new information and communication technologies (ICTs) can provoke eye-rolling these days, but clearly something epochal is going on. For instance, the World Bank's report on Information and Comunications for Development 2012, *Maximizing Mobile*, contains within it a poster showcasing the following nuggets:

- there are over 6 billion mobile phone subscriptions worldwide;
- 75% of the world now has access to a mobile phone;
- the developing world is now more mobile than the developed world, that is most phones are owned by people living in low-income regions of the world; and
- the mobile revolution is only at the start of its growth curve.

The report declares that the "pace at which mobile phones spread globally is unmatched in the history of technology" (The World Bank 2012, 8–9). And if this is only the beginning one can only wonder where all this is going to lead.

The singular contribution of this book is that it asks and seeks to answer a question that has not been properly posed: What does the rapid spread of new information and communication technologies mean in areas of "limited statehood"? The "limited" bit in that formulation contains an important insight. The editors of the volume rightly point out that we are all used to thinking about modern states in terms of the extremes of the spectrum: fully consolidated states like Denmark or failed states like Somalia, but, as they make clear, most states are in between. Most states are neither fully consolidated nor in a state of collapse. As the editors eloquently put, it these are states with "significant deficiencies in rule implementation and the monopoly of force."

The discussion of "areas of limited statehood" as a conceptual category is one of the most fascinating aspects of the book. It reminds me of a moment of illumination I had once in graduate school while preparing for a seminar on Thomas Hobbes's *Leviathan*. After studying the primary text for a while, I was going through a range of secondary literature on the text, and I remember coming across this insight. The idea is that people think about the Hobbesian state of nature as something that, if you live in a modern, fully consolidated state, is ancient history. Yet even in these states, if you are in an environment where you are attacked by a criminal and it takes the police a while to get the message and get to you, then you are in a Hobbesian state of nature. It can be a park, a rural redoubt, an inner city zone with more gangs than cops... the point is that there are Hobbesian pockets even in consolidated modern states. Think, then, about these states that the editors describe as areas of limited statehood. They do not simply have Hobbesian pockets; they have Hobbes regnant. The state is present and strong only in specific places, like the capital, provincial headquarters and so on. In the rest of the territory, well, it is every woman for herself.

What the editors and contributors have done is to examine the impact of ICTs in areas of limited statehood by focusing on three roles. First, are ICTs furthering state consolidation? Second, in the absence of the state, are ICTs contributing to self-governance by citizens? Third, are ICTs helping citizens to hold the state accountable? The book is a careful and thoughtful examination of the evidence via a series of compelling case studies. The freshness of the work and, therefore, the contribution it makes to knowledge derive from the discrimination and care of the contributors. There is much here that will surprise you, particularly on the role of ICTs in state consolidation.

In a sense, what the editors and contributors have done is update a story as old as the building of kingdoms, empires, and states. If, like me, you believe that anything that amplifies the human voice is an ICT, then a variety of ICTs have had an impact on the relationship between human beings and those who have sought to rule them since the dawn of these efforts. For instance, my own father is an African village chief, and the village/town crier still uses a gong to summon the village to a meeting in the village square, even as more and more of these villagers carry mobile phones. In between, other ICTs have played a role: signaling systems in war and peace, drums, papyrus, parchments, the printing press, periodicals, the telegraph, radio, television, and on to our own era of the Internet, satellite, and all the other amazing technologies discussed in the book. Throughout it all, ambitious rulers as well as determined subjects or citizens have deployed these technologies in ways that affect state consolidation, self-governance and accountability.

Finally, if the experts are right, and we are only at the beginning of what Michael Saylor (2012) calls *the mobile wave*, then the contributors to this important volume will have to provide us with another enthralling update in the not-too-distant future.

Sina Odugbemi, PhD
Editor: *People, Spaces, Deliberation*
(blogs.worldbank.org/publicsphere)
Operational Communication Department
External Affairs Vice Presidency
The World Bank
Washington, DC

Contributors

Gregory Asmolov is completing his PhD at the London School of Economics and is a contributor to "Runet Echo," a project of "Global Voices Online."

Philip N. Howard is a professor in the Department of Communication at the University of Washington and, as of this writing, a fellow at Princeton University's Center for Information Technology Policy.

Muzammil M. Hussain is assistant professor of communication at the University of Michigan.

Primož Kovačič is co-founder and the director of operations for Spatial Collective, a technology and development social enterprise company based in Nairobi, Kenya, and a graduate student at The George Washington University.

Steven Livingston is Professor of Media and Public Affairs and International Affairs at the Elliott School of International Affairs, The George Washington University.

Jamie Lundine is the co-founder of Spatial Collective.

Patrick Meier is director of Social Innovation at the Qatar Foundation's Computing Research Institute. He previously co-directed Harvard's Program on Crisis Mapping and Early Warning and served as Director of Crisis Mapping at Ushahidi.

Joseph Siegle is Director of Research at Africa Center for Strategic Studies, National Defense University. He has also held a number of positions with international development organizations around the world.

J. P. Singh is Professor of Global Affairs and Cultural Studies at George Mason University.

Sharath Srinivasan is the David and Elaine Potter Lecturer in Governance and Human Rights and inaugural Director of the Centre of Governance and Human Rights.

Peter van der Windt is completing his PhD at Columbia University where he is a Graduate Fellow at the Center for the Study of Development Strategies.

Gregor Walter-Drop is the managing director of SFB-700, Governance in Areas of Limited Statehood at the Free University of Berlin.

For our children and grandchildren

1

Introduction

STEVEN LIVINGSTON AND GREGOR WALTER-DROP

When considering the effects of information and communication technology (ICT) on politics, scholars tend to focus on parts of the world with relatively consolidated state institutions. As a result, research questions tend to cluster around issues associated with these institutions. For example, scholars have asked important questions about the changing nature of citizenship in a modern nation-state, the possibilities for more robust deliberative democracy, the changing nature of production and economic relations, Internet effects on electoral behavior and outcomes, and of course the role of technology in social change. As important and interesting as these questions are, they overlook the fact that the ICT revolution has reached nearly all parts of the world, including the non-OECD (Organisation for Economic Co-operation and Development) world where state institutions are usually not fully consolidated. In contrast, this book takes up different questions, all centering on the effects of ICT on areas where the state is weak or altogether missing.[1]

We use the term *areas of limited statehood* to describe geographical entities, policy fields, and social groups for which states either cannot maintain a monopoly of force or experience significant problems with regard to rule-making, implementation, and enforcement. In most cases, such limited statehood indicates governance deficits, that is, the undersupply of collective goods such as security, education, public health, and so on. This book therefore considers to what extent, if any, ICT-enabled collective action fills governance voids found in areas of limited statehood. Put differently, can communities use ICT to meet challenges such as indiscriminant violence, disease, drought, famine, crime, and other problems arising from deficient and nonresponsive state institutions?

Theoretically, we are interested in sparking a conversation about the effects of ICT on areas of limited statehood and in exploring why the effects might be greater in some instances than in others. Such a conversation, we believe, would add an important new dimension both to the international relations literature on governance as well as to the new political communication literature on ICT and collective action. In terms of international relations literature, little systematic attention has been given to the effects of ICT on the nature of governance. Various kinds of international organizations, traditional nongovernmental organizations (NGOs), and public–private partnerships have been considered, but not ICT-enabled collaboration as an alternative governance modality.[2]

With regard to new political communication literature on ICT and collective action, the book extends the discussion of digital media and collective action (Bimber, Flanagin, and Stohl 2005). Much of that discussion focuses predominantly on politics and society in the advanced industrialized and post-industrial societies in the Global North. These places share what might be called a *Schattschneiderian* understanding of the significance of new technology on the formation and nature of "pressure groups." E. E. Schattschneider concluded in his 1960 critique of the group basis of politics in the United States that the flaw in the pluralist heaven is that "the heavenly chorus sings with a strong upper-class accent" (Schattschneider 1960, 35). In other words, the "range of organized, identifiable, known groups is amazingly narrow," in large measure owing the costs associated with creating and sustaining an organization, which in turn carries hefty communication and information costs, as Mancur Olson would argue five years later with the publication of *The Logic of Collective Action*. More recently, scholars have postulated that the decline of information costs accompanying the "rise of network society" has led to a concomitant decline in collaboration costs, resulting in the further diminishment of any absolute need for formal organizations, which were once needed to meet the resource demands of collective action (Bimber, Flanagin, and Stohl 2005, 374; Castells 2000a). We analyze the same potential in this book, though applying it to a broader range of collective goods in areas of limited statehood. Rather than address an important though limited discussion of ICT-borne opportunities for broader interest group formation in the pursuit of representation in state and corporate institutions, we address questions about ICT-enabled collective action for the pursuit of the sort of basic collective goods most often provided by consolidated states. Can ICT help fill the gap between pressing human needs and weak states' inability to meet them?

Our contributors, writing about different regions and circumstances, generally offer a qualified "yes." Often, ICT has such a capacity. Yet, one of the major limitations faced in ICT-enabled collaboration, as an alternative governance modality, is found in the nature of the collective good itself. Some goods are more amenable to ICT-enabled governance than are others. On the one hand, strengthening the provision of some collective goods is largely rooted in the provision of faster, often crowdsourced, and interactive information. This is alluded to in our reference to "bits" in the book's title. On the other hand, other types of collective goods are located in material or physical resources. Roads, water wells, sewers, schools, and security forces must be appropriately positioned in proximity to the population in need of them. We allude to this sort of collective good in our reference to "atoms" in the book's title. The array of collective goods provided for by ICT-enable governance therefore ranges from "bits" to "atoms."

In a nutshell, the effects of ICT are uneven because bits do not easily translate into atoms. ICT is best suited to the provision of collective goods that are strongly affected by information. That said, the real-time ability to gather information from ubiquitous or nearly ubiquitous sensors (such as mobile phones) affects the human capacity to generate awareness of need and to manage the distribution of material resources in response. In that sense, bits and atoms are not distinct categories of collective goods as much as they are different phases of their provision.

In the remainder of this introduction we outline the conceptual framework used to bring order and insight into the rich examples offered by our contributors. We then turn to a brief illustration of the spread of ICT in areas of limited statehood. Subsequently, we sketch the theoretical debate on the relationship between ICT and the state and then provide an overview of the chapters that explore the effects of ICT on the state. In a similar fashion, we then review the debate on collective action and ICT and link this to the chapters that highlight the role of ICT for governance. We conclude the introduction with some overarching questions that can guide the reader through the book.

The Conceptual Framework: Governance and (Limited) Statehood

Our conceptual framework rests on a distinction between governance and statehood.[3] Whereas states are usually considered synonymous with governance, *governance is not necessarily synonymous with states*. Alternative governance modalities are not only possible; they are, historically, also more common than other modalities. *Governance* is thus often confounded with *government*, which is also sometimes conflated with *statehood*. It is important to the arguments presented in this book to draw clear distinctions among these concepts.

For *governance* we follow the definition by Risse (2011, 9) as "institutionalized modes of social coordination to produce and implement collectively binding rules or to provide collective goods." For the purposes of this volume, it is important to highlight that governance always requires some form of coordination, collaboration, or collective action for which communication plays a central role. But governance is about creating and sustaining collective goods, usually according to a set of rules and norms. Collective goods include security, economic welfare, education, public health, sustainable infrastructure, and a clean and safe environment. Note that this conceptualization is independent of questions concerning who or what provides these goods. They may be thought of as *governance* services, rather than *government* services. For example, state police and state armies can provide security, as can the United Nations, regional security coalitions, or militias and community policing initiatives. Similarly, either the state or NGOs can finance and provide education. Thus, from this perspective, governance by the *state* is only one modality of governance, a modality that is common in the West but less so in other parts of the world.

In the Western experience, the state forms the core of modern governance activities. Government and governance are thought to be synonymous, despite the fact that, within the West, the role of the state is highly contested, as are assumptions about the extent to which certain collective goods are most properly provided for by the state rather than by private markets. These debates notwithstanding, there is little disagreement about the state's role in the provision of certain core collective goods, such as security. And in addition, there is even less disagreement that the state is to be the institutional forum in which decisions about which collective goods are to be supplied by whom are to be made. But even this view of a tightly conscribed state is linked to certain assumptions about the nature statehood. Most important among these assumptions is authoritative rule in the sense of Krasner's (1999) "domestic sovereignty"—that is, the state's presumptive and fundamental ability to implement and enforce political decisions, including—at its very core—the monopoly of force.

Often overlooked by mainstream governance research is the fact that these are rather bold assumptions. Implementation problems, for example, might be considered a universal challenge; but even consolidated state institutions proper are the exception rather than the rule. What is more, some observers, such as Manuel Castells, argue that consolidated states in the West are themselves straining under the weight of wealth and income inequality, unmet public service needs, and the fraying legitimacy of core institutions (Castells 2012). At the very least, there are clear territorial pockets even within fully consolidated Western states where the state's monopoly of force is contested (such as inner-city slums where police do not go). In most developing or transitional countries, however, such phenomena are much more prominent. State or government control over the use of force is, at best, tenuous and incomplete, and problems of implementation and enforcement are ubiquitous.

Thus, *statehood* is best conceived of as a continuous variable, ranging from fully consolidated states, such as those in Scandinavia, to states that exhibit significant problems, such as Russia or India, to what are usually referred to as *failed* or *fragile* states (Acemoglu and Robinson 2012; Brock et al. 2012). An uncontested example of the latter is the Democratic Republic of the Congo, where central institutions are unable to exercise a monopoly on the use of force, let alone implement political decisions. Yet on a global scale, the outer ranges of the continuum (fully consolidated statehood at one end and failed states at the other) are the exceptions, rather than the rule. About three quarters of the global population live in countries or regions that exhibit varying degrees of *limited statehood*," that is, significant deficiencies in rule implementation and the monopoly of force.

Using the descriptor *areas of limited statehood* rather than *failed states* also allows for territorial variations of statehood *within* the respective country. Typically, states fare better in maintaining the monopoly of force and rule implementation in core urban areas than they do in the peripheries. When one ventures to the edges of Kinshasa or Kabul, one has reached the outer limits of the state's governance reach. Beyond the city borders lies a vast stretch of territory where the state is weak or altogether absent. In fact, in some places one does not have to venture from the center to find little to no evidence of the state. Urban slums such as Kibera and Mathare in Nairobi offer examples of areas of limited statehood at the heart of the territorial state. *Areas of limited statehood* thus exist *wherever* the state's ability to implement and enforce the monopoly of force and political decisions is deficient.

The purpose of this book is to explore the role of ICT in such areas of limited statehood. On the one hand, the contributions in the first part focus on the effects of ICT on the institutions and capabilities of the limited state structures themselves. The second part, on the other hand, explores ICT's effects on governance—under the conditions of limited statehood. The central point here is that limited and even failing *statehood* does not *necessarily* translate into the absence of *governance*. Governance may instead take different forms, involve different actors, and follow different procedures than the Western, state-focused model implies. Today, technologically enabled collective action for the purposes of governance may play an important role in such forms of governance. The guiding hypothesis for the contributions in the book's second part is that in the absence of strong state institutions, the availability of ICT makes a significant difference for the possibilities and forms of nonstate collective action, which in turn, is a prerequisite for governance.

ICT in Areas of Limited Statehood

Situating our analysis in areas of limited statehood also allows us to expand the consideration of "new media" beyond the more common discussion of the Internet, to date concentrated in the Global North, to digital technologies and applications that are most relevant to less developed regions. This includes mobile telephony (and mobile-based Internet access), remote sensing satellites, and geographical information systems (GIS).

Chief among them is *mobile telephony*. In 2000, almost three-quarters of global mobile phone subscriptions were found in the developed world. A decade later the proportions were reversed, reflecting much more the actual distribution of the world population. By mid-2010, there were over five billion mobile phone subscribers around the globe. Just one year later, the global total reached 5.6 billion subscriptions (Gartner 2011). In India, cell phone ownership has become nearly ubiquitous. By 2014, cell phone penetration is expected to reach 97 percent of the country's population of 1.26 billion persons (Rebello 2010).

In Africa, the number of mobile phone subscribers has increased tenfold in the last decade and has reached well over a third of the entire population. India,

Africa, and other regions of the less-developed world consistently exhibit the highest growth rates (Livingston 2011). The growth rate of mobile phone subscriptions, for example, is now among the highest in the world. Africa has seen a 20 percent rate of growth each year for the past five years, soaring from 2 percent of the population in 2000 to 28 percent by the end of 2009.[4] By the year 2015, sub-Saharan Africa will have more people with mobile network access—some 138 million people by 2015 (Rao 2011, 11)—than with access to electricity at home. By 2020 there will be at least one SIM card for every person on the continent (Salz 2011). MTN, a leading provider of mobile telephony service, offers an example of this phenomenal growth. In 2010, it announced a 22 percent increase (116 million in 2009 to 141.6 million in 2010) in its subscriber base. In South Africa, Ghana, Gabon, and Kenya, there are already nearly as many SIM cards as there are people.

Although growth rates are slower, *Internet access* is also available to increasing proportions of the population. About 80 percent of global data transmission uses undersea cables. As of mid-2009, 40 percent of continental Africa was without a direct high-bandwidth cable connection. Satellite uplinks were used instead but at rates that were twenty times more expensive than bandwidth prices in the United States. New sub-sea cable systems alter that pricing structure, opening up new opportunities for the growth of high-speed Internet and better cellular telephony. The digital divide between the Global North and Global South has begun to narrow, as is evident in the data provided by the International Telecommunication Union's International Development Indicators (ITU 2010).

Remote sensing satellites are also important to areas of limited statehood. Since 1999 a fleet of commercial high-resolution remote sensing satellites have come on line. Public availability of data from high-resolution remote sensing satellites has empowered nonstate actors with a technical capability that was once the exclusive preserve of a few powerful states. For example, the Satellite Sentinel Project (http://www.satsentinel.org/) uses high-resolution remote sensing images provided by DigitalGlobe, one of the premier remote-sensing firms, to monitor human rights violations in Sudan. From about 420 miles in space, each satellite captures images of objects on the ground as small as a typical microwave oven. Where roads systems are rudimentary and populations scattered, the ability to see phenomena on the ground from space enables new forms of governance. It allows for an entirely new image of the world to emerge and creates new technical possibilities when combined with other technologies.

Another new politically significant capacity is found in widely available *geographical information systems* (GIS). In the West, scholars, technologists, and social critics grapple with the significance of GIS in terms of privacy, social media, marketing, and navigation. In areas of limited statehood GIS is particularly interesting in the context of crisis- or event-mapping—the use of crowdsourcing to populate significant events on a digital map in the context of a natural disaster or political event. People who are caught up in crises use mobile phones and other communication devices to share awareness of local circumstances with a central aggregating platform, such as Ushahidi.com.

Ushahidi exemplifies that the technologies prevalent outside the Western world can best thought of as nested technologies that create a "system of systems" array of capacities. For example, GIS and GPS constitute the foundational capacity for the use of mobile telephony in crowdsourced event-mapping platforms such as Ushahidi. Put differently, mobile phones are used to populate open source digital maps with markers of significant events or phenomena, much in the same way Google Maps marks locations of interest to users.

The result of these technological developments is not found in any single technology or gadget. Instead, the major effect is found in the costs of information and the subsequent effects of lower information costs realized by advances in ICT on collaboration costs. The non-Western world is witnessing the diffusion of different information and communication technologies at a pace no less rapid than is found in the West.

At the heart of the argument made in this volume is that ICT lowers collaboration costs. Lower costs help realize new forms of collaboration by nonstate actors which, in turn, may strengthen nonstate actor efforts to bolster weak state capacity, or perhaps even fill some of the governance void created by failed states. A consolidated state, one that is supported by compulsory revenue generation and held to account by a free press and regular and fair elections, no doubt constitutes a preferred governance modality, at least to most observers. In the absence of this alternative, might ICT help fill the governance void?

The Contributions to This Volume

OPPOSITION, CONSOLIDATION, AND SIMULATION: ICT AND THE STATE

Scholars studying digital technology have tended to focus on some parts of the globe while neglecting the rest. There are two reasons for this. The first is rather obvious: North America and Europe are where key technologies were first located and where, even today, they are most heavily concentrated, at least in their more advanced forms. But this also implies that the kinds of questions asked and the assumptions behind them have tended to reflect the political and economic context of the technology, as much as they have mirrored the inherent qualities of the technologies themselves. But as outlined above, different patterns of technological diffusion have occurred (and are occurring) in Africa, Latin America, and parts of Asia. The political context in which this is happening is equally divergent from the Western experience.

One of the core differences emerging in this context is found in the role of the state. In the West, the state has been both an enabler of technological development and a conceptual anchor for social science theory building. With respect to the state as an enabler of technological development, one need only recall that the Internet's direct predecessor, the ARPANET, was the product of research commissioned and supported by the United States Defense Department. Bell Labs, Sarnoff Labs, IBM, and other technology innovators pursued projects that were directly connected to state objectives, especially concerning national defense. It was an era of big science funded by government research initiatives (Arthur 2009; Wagner 2008). The connection between the state and technological development is not nearly as strong in much of Africa today, especially after the liberalization of the telecommunications sector beginning in the last decade of the twentieth century (Harsch 2000; Petrazzini 1995).[5] The source of much of the innovation seen in Africa today comes from the private sector, sometimes in partnership with nonprofits such as iHub in Nairobi.

Of greater importance to our present argument is the second role of the state. The state serves as a *conceptual* cornerstone of social science theory building. Either implicitly or explicitly, it is at the center of paradigmatic statements concerning political communication. This is of course understandable, given the geographical focus of the research. The theory, like the technology, is rooted in the North American and European political experience. In this context, the state is fully consolidated; in other words, its monopoly of force is often uncontested, its abilities to implement, and enforce whatever regulation is passed is largely intact, and in addition, the state as such enjoys a sufficient degree of legitimacy. In sum, the Western state casts a long and dense "shadow of hierarchy" over society and is ready to step in whenever and wherever it deems necessary.[6] But this experience is hardly universal. As outlined above, *limited statehood* is in fact much more common than are consolidated states. To varying degrees, most of the states in the world experience problems with rule implementation and the monopoly of force. The chapters in the first part of the book explore what the rapid diffusion of the technologies means under these conditions of limited statehood. Three major phenomena will be considered in the book: ICT's oppositional role, its consolidation role, and its simulation role.

A common form of limited statehood is marked by a state's disproportional concentration of what limited capacity it has for coordination. In a sense, it is unbalanced, simultaneously too strong and too weak. Such states are preoccupied with maintaining the monopoly of force and a version of security provision, often including violent persecution of any internal opposition. Because of their ability to marshal force, these states are usually not considered weak, per se, despite their other deficiencies. Put another way, states of this sort are characterized by extractive political and economic institutions. They concentrate power and opportunity in the hands of a minority and use the monopoly of force to protect the elite (Acemoglu and Robinson 2012). Not surprisingly, such states often feature severe legitimacy problems fueling internal opposition and making the entire state significantly more brittle than it might appear from the outside. Examples of this constellation include most of the post-soviet countries and many Arab states. In fact, the Arab Spring highlights the weaknesses of some of the states that were hitherto widely considered mostly consolidated.

At the same time, the Arab Spring also provides a fascinating example of the role ICT can play under these circumstances. In Chapter 2, Philip Howard and Muzammil M. Hussain explore the extent to which ICT in the Arab Spring served as a *tool in the hands of the opposition*, which allowed the movement to spread, to organize, and to deliver their message abroad, while state institutions, ultimately, failed to suppress the use of technology. They find that mobile phone use in particular plays a decisive role in explaining the success of protest movements.

The more general question is under which conditions ICT favors the opposition more than it does the state. Although the political opposition can use ICT, it can also be an equally powerful *tool in the hands of state institutions*. In Chapter 3, Gregory Asmolov uses the example of Russia to exemplify how ICT can be used as a tool to simulate transparency and accountability and thus to construct symbolic (rather than functional) statehood. The same technology, however, also enables the opposition to expose the synthetic nature of these efforts.

The next two chapters, by J. P. Singh and Joseph Siegle, respectively, take different perspectives. In Chapter 4, Singh examines the role of ICT in improving the governance capabilities of limited states. Under the conditions of limited statehood, he asks whether ICT-based services can make a difference in service delivery by state institutions. The chapter explores the potential of ICT to improve state services and arrives at a different picture that shows both success and failure.

Chapter 5, by Joseph Siegle, takes it cues from the Western debate on ICT's influence on the changing landscape of civil society and the new, technology-based possibilities for communication between state and society, exploring the potential ICT has for improving accountability. Although the accountability of state structures if often deficient in areas of limited statehood, ICT can facilitate the development of civil society, which, *in turn*, can offset or balance some of typical deficits in state accountability. Two aspects of this are of particular importance: ICT's ability to greatly increase the accessibility of information and the facilitating of linkages between societal actors. A telling example is provided by crowdsourced corruption monitoring systems such as http://www.ipaidabribe.com in India or http://www.stopthebribes.net in Nigeria. The latter allows citizens to submit anonymous reports of petty bribe solicitation by police.

SUBSTITUTION: ICT AND GOVERNANCE

In areas of limited statehood, the state's governance capacity is deficient. Yet limited statehood does not necessary result in the absence of *governance*. In fact, even in macro-quantitative studies, the relationship between statehood and governance is remarkably inconclusive (Lee, Walter-Drop, and Wiesel 2013). Rather than being absent, governance can take on different forms, involving a different set of actors and different modalities from the standard Western state-based model of "governance by government." In our context, of particular interest are forms of self-governance where collective goods are produced by collective action. In other words, the governance constituency (the stakeholders) organizes to provide collective goods that the state is unable to deliver. They thus substitute for the deficiencies in state governance. The contributions in the second part of the book specifically explore the role of technologically enabled forms of collective action. Two aspects of this approach merit a closer inspection: (1) the focus on collective action in the absence of strong state institutions, and (2) the focus on the role of ICT.

(1) In different ways, various tributaries of collective action and social movement theory came together around a shared assumption concerning the centrality of the state. For the mainstream theories of contentious politics, nation-states serve as preconditions for social movement formation and collective action. A major influence on this thinking has been the important work of Charles Tilly (1978), who argued that collective action interacts with a set of necessary conditions for mobilization, chief among them was the rise of the consolidated national state. In a more recent contribution, Tarrow (2010, 18) confirms the centrality of the state for the formation of social movements. He sees the state as the "fulcrum" for the emergence of such movements. The contributions in part two of this volume, however, look at social movements and collective action in the absence of strong state institutions. The respective processes do not engage the state. Instead, they engage the absence of governance because of the absence of the state.

(2) The central characteristic of ICT is its effect on information and transaction costs. These costs, however, are central to collective action. Max Weber sees the reason for large hierarchical institutions in the nature of information. Where information is hard to gather, manage, and distribute, one is more likely to find specialized command-and-control hierarchical institutions—bureaucracies—to manage it. The classical Weberian conception of bureaucracy is a "body of arrangements for organizing information and communication into a system for rational decision making and administration" (Bimber 2003). Weber's argument assumes that information is inchoate and inherently difficult to organize, making it costly to assimilate and manage over time. Olson has made similar assumptions in his classic analysis of collective action. Meeting the burdens of collective action requires agreement and organization, writes Olson, "These are the costs of communication among group members, the costs of any bargaining among them, and the costs of creating, staffing, and maintaining any formal group organizations" (Olson 1965, 47).

Resource mobilization theory in the 1970s and 1980s argued along these lines when claiming that collective action occurs only where and when adequate resources are available (Zald and McCarthy 1997). The resource mobilization perspective maintained that professionalized membership-based organizations with full time, professional staff base were central to movement mobilization, stability, and maturation.

With the rapid diffusion of digital technology in the West at the turn of the century, political scientists and sociologists began seeing interesting new patterns in social protest movements. Groups and interests that, according to traditional models of collective action, would not be present began appearing at antiglobalization protests across Europe and the United States. Among the many things that were interesting about these new groups was their under-resourced, yet still sizeable, presence at various protest actions. According to the assumptions of collective action, this wasn't supposed to happen. Yet mostly leaderless and loosely organized—if organized at all, relative to expected requirements—were clearly present as early as the anti–World Trade Organization (WTO) protests in Seattle 1999. What explains this?

The key explanatory variable seems to be the information characteristic of the environment. Whether we speak of "post-bureaucratic politics" (Bimber 2003), "organizing without organizations" (Shirky 2008), or "leveraging affordance" (Earl and Kimport 2011), the conclusions are generally the same: The information environment affects the nature of organizations and the opportunities and constraints they face in collective action. Advances in various information technologies lower the cost of gathering, creating, storing, retrieving, and distributing information. That in turn creates opportunities for groups and identities to coalesce and coordinate with much lower costs than would have been the case in an earlier age. In the words of Bimber, "the contemporary information revolution has the capacity to alter organizational structures. The result is a diminished role on many fronts for traditional organizations in politics" (Bimber 2003, 21–22).

We extend this possibility to our consideration of areas of limited statehood in the contemporary information environment. Again, this type of collective action is not about the articulation and organization of demands on states (or corporations); rather it is about the pursuit of basic collective goods. The individual chapters offer different examples of how such technologically enabled forms of collective action can look.

FrontlineSMS, for instance, introduced by Sharath Srinivasan in Chapter 6, is an-open source software that is used to collect and distribute mobile phone text messages. It allows users to connect a range of mobile devices to a computer to send and receive SMS text messages. If Internet access is available, FrontlineSMS can also be connected to online SMS services and set up to feed incoming messages to other web or e-mail services. It has been used in a variety of circumstances, all characterized by the remoteness of the users, a lack of state services, and an otherwise isolated and scattered population. For example, in the absence of a state agricultural assistance service, common in the United States and Europe, a variety NGOs have established farmer information services.[7] The

Grameen Foundation's Community Knowledge Workers Initiative, for example, provides farmers with information about crops, international market prices, and other services via mobile phones (Grameen Foundation 2012). The chapter concludes by explaining technology is less used for self-governance but rather as a tool for nonstate governance provision by NGOs.

The three subsequent chapters are devoted to the role of crowdsourcing and event-mapping. Ushahidi, the most commonly used open source geographical information systems mapping platform, emerged in 2008 in the midst of the post-election violence in Kenya. Kenyan bloggers and technologists created a mash-up of open source GIS-mapping to record and aggregate various kinds of violence. Since then, Ushahidi has been used in a wide variety of circumstances, including the tracking of anti-immigrant violence in South Africa in 2008 and the tracking of pharmacy stocks in several East African countries and for election-monitoring in Nigeria in 2011 (Banks 2009). In Chapter 7, Gregory Asmolov illustrates the use of Ushahidi for monitoring wildfires and coordinating nonstate relief efforts in Russia in 2010 that counterbalanced the deficiencies in state disaster relief.

In Chapter 8, Primož Kovačič and Jamie Lundine analyze the role of mapping platforms for the empowerment of residents in urban slums in Africa. Such informal settlements are usually marked by the absence of any detailed geographical information (with official maps of Nairobi marking the slum areas as "woods"). The authors show that user-based geographical information gathering on infrastructure, health, education, security, and so on, played an important role to improve the effectiveness and efficiency of nonstate governance initiatives.

In Chapter 9, Patrick Meier compares various deployments of Ushahidi (ranging from post-earthquake Haiti via Egypt to Libya) in search of the (online and offline) conditions for its success. The chapter concludes that the success of live crowdsourced maps depends on pre-existing social capital. In turn, however, such online cooperation greatly enhances social capital fostering online *and* offline capacity for social action.

Finally, in Chapter 10, Peter van der Windt takes the idea of ICT-based empowerment a step further. Most mapping efforts are based on crowdsourcing, which in turn, presupposes a technologically enabled "crowd." By contrast, "crowdseeding" makes the technological enabling of the governance constituency part of the process. In his example from the Democratic Republic of the Congo, mobile phones are distributed to village resident in rural Eastern Congo, enabling to internationally report security relevant events.

Guiding Questions

By now, the ICT revolution has reached all parts of the globe, including the vast majority of states outside the West that can be described as "areas of limited

statehood." Up to now, the academic debate has largely neglected this development, focusing instead on the part of the world where in the context of fully
consolidated states broadband technology is changing much of the political landscape. The intention of this book is to draw attention to the fact that ICT in areas
of limited statehood has equally significant effects. For this purpose, the contributions to this volume draw on examples from around the globe to provide a more
complete picture of what ICT can do.

Although we leave the conclusions of this exercise to the book's final chapter,
we want to offer the reader a set of guiding questions to consider while going
through the individual chapters. In Chapter 11, we return to these questions and
consider them on a more abstract level based on the insights of the contributors
to this volume. The questions are organized around the two main topics of the
book: the effects of ICT on statehood and on governance.

The specific condition of areas of limited statehood has three central charac-
teristics: (1) weak statehood—that is, challenges to the monopoly of force and
significant difficulties with regard to rule implementation and enforcement, (2) a
state governance record which—across the different governance services—falls
between patchy and poor, and finally (3) significant problems of input and output
legitimacy. On the output side, (3) is the logical corollary of (2); on the input side,
we find that some political systems compensate for (1) and (2) by repressive security policies and authoritarian structures. When we consider the rapid diffusion
of advanced ICT in this particular context, two main questions arise:

(1) Under which conditions can ICT improve statehood and the governance
record of the respective state institutions?
(2) Under which conditions can ICT improve state legitimacy? Or, if this is not
an option, and the legitimacy deficit translates into political struggle and turmoil: Under which conditions does ICT favor government, under which conditions the opposition?

In a Western context we consider governance the domain of the state; it is
not an accident that *governance* and *government* are often conflated. In areas of
limited statehood, the weakness of the state can give rise to alternative forms
governance. This implies that different actors and different processes can involve
themselves in a governance process. The political potential of ICT lies in the low-
ering of information and transaction cost, which in turn facilitates collective
action in pursuit of public or collective goods. This can be thought of as "governance without government" (Rosenau 1992).[8] However, many of the goods of
governance involve material resources and tangible costs rather than information
alone. In other words, collective goods often involve not only information but also
the provision of tangible resources. Information about security threats may be
made more readily available by crowdsourcing or crowdmapping, but, ultimately,
credible and accountable security forces of some sort must be deployed to address

the threat. It may be true that ICT makes it easier to organize but does it feed hungry mouths? This gives rise to the main question with regard to governance:

(3) Under which conditions do technologically enabled collective action initiatives in areas of limited statehood rise to the level of governance?

Notes

1. The editors gratefully acknowledge the generous support for developing this book provided by the Collaborative Research Center (SFB) 700, funded by the German Research Foundation (DFG) and hosted at Freie Universität Berlin. For further information please consult http://www.sfb-governance.com.
2. For a review, see Risse (2011).
3. This concept of governance and statehood was developed at the Collaborative Research Center (SFB).
4. Most Africans use prepaid SIM cards. This creates some ambiguity as to what these numbers mean. For example, one can have a mobile phone subscription without having a mobile phone; or one can have multiple mobile phones and multiple subscriptions; or one can have a subscription without any minutes, and therefore effectively be without a phone (see James and Versteeg 2007; Harwood 2012).
5. As with some many other things, this claim is less true of South Africa where the state has been more involved in scientific pursuits, including nuclear research and development.
6. Shadow of hierarchy is a term found in the international relations literature that refers to the presence of hierarchical or state institutional structures in forms of governance that do not immediately involve the state (see Héritier and Lehmkuhl 2008).
7. A similar technology, RapidSMS, was developed as a communication tool for UNICEF's Global Operations Center. In Somalia exists RapidSMS project for emergency response monitoring. In Kenya, it is being used to address mortality rates of children under five years of age at a community level. In Nigeria, RapidSMS was piloted in the first phase of a 70 million "long lasting insecticide-treated nets" distribution campaign (see RapidSMS 2013).
8. The *locus classicus* of this term is Rosenau (1992), not accidently a major contribution to International Relations after the end of the Cold War.

Part One

SIMULATION, CONSOLIDATION, OPPOSITION

ICT and Limited Statehood

2

Information Technology and the Limited States of the Arab Spring

MUZAMMIL M. HUSSAIN AND PHILIP N. HOWARD

Introduction

One of the core arguments of this collection of essays is that the state and governance are not necessarily synonymous.[1] Highly consolidated states are but one of several governance modalities. Moreover, there are different ways in which statehood can be limited. Before the Arab Spring of 2011, the region of North Africa and the Middle East was replete with example of such forms of statehood. In some countries, the state was able to make political decisions, but with a limited range of enforcement. In others, the state had such a limited capacity to sense and respond to public needs that people made other institutional arrangements, relying on professional unions or religious groups like the Muslim Brotherhood to provide healthcare services, dispense justice, and provide collective security. In some, the state was limited because its primary task was to protect ruling elites and their assets, rather than to provide for collective welfare. In the years prior to the Arab Spring, digital media allowed spatially distant communities to realize that their grievances were shared and their oppressors proximate. More important, it was through digital media that people were able to discover and document the weaknesses and limits of their states. Thus, information and communication technologies (ICTs) primarily extended the capacity of these other political actors and were not effectively used by states to improve governance in the areas—territories or policy domains—in which they were limited.

In an important way, it was the condition of limited statehood that made so many Arab Spring regimes surprisingly brittle in times of crisis. Over the course of a year, popular movements for democracy cascaded across the Middle East and North Africa. These were not Marxist or Islamist or nationalist movements, and while there was great diversity in the expectations for what democracy could look like, there was a shared fatigue with authoritarian rule. In the early days of protest in each country, the participants were unusual: they were not the urban poor, unionized labor, existing opposition party members, radical Islamists or minorities with grievances. They were middle class, educated, and underemployed, relatively leaderless, and technology-savvy youth. The gender balance also surprised many Western observers. Four dictators were successfully deposed, a dozen other regimes made major political and economic concessions, and political turmoil devolved into civil war in several others.

By 2013, Egypt, Libya, and Tunisia had run elections and were in the difficult process of building new constitutions. There were also new parliaments and cabinets in Morocco and Jordan, with significant commitments to extend franchise. Even in constitutional monarchies where ruling families remained in control, a greatly expanded welfare state was the cost of the stability. Transitional governments with imperfect constitutions and predatory militaries now govern several countries. It will be years before we can judge the democratic practices of the new governments. But even in countries where Islamism is on the rise, the most viable Islamist leaders are competing in elections and advocating different brands of Islamic constitutionalism. And what is surprisingly important is the powerful role of digital media in both socializing young people into the existing tropes of political dominance or revolution and in allowing young people to create new rhetorical tools—and often logistical tools—for perpetuating or challenging ideological control (Singh 2013).

There are several ways that limited statehood is linked with popular uprising. Limited statehood can be the reason for civic unrest, in that a dissatisfied public may be more likely to take to the streets. Limited statehood can be the reason for a weak government response or the speed of collapse. Limited statehood can also be the outcome of civic unrest, in that once challenged for its failures in one policy domain, the regime may even have less credibility and capacity to act. For many observers, digital media appeared to have an important role in the ignition of social protest, the cascade of inspiring images and stories of success across the countries of the region, and the peculiar organizational form that Arab Spring uprisings had (Tufekci and Wilson 2012). For scholars of comparative politics, the distribution of outcomes suggest a need to take information technology seriously as a potentially causal factor: the two Arab Spring countries in which dictators were deposed relatively quickly, Tunisia and Egypt, had the most tech-savvy civil society and largest Internet-using population in the region; the two Arab Spring countries in which dictators were deposed only after months of protracted civil war, Libya and Yemen, had no such character.

We build on a six-stage framework for political change observed during the early aftermath of the Arab Spring to understand the contextual variables that were in-play *before* the Arab Spring in countries with varying degrees of limited statehood (Howard and Hussain 2012). The most successful cases of sustained and peaceful protest, with deposed despots were Tunisia and Egypt. Both cases exemplified a pattern that can be seen, with different degrees of strength, across the region: a *preparation* phase, involving activists' use of digital media across time to build solidarity networks and identification of collective identities and goals; an *ignition* phase involving symbolically powerful moments that ruling elites and regimes intentionally or lazily ignored, but galvanized the public; a *protest* phase, during which, by employing offline networks and digital technologies, small groups strategically organized on large numbers; an *international buy-in* phase, during which digital media networks extended the range of local coverage to international broadcast networks; a *climax* phase, during which the regime maneuvered strategically or carelessly to appease public discontent through welfare packages or harsh repressive actions; and finally, a *follow-on information warfare* phase, during which various actors, state-based and from international civic advocacy networks, compete to shape the future of civil society and information infrastructure that made it possible. But this narrative of political change, though generalizable to many Arab Spring cases, does not account for some important technology related factors that were in play as well.

Citizen journalism videos and blogs were important vehicles for the spreading of news about self-immolations in Tunisia, Egypt, Saudi Arabia, and Algeria (Lim 2012). More formally organized networks of citizens and civic organizations have also led to the entrenchment of civil society, albeit in some cases, mostly online. These civil society groups, like the April 6 Youth Movement in Egypt, and banned but preeminent political parties, like the Muslim Brotherhood, have all successfully used information infrastructure to do political organizing and capacity building *over time*, not simply during the phase of street protests. The April 6 Youth Movement has been active since at least 2008, and the Muslim Brotherhood has built a massive online blogging and news production ecology outweighing any other Egyptian party or movement. Lastly, especially in the case of women in the Middle East, many, including but not limited to feminist movements, have expanded the range of political inclusion from suffrage rights to driving, particularly in Saudi Arabia—and they have done so through online advocacy movements and awareness campaigns. Media has been particular important to "pink hijabis," who integrate their faith with the pursuit of women's rights by circulating films about female genital mutilation to friends and family, organizing workshops about technology strategies, and learning about successful digital strategies from like-minded groups in other countries (Wright 2011).

There has been no global study of the contribution of different kinds of information technology towards regime transparency or state capacity generally. In one of the largest of public opinion analyses, Nisbet and colleagues find that Internet drives democratic expectations, especially in countries that already have a few democratic habits (Nisbet, Stoycheff, and Pearce 2012). Ever since the Zapatista rebels used the World Wide Web to promote their struggle for indigenous land rights in 1994, international analysts have been engaged in explaining the uses of digital technology by grassroots activists and social movements and determining the technologies' effects on political outcomes (Garrido 2003; Meikle 2002; Russell 2001; Russell 2005). In years since, many distinguished scholars have contributed valuable insights on this phenomena in specific geographic and temporal contexts, sometimes focused on moments of heightened contention, such as national elections or social justice campaigns (Earl and Kimport 2011; Howard 2010b; Margolis, Resnick, and Tu 1997; Pedersen and Saglie 2005; Sreberny and Khiabany 2010). Others have taken a thematic approach, viewing a specific phenomenon, such as digital authoritarianism, across a group of representative countries (Kalathil and Boas 2003b). These scholars have drawn on qualitative and quantitative data and have written from a variety of subject perspectives, including sociology, communications, political science, computer science, and area studies. Yet all have been limited to a specific country or region and have a fairly limited time horizon.

However, major protest movements around the world, most recently the Arab Spring, have demonstrated that the phenomenon of digital activism is of great (and increasing) importance. In 1998, Suharto's rule over Indonesia was broken by a student movement that successfully used mobile phone infrastructure to organize their protests (Barendregt 2008; Hill 2003; Hill and Sen 2005). During Kyrgyzstan's Tulip Revolution of 2005, democratic leaders used mobile phones to organize at key moments to throw out a dictator (Beissinger 2007; Chen 2011). When the authoritarian government of Kazakhstan shut down opposition websites, democratic organizations moved their content to servers in other countries. Threatened political elites in authoritarian regimes and emerging democracies often try to strip social movements of communications tools: Iran and Albania have blocked Internet gateways and mobile phone networks during politically tumultuous periods. In Iran, Saudi Arabia, and Syria, blogs and YouTube submissions are nascent deliberative democratic practices and reflect the real opposition there (al-Saggaf 2004; Deibert, Palfrey, Rohozinski, and Zittrain 2008, 2010). In many Arab Spring countries, the Internet is the primary place for open dialogues about race, gender, and the interpretation of Islamic texts (Howard 2010b; King 2011; Wolcott and Goodman 2000).

Studies suggest that along with wealth, telecommunications and information policy can contribute to democratization (Howard and Mazaheri 2009; Milner 2006; Norris 2001). Many have hypothesized that increased internet usage supports the growth of democratic institutions (Abbott 2001; George 2006; Hogan 1999). Yet both democracies and dictatorships have fast-growing numbers of Internet users, Internet hosts, mobile phones, and personal computers. Authoritarian regimes may develop their digital communication infrastructure specifically to extend state power (Kalathil and Boas 2003a). There is significant research on the censorship strategies of the most authoritarian of Islamic states, but also evidence that a significant amount of digital content is beyond the reach of state censors (Deibert 2008). In democracies, there is some evidence that effective state services online breeds trust and confidence among citizens in their government (Hasan 2003; Tolbert and Mossberger 2006; Welch, Hinnant, and Moon 2005). As Iran's experience suggests, it may be the social media that is most difficult to censor consistently.

Indeed, there are lessons about civic action from Iran that may well be consistent with the Arab Spring and the Occupy Movement: digital technologies provide the entry points for young activists to explore democratic alternatives, an action landscape such as cyberspace that allows for political discourse and even direct interventions with state policy, and coordinating mechanisms that support synchronized social movements through marches, protests, and other forms of collective action (Abdulla 2007; Abdulla 2005; Kirsh 2001; Shapiro 2009; Warschauer, Said, and Zohry 2002). Perhaps the clearest signs that ICTs have changed the dynamics of political communication comes from the awkward ways that authoritarian regimes have responded to its own tech-savvy activists. In pre-revolutionary Egypt, when Muhammad Khaled Said posted an online video incriminating the police in a drug deal, he was beaten to death outside of his Internet café, an event that precipitated a Facebook group that was critical in mobilizing elites during the revolution (York 2011).

While "terror on the Internet" and transnational Islamic identity has been well explored in the security studies literature, relatively little research has been done on the specific mechanisms of technology use and repurposing by civil society actors (though see Chapters 3, 7, and 9 in this volume). As mentioned in the opening chapter of this collection, the primary instinct of political researchers has been to look for the impact of technologies on existing, hierarchical organizations. Network organizational forms, made resilient and expansive through ICTs, have recently become interesting, but for the most part the networks that international relations scholars have studies have been terrorist networks. Understanding such mechanisms would help us answer broader questions about the nature of contemporary regime change, online participation, and the security implications of information policy (Bunt 2000; Bunt 2003; Bunt 2009; Weimann 2006). Some area-studies and Islamist scholars have studied information technology diffusion and political practices in particular countries, or investigated the impact of al Jazeera on news cycles and sourcing (Alavi 2005; George 2006; Rugh 2004; Wheeler 2006). Information technologies are also the infrastructure for antidemocratic movements and the site of what some have called "cyberconflict" (Karatzogianni 2006). However, rigorous social science can build more transportable theories about the role of social computing during political crisis and the role of social computing in civic life in the Muslim world. Cyberwar and cyber-terror are not the only form of social computing in the service of political discourse (Stohl and Stohl 2007).

Fuzzy Logic for Comparative Problems

It would be wrong-headed to debate how many bloggers it takes to make a democracy. In the analytical discourse so far, there are two ways of describing the causes and consequences of the Arab Spring. The first analytical frame is to think about the limited statehood of the regimes that faced social unrest, the lacking capacity that made them susceptible to popular uprising. It is plausible that limited statehood was both a source of grievance for citizens—who wished their government could be more effective—and a feature of the regime that made regime response so weak. The second is to identify the things that might explain a successful uprising. Rather than looking for simple or singular causal explanations for what made a country susceptible to popular uprisings or what allowed a popular uprising to achieve its goals, we should expect that there would be complex causal patterns, or even several causal combinations that would provide analytical purchase over several sets of cases. Moreover, knowing what we know about social movements and regime change, it makes the most sense to look for conjoined causal conditions—the set of multiple indicators that together provide a fulfilling narrative for understanding political outcomes.

There have been a significant number of single-country case studies in which information technologies have been part of the contemporary narrative of both democratic entrenchment and persistent authoritarianism. The comparative perspective taken in this investigation will not be limited to the standard cases, or even to situations that stand out as incidents of technology-driven, -enhanced, or -enabled regime change. Instead, this comparative perspective embraces cases in which information technologies had little to no role in democratic promotion, as well as situations in which information technologies were carefully used by authoritarian elites to become better bullies, and situations in which information technologies played a critical role in sudden democratic transitions. Thus, the comparative approach is anathema to those who would generalize from singular studies in which information technologies had a central role in a grand democratization project and those who would generalize by only relying on statistical models of international data on government effectiveness in terms of Internet penetration.

Methodologically, the comparative approach is powerful and productive in that it confronts theory with data. Sometimes this approach is called "set-theoretic" in that attention is given to consistent similarities or differences across a set of cases, especially the causally relevant commonalities uniformly present in a given set of cases. The set of cases at hand is the population of Arab countries with large Muslim communities, and there are twenty of these. The argument of this investigation is that in recent years, information technologies have opened up new paths to democratization and the entrenchment of civil society in many Arab countries. Large-N quantitative researchers often turn "democratization" into an indicator for which the Western democracies are the standard. In our set-theoretic approach, we assume that democratization among these twenty countries is best calibrated according to a more regionally relevant standard, set by countries such as Lebanon at the high end and Saudi Arabia at the low end. This calibration does not preclude the theoretical possibility of an Islamic democratic ideal type. But a grounded approach does assume that healthy, functional Muslim democracies may not look like Western democracies. Set-theoretic reasoning allows for fine gradations in the degree of membership in the set of successful democratic outcomes, and it requires evidence about each country's degree of membership in the set of countries that have experienced democratic transition or entrenchment during or since the Arab Spring. For more on the use of fuzzy logic in comparative analysis of the Arab Spring (see Howard and Hussain 2012).

FUZZY CAUSAL VARIABLES

Several contextual factors might exacerbate or mitigate the causal role of particular aspects of technology diffusion, and reducing the set of causal attributes to a few important ones must also respect the significant diversity among these countries. The cases involved in the Arab Spring differ in important ways, yet there may still be causal patterns and shared attributes that explain membership in the set of countries that have democratized or not. Along with the impact of technology diffusion on the system of political communication involving states, journalists, political parties, civil society groups, and cultural elites, additional contextual conditions should also be evaluated on a case-by-case basis:

- *Average incomes within country (gdppc)*. Measured as GDP per capita (adjusted for purchasing power parity), this factor accounts for the large diversity in the economic productivity across the region. The high end of this scale includes rich countries like Qatar, the United Arab Emirites (UAE), Kuwait, and Bahrain (average range of $7,000 to $20,000); the low end includes countries like Mauritania, Iraq, Comoros, and Somalia (average range of $200 to $800).
- *Wealth distribution (gini)*. Measured as Gini coefficients for income distribution, this indicator reveals the relative deprivation of the poor in society. It captures the distinctions between countries like Lebanon and Qatar, where wealth is comparatively well distributed, and Egypt and the UAE, where wealth is highly concentrated.
- *Levels of unemployment*. Access to jobs may have been a primary source of discontent in Arab Spring countries, particularly in countries like Tunisia and Yemen where the formal unemployment rates topped 15 percent. Employment may also be a comparatively important variable because some of the countries with weak protest turnout had low unemployment rates. In Saudi Arabia formal employment was hovering around 5 percent, and it was even lower in Kuwait. Youth unemployment is also a useful variable to include because of anecdotal evidence that the political uprisings were led by disaffected youth.
- *Demographic variables (unemp, urban)*. The causes of political unrest during the Arab Spring could be plausibly related to having large groups of youth in densely packed urban settlements, so it is important to include measures of

the size of the country in terms of population, the degree of urbanization, and youth bulge. Almost the entire population of Qatar and Kuwait lives in urban centers, while less than 40 percent of Yemen and Somalia's population does so. Yemen and Somalia also have the largest proportion of population under twenty-five years old—some 45 percent of the total population—while less than 25 percent of the population of Qatar and Kuwait is under twenty-five years old. Overall, the Arab Spring countries include both small island states with a few million inhabitants and countries like Egypt, with large populations. Population rarely appeared in the causal solutions, while the size of the youth population and level of urbanization was often relevant.

- *Mobile and Internet connectivity (mobile, internet)*. We measure digital connectivity in the diffusion of mobile telephone and Internet use. Interestingly, more than half of Arab countries have mobile penetration well over 100 percent, including several of the countries where Arab Spring protests were most successful. Internet penetration rates do not always mirror mobile phone penetration rates, however. While 54 percent of the population of Bahriain has Internet access, it is a country where the popular uprising was quickly crushed. Only 15 percent of Egyptians have access to the Internet, but in that country the dictator was quickly removed.
- *Regime type (pol)*. We used the Polity IV scores of regime type, which rank countries on a simple index of how authoritarian or democratic each regime is.
- *Fuel dependent economy (fuel)*. Having access to the wealth generated by a fuel-dependent economy can allow ruling elites to maintain social control. Not having this wealth means authoritarian rules may not have the resources to maintain internal security services and co-opt political opponents. To account for this significant variable, we included countries' level of oil production and its share in the global oil resources available. Saudi Arabia, the UAE, and Kuwait ranked most highly.

REGIME FRAGILITY AS THE FUZZY OUTCOME

Because our key research questions deal with the contextual factors and variables at play during the Arab Spring, many of our predictive variables listed above come from the latest data points available at or just before the protest periods. However, our overall objective is to find a parsimonious set of causes or conjoined causes that explain what made some Arab Spring regimes fragile to popular uprisings, and then what made some popular uprisings successful. Regime fragility was evaluated by the relative numbers and impact of protest mobilizations in each of the countries of the Arab Spring (*fragile*). Full membership in the set of fragile Arab Spring countries was given to the countries where street turnout was surprisingly large, attendance was consistently high over several days, domestic media attention unusually interested, and protests took place in an unexpected number of diverse locations. Lower scores went to cases where protest turnout was small, concentrated in only a few locations, or protesters themselves were quickly dissuaded.

We used data from 2011 or the best available year. When the data taken from large datasets were incomplete, supplementary data from secondary sources were used. Patching these gaps by hand significantly reduced the number of missing cases and provided for a more robust and meaningful ranking system. Preparing data for treatment as a fuzzy set required several steps. First, we computed indices for the plausible causal factors. Then we calibrated the indices, a process that evens out the distribution of cases between the thresholds for full inclusion in each set, full exclusion from the set, and the crossover point at which cases go from being partially in the set to being partially out of the set.

The variable of population size provides a useful example of how the calibration process works. Among the twenty countries, there are a few very populated countries and many countries with a small population. Egypt, Iraq, and Saudi Arabia are at the top of this set, and obviously helps define the category of "populated Arab Spring country." In fact, Egypt has such a large population that if the set were left uncalibrated, Tunisia and Syria would be barely in the set, and most of the countries would be fully out of the set. Yet the important attribute is that some countries are comparatively more populated than others, so calibration makes the differences between the populous countries more intuitively comparable to those between smaller countries. The very populated countries still define the set by being almost full members, while the rest of the cases get graded by their degrees of membership in the set. In this example, the threshold value for full membership in the set of populated countries is established just below the actual population of Iraq. Bahrain, Qatar, and Oman are definitely not populated Arab Spring countries. So the threshold for full exclusion is set at 3 million people because these countries have even smaller populations than that. The crossover threshold for set membership was set at 10 million people, which roughly splits countries into two groups. Since Somalia and Tunisia have barely 10 million citizens, these two countries are just barely in the category of "populated country." The recalibration around these thresholds allows for fuzzy set values that more meaningfully reveal the degree to which each country can be included in the theoretical set of populated countries.

The index for regime type required some direct calibration. Polity IV identifies Somalia as a failed state in 2010. This case is not likely to teach us much about a theoretical relationship between political institutions, technology diffusion, and popular movements for democracy, so it was given a fuzzy score of 0.50. This is a special score designating a case that is neither in nor out of the theoretical set of democracies. A score of 0.51 would mean that a country is very slightly in the theoretical set of democracies, and a score of 0.49 would mean that a country is just out of such a set. But the transition score signals that if regime type is important, Somalia is not a good instance of either a democracy or an autocracy.

The full dataset of all variables in the causal recipes described in this investigation is available at http://www.pITPI.org, as are the technical scripts for secondary solution sets not described here and the calibration points for specific membership sets. For more on fuzzy set calibrations see the codebook for the fs/QCA 2.0 software and Ragin (2000). The fuzzy scores used in this analysis appear in the Appendix.

Fuzzy Recipes for Fragility

Each Arab Spring country could be described with its unique combination of causal factors. Certainly, there are more complex formulations of conditions that would also explain the susceptibility of a regime to a popular uprising or the chances such an uprising would be successful. The combinations reported here are not the only plausible ones, but they plausibly explain multiple cases with good coverage and consistency. Coverage refers to the percentage of cases explained by that recipe. Consistency refers to the degree to which cases adhere to a particular causal recipe. Since the goal of comparative work is sensible, parsimonious explanations, Table 2.1 presents the parsimonious models with the best balance of case coverage and solution consistency.

Table 2.1 reveals that there is a strong causal connection between having low levels of mobile phone and Internet use and regime durability. In other words, the countries experiencing low levels of protestor turnout, and relatively modest interest in social movement organizing, were those without many Internet or mobile phone users. Indeed, regimes appear to be most durable when there are no extreme contrasts between rich and poor—low Gini coefficients are a consistent ingredient all of the parsimonious recipes. Causal recipes can explain several countries, and the events in several countries can be understood through several causal recipes. Of the best instances defined in these reduced solutions, Iraq is the country where events may be best explained by urbanization and youth bulge rates over technology diffusion patterns. Outcomes in Somalia, Algeria, Egypt, Syria, Libya, and Saudi Arabia—all with areas and domains of limited statehood—should be understood in the context of the distribution of wealth, technology use patterns, urbanization, and youth bulge.

Digital media were very important during the short-term cascade of street protests across the region. For example, we know that online conversations spiked before major events on the ground in both cases, as well as many others, across many of the Arab Spring cases (Howard et al. 2011). This was possible because social media helped democratic ideas spread across borders, through informal networks of families, friends, and interested onlookers. The intensity of political conversations that took place preceding major street protests supports the idea that virtual networks materialized before street protest networks. For example, detailed maps and guides were widely available before protests began and

Table 2.1 **Parsimonious Model Explaining Regime Fragility**

Causal Recipe	Raw Coverage	Unique Coverage	Consistency	Best Instances
~internet*~gini	0.56	0.02	0.81	Somalia (0.99,0.01), Algeria (0.63,0.53), Egypt (0.63,0.74), Syria (0.58,0.84), Libya (0.58,0.95), Saudi (0.53,0.63)
~urban*~gini	0.58	0.1	0.84	Somalia (0.89,0.01), Egypt (0.74,0.74), Iraq (0.58,0.84), Syria (0.58,0.84), Algeria (0.53,0.53)
~mobile*~gini	0.53	0.2	0.80	Somalia (0.99,0.01), Egypt (0.63,0.74), Iraq (0.58,0.84), Syria (0.58,0.84), Algeria (0.53,0.53)
youth*~gini	0.61	0.3	0.83	Somalia (0.99,0.01), Iraq (0.89,0.84), Syria (0.58,0.84), Egypt (0.58,0.74), Saudi (0.53,0.63)

Note: The consistency cutoff for the solution set was 0.97, the solution coverage is 0.72 and solution consistency is 0.83. Variables tested include wealth per capita (gdppc), wealth distribution (gini), unemployment (unemp), urbanization (urban), size of youth population (youth), mobile phone diffusion (mobile), internet access (internet), economic dependence on fuel exports (fuel), and regime type (pol).

provided would-be participants with strategies and nonviolence goals to sustain periods of dissent that disabled authoritarian regimes' past coercion and suppression techniques. Indeed, Facebook pages and Twitter conversations were essential for designing and trying out new strategies as events took place on the ground. Political blogospheres, many based nationally, but others also based more regionally, brought together political diaspora communities from France, the United Kingdom, and other Western democratic countries (Etling et al. 2010). The ability to produce and consume political content was important because it created a sense of shared grievances and strong political efficacy that had not led to such sizable, diverse, and quick mobilization before the Arab Spring.

Conclusion: The Digital Scaffolding for Social Movements

What might have made several of these limited states more susceptible than others to popular uprisings? What role does information technology have in the modern recipe for democratization? Weighing multiple political, economic, and cultural conditions, we find that information infrastructure—especially mobile phone use—consistently appears as one of the key ingredients in parsimonious models for the conjoined combinations of causes behind regime fragility. Internet use is relevant in some solution sets, but it causal logic it is actually the absence of internet use that explains low levels of success by Arab Spring movements.

Fung and colleagues argue that there are two distinct models for how information technologies might have a role in democratic politics (Fung, Gilman, and Shkabatur 2013). Rapid transitions towards democracy might come from a newly emboldened public sphere, the displacement of traditional organizations by new digitally self-organized groups or digitally direct democracy. Long-term, democratic entrenchment might come from truth-based, online advocacy, constituent mobilization, and crowdsourced social monitoring. They find more intellectual promise in the second suite of possibilities, and until the Arab Spring much of the scholarly research on the political impact of digital media over the last decade supported this perspective (Howard 2010a). But this comparative analysis demonstrates that digital media may also have a role in rapid political transitions.

Since the Arab Spring, perhaps some of the best evidence that digital media altered the system of political communication in several countries is in how political candidates have campaigned for office, emboldened by successful digital tactics, and have continued to use information technologies in running for office. In both Egypt and Tunisia, the initial rounds of elections were notable for how candidates wooed voters with social media strategies. Interacting with voters face to face was most important for reaching the many new voters who were not online and had little experience with campaign politics. But competitive candidates also took to the Internet and independent candidates not allied with Islamist parties, such as Mohammed El Baradei in Egypt, but also relied heavily on Facebook to activate networks of supporters. Digital media have had a crucial causal role in the formation, enunciation, and activation of coordinated opposition in several countries in North Africa and the Middle East. Now there is more evidence to suggest that this information infrastructure continues to be important after the dictators fell—further supporting the need to develop our theory to go beyond seeking linear relationships and towards parsimonious recipes grounded in limited but real case contexts.

In an important way, authoritarian regimes are limited states precisely because resources must be directed into maintaining social control. Public services become fragile, and in fact a weak state may become an important source of grievance for protestors. ICTs have been used by authoritarian regimes to empower security services, but in the years leading up to the Arab Spring ICTs were also used to collective evidence of limited statehood. Their governance capacity is imbalanced in the sense that whatever capacity and resources that are at hand go into the service of a "security" apparatus that has as its primary function the preservation of the states, and not service delivery to the general population. Indeed, maintaining the loyalties of local elites, or a network of sycophants, becomes one of the primary functions of the state and one of the primary ways that public resources get spent.

Appendix: **Comparative Scores for Set Membership**

Country	gdppc	gini	unemp	urban	youth	mobile	internet	fuel	pol	fragile
Somalia	0.01	0.01	0.95	0.11	1	0.01	0.01	0.16	0.5	0.01
Sudan	0.26	1	0.79	0.16	0.79	0.11	0.21	0.74	0.67	0.01
Djibouti	0.16	0.74	1	0.63	0.74	0.05	0.16	0.01	0.83	0.11
Qatar	1	0.79	0.01	0.95	0.01	0.74	0.95	0.63	0.01	0.16
Kuwait	0.89	0.01	0.05	1	0.16	0.84	0.74	0.89	0.28	0.21
UAE	0.95	0.11	0.11	0.79	0.05	0.79	1	0.53	0.11	0.21
Bahrain	0.84	0.42	0.58	0.89	0.26	0.68	0.89	0.58	0.11	0.32
Lebanon	0.63	0.95	0.32	0.84	0.21	0.26	0.58	0.11	1	0.32
Jordan	0.53	0.58	0.47	0.01	0.63	0.63	0.47	0.05	0.56	0.42
Morocco	0.42	0.79	0.37	0.37	0.37	0.53	0.68	0.21	0.44	0.42
Algeria	0.58	0.37	0.42	0.47	0.32	0.47	0.32	1	0.83	0.53
Tunisia	0.47	0.79	0.53	0.53	0.11	0.58	0.63	0.32	0.5	0.53
Mauritania	0.11	0.68	0.84	0.21	0.84	0.32	0.05	0.26	0.67	0.63
Saudi	0.74	0.21	0.16	0.74	0.53	1	0.47	0.79	0.01	0.63
Egypt	0.32	0.21	0.26	0.26	0.58	0.37	0.37	0.42	0.56	0.74
Oman	0.79	0.21	0.58	0.58	0.47	0.89	0.84	0.68	0.11	0.74
Iraq	0.05	0.11	0.74	0.42	0.89	0.42	0.79	0.37	0.94	0.84
Syria	0.37	0.42	0.21	0.32	0.68	0.21	0.42	0.47	0.28	0.84
Libya	0.68	0.42	0.84	0.68	0.42	0.95	0.11	0.95	0.28	0.95
Yemen	0.21	0.58	0.58	0.05	0.95	0.16	0.26	0.84	0.67	0.95

Notes

1. This research was supported by the Center for Information Technology Policy of the Woodrow Wilson School for International Affairs at Princeton University, the US Institutes of Peace, and the National Science Foundation under award IIS-1144286, "RAPID—Social Computing and Political Transition in Tunisia." Any opinions, findings, and conclusions or recommendations expressed in this material are those of the author and do not necessarily reflect the views of the National Science Foundation or the US Institutes of Peace. For useful comments on earlier drafts of this work, we are grateful to Lance Bennett, Andrew Chadwick, Larry Diamond, and Steven Livingston. Please direct correspondence to Mr. Muzammil M. Hussain, Department of Communication, University of Washington, 102 Communications Building, Box 353740, Seattle, Washington, United States, or by email to muzammil@uw.edu. Replication data is available at the website of the Project on Information Technology and Political Islam, www.pITPI.org.

3

The Kremlin's Cameras and Virtual Potemkin Villages: ICT and the Construction of Statehood

GREGORY ASMOLOV

The Collapse of the Soviet Union and Limited Statehood

Even after the collapse of the Soviet Union in 1991, the Russian state constituted the largest sovereign landmass in the world. It also inherited from the Soviet Union the major elements of state power, including a nuclear weapons arsenal and a large standing army, and oil reserves that positioned it as one of the world's superpowers. However, having a huge territory, nuclear weapons, and rich energy resources does not necessarily guarantee a high degree of statehood. On the contrary, the size of the state makes preserving the degree of statehood more challenging. In the introduction to this volume, Livingston and Walter-Drop point out that some states, "are usually not considered weak, per se, despite their inability to provide basic collective goods." due to "their ability to marshal force." The limited statehood framework allows us to conceptualize an ambivalent political situation when a state is "simultaneously too strong and too weak" (see Chapter 1, p. 8).

Russian is an example of this type of political ambivalence. Beginning in the period of the Russian empire, power holders in Moscow and St. Petersburg struggled over how to control the country. The collapse of the Soviet Union, which can be understood as the result of increasingly limited statehood in the Soviet Republics, led to a new crisis of statehood for the Russian Federation. The new Russian state had to repair immediately an uncertain command and control system, a requirement made all the more urgent given the unstable political, social, and economic circumstances. Yet, more than twenty years since the collapse of the Soviet Union, the state's ability to implement political decisions and enforce them is still deficient, in particular in areas distant from Moscow, and during crises. One of the most significant—although not the only—indicators of statehood is endemic corruption; in Russia entire budgets disappear before reaching their destination. What is more, decisions made in the center do not reach outlying districts.

In response, one of the major initiatives of Vladimir Putin's rule has been the development of "power vertical," a centralized management system that enables full control of the entire country by the person at the top of the pyramid. It includes, for example, a reform of governors' election that allowed the Kremlin to control who is going to rule Russian regions. Questions of democracy aside, many experts question the efficiency of this approach. Russian sociologist Michael Dmitriev speaks of a deep institutional crisis, one in which traditional institutions are not able to fulfill their functions (Dmitriev and Belanovsky 2012). According to Shevtzova (2010), the system is in fact an imitation of a system; maintaining the façade of fulfilling various governance functions has become a substitute for real action. One can argue that the imposition of vertical power eventually led to the opposite result. While the distributed semi-autonomous system of control was neutralized, it is questionable whether the vertical system has been able to substitute for it and strengthen statehood.

This paper argues that information and communication technologies (ICT) are used by the Kremlin as a part of the effort to build a "power vertical" in order to enhance its governance capacity. Yet the Russian case study also demonstrates the ambivalent nature of ICT's role for governance. ICT can just as well be used for contradictory purposes. It can serve to enhance transparency and accountability, on the one hand, or be used as a means of manipulating public opinion and to conceal the limited capacity of the state on the other hand.

The latter is not a new phenomenon. Russia has a long record in the construction of spectacles as a political strategy. Perhaps most famously, Russian Minister Grigory Potemkin is alleged to have created a series of painted façades to mimic real villages to impress Empress Catherine II during her visit to Crimea in 1787.[1] This chapter presents how ICT provides new methods for creation of virtual Potemkin villages. In this case, ICT is not used to improve the state's capacity to implement decisions and provide governance to its citizens, but rather to conceal the state's inaction in response to emerging problems.

However, monopoly of the state over construction of social reality as a substitute to governance is challenged by the same technologies that are used by the state in creating the manipulation. ICT (e.g., social media and crowdsourcing), as technologies of mass self-communication, enable emergence of a new citizens' surveillance power (Castells 2007). This power continuously deconstructs the "virtual Potemkin Villages." As consequence, what is appeared to be a strategy for manipulation is transform into a contest, one that demonstrates the duality of ICT and its role as a tool for empowering the state, and, at the same time, a source of countervailing power.

Statehood and the Power of Sensors

One of the major attributes of statehood is the capacity to monitor and evaluate conditions in the reach of its sovereign territorial boundaries. To know what decisions should be made, appropriate state institutions must know something about the social conditions that at least some regard as pressing problems. Second, they must be able to determine whether decisions were actually implemented in response to that awareness. Finally, the state must be able to say whether the results constitute at least an approximation of a solution.[2] These features can be conceptualized as *feedback* capacity. Feedback depends on the availability of *sensors* that collect data and *analytical resources* that are able to conduct data analysis.

A century ago, Max Weber underscored the political importance of feedback and sensors. Weber emphasized the central role of information flow and feedback for the bureaucratic process and defined bureaucracy as "body of arrangements for organizing information and communication into a system for rational decision making and administration" (Bimber 2003, 95). Livingston and Walter Drop explain: "Where information is hard to gather, manage, and distribute, one is more likely to find specialized command-and-control hierarchical institutions— bureaucracies—to manage it" (see Chapter 1, p. 10). This degree of statehood depends on the capacity to collect and process information by decision-makers. The more territory that must be monitored, the more challenging it is to collect and evaluate information about it.

A distributed model of monitoring evaluation suggests that the central government would transfer monitoring and evaluation responsibility to local authorities. However, that requires a certain degree of trust of the regional authorities by the central government. That is missing in Russia. As consequence, the data need to be collected directly by the center. Moreover, the regional authorities themselves are a subject for surveillance by the center.

Another system of sensors is the traditional media. However, if the government controls traditional media, their capacity to provide relevant and valuable information is debatable. Censored media tend to provide skewed, unreliable, and mostly positive feedback. As consequence, a system of sensors must be created to transfer information directly to the center. It requires both an elaborate network of sensors and a significant analytical capacity to evaluate the constant information flow.

The center-oriented autocratic model of information collection is reminiscent of Jeremy Bentham's Panopticon, used metaphorically by Michel Foucault, in which the center surveys the entire system (Foucault [1975] 1995, 195–228). But to what extent is the state capable of surveying the entire system from the top, especially when it is a big country with a high degree of corruption and weak institutional accountability? The purpose of this chapter is to consider whether ICT can strengthen a weak state's monitoring and enforcement capacity by compensating for deficiencies of the classical state bureaucracy, and consequently strengthen statehood.

ICT: Human and Nonhuman Sensors

Mechanism of monitoring and evaluation rely on two types of sensors: human and nonhuman. *Human* sensors are simply people who collect information about the surrounding environment. ICT allows for rapid and low-cost distribution of information collected by individuals to a wider audience (Castells 2007).

Nonhuman sensors are various types of technical devices that can collect information and send it to a central hub. At this point of technological development, the nonhuman sensors are separate devices that were created as dedicated sensors, such as web cameras. In the future, however, with the development of the "Internet of Things," we can assume that things themselves will contain many sensors that are connected to a worldwide network. According to an analysis by Cisco Systems, there will be 25 billion devices connected to the Internet by 2015 and 50 billion by 2020.

The sensors can be deployed on the basis of a central decision in order to collect specific information or cover specific areas. It means that in order to strengthen statehood, a state can deploy or activate human *and* nonhuman sensors.

This chapter provides a number of case studies for deployment of a system of sensors in areas of limited statehood. These cases allow us to analyze the role of ICT-enabled sensors for statehood. The case studies demonstrate how the Russian authorities use ICT to collect and evaluate data relying on human sensors (bloggers, crowdsourcing) and nonhuman sensors (web cameras).

HUMAN SENSORS: CROWDSOURCING AND SOCIAL MEDIA

Research of the Russian blogosphere conducted by the Berkman Center demonstrates the dissonance between traditional media and the space of mass self-communication (Etling et al. 2010). According to other research that was conducted by Medialogy, a data analytics firm, while traditional media tend to focus on "good news" that provides positive feedback to state policies, the Russian blogosphere content has primarily focused on problems and challenges to the state's governance capacity.[3]

If the degree of Internet freedom allows for the sharing of information online, in comparison to the major traditional media that are controlled by government, the Internet turns out to be the most significant resource for negative feedback.[4] This is in keeping with the conclusions reached by Castells: "Mass self-communication provides the technical platform for construction of the autonomy of the social actor, be it individual or collective, vis-à-vis the institutions of society. This is why governments are afraid of the Internet" (Castells 2012, 7). Consequently, as a "negative feedback resource" the Internet can have a crucial role in decision making. The human sensors that might have a political function can be defined as *"citizen sensors."*

There are two types of citizen sensor systems that can be identified online. The first type is the blogosphere and social media. People write blog posts, Facebook updates, tweets, and so on, about various events all over country, including information and opinion about actions by officials and various types of governance services. This type of sensor can focus on a particular institution or particular type of problem.

The flow of mass self-communication provides new opportunities for monitoring the situation all over the country and collecting feedback. Consequently, the government should be able to identify, collect, and analyze the relevant information. In this case the citizen sensors are already deployed and active. The only thing that the authorities need to do is to use the information that is already there.

Collection of feedback from the user-generated content platforms requires development of special media-monitoring software for data mining. In the Russian case, this software was developed by the firm Medialogy and included an iPad application that was able to compare information from social and traditional media about a particular topic and divide it into positive and negative information based on sentiment analysis (Samigullina and Badanin 2010).

A second type of citizen sensor relies on crowdsourcing. Unlike blog monitoring, the state created a dedicated system for the purpose of collecting information from citizens about various fields of policy. An example of crowdsourcing of negative feedback is the website "Rossiya bez durakov" (Russia without fools), which was created by the Russian presidential administration (http://россиябездураков.рф/). The website is actually a countrywide complaint book, where anyone can report problematic decisions or actions by state and regional officials.

The presidential blog and Twitter were also used as tools to collect feedback from citizens. Dmitry Medvedev has said that he reads at least fifty messages a day that have been sent to him through Facebook, Twitter, and other websites. He also said that he uses information from social media for giving direct orders: "Sometimes, when I am preparing to go to work in the morning, I go online and see something very problematic for our country. Then I print the document and write my orders directly on it" (Medvedev 2012).

Even in relatively authoritarian countries, authorities can approach social media not only as a threat, but also as an opportunity to improve monitoring. Citizens who share information online can be seen as a human-based network of sensors. If the classical Panopticon model says that government follows citizens, the new model suggests that the central government could use the citizens as sensors to follow the local government.

Approaching the blogosphere as a network of sensors and a new opportunity for collecting feedback can increase the degree of statehood. At the same time, one can argue that if the president needs Twitter to know what is happening in the country, it demonstrates the failure of the traditional bureaucratic system and, as such, is a symptom of limited statehood. It can be also argued that public engagements with social media and response to complaints can be a part of a public relations strategy that emphasizes that the leaders care about the citizens and are personally involved in the solution of problems (an illustration of vertical power in action).

NONHUMAN SENSORS: WEB CAMERAS

One of the more common types of nonhuman sensor is a CCTV camera. A web camera is any camera connected to the Internet that sends information online. Webcams have a number of unique features:

1. Deployment of sensors and transferring information is relatively inexpensive and easy.
2. Information collected by sensors can be transferred any distance in real time.
3. The information from sensors can be made available to a wide public in real time.

One of the first examples of using web cameras for participatory governance was launched in the United States in 2006. The state of Texas launched an initiative that allowed citizens to participate in watching the border of Mexico for illegal immigrants through a network of surveillance cameras that were connected to the Internet. The watchers were able to follow the cameras through a special website (http://texasborderwatch.com) and e-mail the authorities if they saw any suspicious activities. The initiative was continued through BlueServo.net, a public-private partnership that created "Virtual Community Watch," where individuals could join virtual surveillance teams and alert the nearest sheriff if suspicious activity was identified (NBCNews 2010).

Borderlands are ambivalent areas where the statehood is defined and challenged at the same time. Borders are remote from the center, are close to areas beyond control of the state, and have high degree of security and criminal threats. ICT allows an increasing presence of the state in border areas. The BlueServoSM system includes two elements. The sensors are the webcams that survey the border areas and broadcast real time video online. The analysis of data that is collected by the sensors is crowdsourced through creation of the "Border Watch" community.

However, the role of nonhuman sensors in area of limited statehood can be much more complex than just increasing the capacity of the state to collect and analyze information. That is demonstrated in following case studies that focus on the role of webcams in Russia.

Case Studies

WEB CAMERAS AND FUNCTIONAL GOVERNANCE

In 2005 the Kremlin announced the "national projects" initiative. This initiative designated that some of the projects considered by the central government to be of special importance would get funding from Moscow and would be placed under direct control of the government and the president. This would ensure that they would be implemented and the budget would not be abused.

Two years later, in April 2007, the Russian government released a special directive entitled "A concept for creation of the state's automatic system for informational support of management of the prioritized national projects." One of its stated goals was the collection of audio and video information that would be used to confirm the realization of specific projects. It also designated a number of methods for collecting information and providing it to decision-makers. One of the tools described in the directive is the "mobile multimedia systems" that was to be installed in the office of the president and prime minister. The directive also said that some of the information could be shared with the public "on the official national projects website on the Internet in order to inform the public about how these national projects are realized" (Business Pravo 2009).

In 2007 web cameras were installed on the construction site of the Federal Center for Heart Medicine in Astrakhan. This would allow authorities in Moscow to monitor the pace of construction. Another ten web cameras were also installed in a number of construction sites in several remote regions. According to unconfirmed sources, some of the cameras were deployed without the knowledge of the local authorities.

A story shared by one of the Russian officials shows how the deployment of an Internet-based network of sensors could empower the "power vertical" and increase the degree of statehood. On one occasion, a governor came to meet with President Medvedev to tell him about recent developments in his region. Medvedev asked him about progress on the building of a new hospital that was being funded by federal money. The governor responded that the construction was moving forward fast and would be completed soon. Then Medvedev turned the screen of his computer towards the governor to display the web camera based live broadcast from the construction site. The site on the screen was empty.

It might be argued that the cameras are an indicator of limited statehood. A functioning state does not need cameras to verify that its bureaucracy is doing what it is supposed to do. However, the cameras can also be understood as an innovative part of a solution. The case demonstrates that deployment of networked sensors, and web cameras in particular, can strengthen a weak state's governance capacity and increase the state's ability to implement and enforce political decisions. At the same time, as the following case studies demonstrate, the functional role of the web cameras for increasing statehood can also be secondary and limited.

WEBCAMS AND WILDFIRES: ICT AS A MEANS
FOR SYMBOLIC STATEHOOD

While the Russian government has used cameras for monitoring since 2007, the first use to attracted broad public attention was in 2010. In late July 2010, Russia experienced unprecedented wildfires that killed more than sixty people and destroyed dozens of villages. A thick smog blanketed a number of cities, including Moscow.

In addition to the devastation that was caused by the fires, the natural disaster also led to citizens' increasing distrust of the government.[5] Citizens also personally verbally attacked Prime Minister Putin during his visit to one of the villages that was heavily damaged by the fire. During a meeting with victims of wildfires on August 3, Putin said this about the reconstruction process: "One of the most efficient methods of control is 24-hour surveillance. Therefore I gave an order to place cameras on every significant construction site and three monitors: one in the White House (the Russian government compounds—G.A.), one at my home, and one more—on the government website." Putin emphasized that this would allow citizens to follow what happens at construction sites (Dni.ru 2010). Following Putin's order, a special dedicated page was launched on the prime minister's website, where anyone could follow one of thirty-five cameras located in twenty-eight villages.

The cameras were presented as a measure to increase transparency and accountability in post-emergency responses. However, the fact that the installation of cameras was presented as a symbol of accountability does not necessarily mean that the content that is provided by them led to that result. To what extent can thirty-five web cameras that broadcast twenty-four hours per day online really provide information about emergency relief and the progress of the work? One may question the significance of the scope of reality that is represented by a few dozen cameras.

Some citizens did not trust the cameras and suggested that the initiative's purpose was the creation of an impression of accountability. A cartoon that was distributed online following Putin's initiative showed a webcam installed opposite a painting of a beautiful green and sunny village house. Both the camera and the picture are surrounded by wildfires, and a human skeleton sits under the column supporting the webcam.[6] Other citizens argued that the cameras were a distraction that were used to cover up inappropriate usage of the reconstruction budget. "The cameras should be placed in the office of officials where they share money," wrote an anonymous Internet user.

While ICT can provide a decision enforcement mechanism and increase the degree of statehood, at the same it can be used for the symbolic construction of transparency and accountability that substitute for real measures of transparency and accountability. The thirty-five webcams that broadcast live images represent a narrow and selected part of reality. Eventually, ICT enabled a new method to create virtual Potemkin villages. ICT is able not only to contribute to transparency, but also to create an illusion of transparency. One can argue, that in this case, the medium (web cameras) is the message (transparency and accountability).

The web cameras have an additional role for statehood. Prime Minister Putin emphasized that he would follow the information from the cameras personally via special monitors. The webcam system was used to send a message that the president is keeping the situation under his personal control. A capacity to enforce decisions is substituted by the construction of a symbolic statehood through the image of control. The symbolic function of web cameras as an image of statehood is reminiscent of the function of the Panopticon for power, as described by Foucault. What is really important in the Panopticon is not the actual capacity to see everything, but the design of the system in such a way that it sends a message that everything is under control. To some extent, the Panopticon is more powerful as a symbol of surveillance than the methodology of surveillance. However, if in the classical case the Panopticon is used for suppression of individuals, in the case of limited statehood it is transformed into a strategy for deception that seeks to convince the citizens that the state is still able to govern. Deployment of sensors is a symbolic act of statehood that substitutes policy-making and decision enforcement for show. Any project for deployment of networked sensors can serve both functional and symbolic purposes, but the balance between these two can be different in various political systems.

SENSORS AND LEGITIMACY: THE CASE OF THE RUSSIAN PRESIDENTIAL ELECTIONS OF 2012

The next big state-backed project that used web cameras was the monitoring of presidential elections. This time it was not only a question of control over the bureaucratic system or accountability, but also the existential issue of legitimacy of the political leadership. Following the questionable results of elections to the Russian parliament, the Duma, in December 2011, the presidential elections took place in a sensitive political situation. Thousands of Russian citizens protested against election fraud and demanded fair presidential elections.

ICT played a significant role in exposing the degree of fraud. A special crowd-sourcing platform, "Map of Violations" (http://kartanarusheniy.org), collected reports for citizens about a variety of election frauds. Mobile phones and cameras were actively used to create visual proof of falsifications, which were immediately shared online. Many activists who had witnessed fraud, either while voting or while working as observers, posted their testimonies online. The significant increase in the number of human and nonhuman sensors following the elections created a critical mass of evidence that brought into question not only the legitimacy of the parliamentary elections, but also the upcoming presidential election (Asmolov 2011a). Crowdsourcing platform, as one of the forms of mass self-communication, allowed challenging the balance of power and questioning the capacity of the state to control information about elections fraud.

The Panopticon as a conceptual model helps us to understand the nature of this change. In Jeremy Bentham's original prison design, prisoners inhabit an outer ring of cells, all cut off from one another. At the center of the ring is an observation space occupied by the guards. The guards can see each of the prisoners without themselves being seen. Thus, the prisoners never know whether they are being watched. ICT attenuates the centralized observational power of centered authority by offer an opportunity to those on the periphery to communicate and share information among themselves. Networked surveillance has reversed the power relationship such that the center is now observable by a citizen-based network of sensors.

Fredrik Sjoberg argues that because ICT has increased the cost of election manipulation, authoritarian states must now find new election strategies (Sjoberg 2012). The government has to protect the legitimacy of the elections and respond to the emergence of the counter-power of citizen-based sensors. It can restore the balance either by restricting the citizen-based system of sensors or by harnessing the citizen's sensors to the state-backed system. Both options unfolded in Russia.

A few days after the parliamentary elections, Vladimir Putin (this time the Russian presidential candidate) offered to put webcams on all polling stations in Russia. He explained that the country should see what happens at every polling box, as a way to eliminate fraud as well as to minimize the capacity to argue after the elections that the voting process was unfair.

It was not the first time that web cameras were used for election monitoring. The pioneer in this regard was Azerbaijan, which introduced a webcamera real-time monitoring system in their 2008 elections. The cameras there were deployed in 10 percent of polling stations (Sjoberg 2012). However, the scale of Russia's project was unprecedented. In less than three months, Russian authorities wanted to construct what could probably be considered the largest network of visual sensors in human history to cover the territory of the biggest country of the world.

Russia had approximately 95,000 polling stations. The number of polling stations that were covered was 91,000, with more than 180,000 cameras (every station had two cameras). Of these, 80,000 cameras broadcasted live-stream online. The rest recorded videos that were supposed to be available on request following the elections. One camera in a station was focused on the polling box, and another camera showed a general view, including the registration table. After the voting was completed, the cameras broadcasted the votes being counted.

The project, with a budget of about 13 billion rubles (around half a billion dollars), was given to the state's telecommunication company, Rostelecom. The most expensive part of the project was development of infrastructure to allow connecting all the stations. It also included creation of nine centers for data collection, where the video archives were stored after the elections.

On the day of elections Internet users could access a special website http://Webvybory2012.ru. It had a big map of Russia covered with dots of polling stations. One could zoom in to a particular region or find a particular polling station through a search engine. Once a user had chosen a particular polling station, he could switch between the two cameras and follow the events there not only visually but also with sound.

In addition to the website, two big video walls were constructed to demonstrate the video on the day of elections. One video wall with twenty LCD monitors was installed in the main office of the Central Election Committee. Another wall with thirty-six monitors was placed in the "Elections 2012" information center. The head of the Russian election committee, Vladimir Churov, praised the technology: "For the first time in history we can see in real time the opening of the polls in Chukotka, which is eight time zones away from us. For the first time in history we can see everything in the polling station" (RIA Novosti 2012a).

According to the Under Development company that was responsible for the http://Webvybory2012.ru website, 3.5 million Internet users visited the website and watched about 7.9 million video streams. Among them, 914,000 were from Moscow and the Moscow region, 308,000 from Saint Petersburg and its region, and 112,000 from the Krasnodar region. Four million hours of video were recorded (1,350 TB). The most viewed regions included Moscow (3 million streams), the first region that started to vote—Chukotka region (2.1 million), and Chechnya (1.3 million streams). The most popular polling station for video streaming was a private house in Mesedoy village in Chechnya (RIA Novosti 2012b).

On March 5, the day following elections, Putin summarized the role of the project as follows: "I think that - not 100 percent, but to a certain extent - they (web cameras—G.A.) played a role and increased the transparency of the process." Putin noted that no other country in the world has created this type of system, and promised to continue "improvement of the electoral procedures, increasing transparency and minimizing, reducing to zero violations" (RIA Novosti 2012c).

Experts and citizen activists, however, questioned this evaluation of the role of the system and argued that the cameras were not able to identify a number of potential and significant types of manipulation, that is, illegal changes in the protocols of voting or multiple voting by the same people.

In his analysis of web cameras in the Azerbaijan elections, Sjoberg (2012) argues that "authorities adjust their fraud strategies in the presence of a particular monitoring technique." He suggests that the ruling power is able to introduce compensation mechanisms that "are able to prevent vote share losses, while contributing a veneer of legitimacy by self-initiating anti-fraud measures."

The case of Russia is different from the case of Azerbaijan, first because—according to Sjoberg—the major compensation mechanism was selective allocation of web cameras in "less fraudulent precincts." However, in Russia cameras covered the majority of polling stations, and therefore allocation bias was not possible. Second, in Russia, in comparison to Azerbaijan, the degree of Internet penetration as well as Internet activism is higher.

In the Russian case, however, we can see more complicated compensation mechanisms. Even if people could see illegal activity occurring on their screen, there was little they could do about it. The system had not provided any mechanism for submission of complaints if something wrong were to occur. It also had no mechanism for recording the broadcasts. The recordings from cameras were stored in data centers and the public could submit an official request to get a limited amount of video footage. However, the process was complicated and time consuming.

Furthermore, the legal status of video recording in the courts was not defined. When an oppositional politician from Astrakhan, Oleg Shein, collected evidence of falsification from webcams in his city, the head of the central election committee responded that there were "procedural problems" and the court refused to cancel the results of voting. Ultimately, none of the 4 million hours of video footage led to a criminal conviction of election fraud or revision of election results in any of the polling stations. Deputy director of the independent monitoring organization Golos, Grigory Melkonyantz, says that in some cases judges refused to request webcam footage or accept it as legitimate evidence in fraud investigations.[7]

The large number of cameras that were available for surveillance via the Webvybory website made it difficult to focus on a particular place. An offline observer has usually one polling station to monitor for the entire day. But when people have access to 80,000 stations, it is more difficult to achieve meaningful results. Information overload reduces the efficiency of surveillance. Unlike the classical Panopticon, in this Panopticon the citizens had access to the governmental network of sensors. However, the system's architecture led to sporadic gazing instead of meaningful systematic observation that could lead to viable outcomes.

Online activists addressed some of these challenges. Tech-savvy Internet users developed a few methods for recording the webcasting from polling stations. Following the elections, some groups tried to conduct analysis of data that was collected. However, doing so proved to be time consuming. Still, despite this handicap, the analysis revealed many examples of elections fraud. For example, one video captured images of the same handful of persons voting many times in Chechnya. Even members of a local elections committee could be observed doing so.[8] Despite these limitations, according to Grigory Melkonyantz, the Webvybory system engaged the public in monitoring, limited the scope of potential manipulations, and provided proof that the state was not willing to investigate strong evidence of fraud.

At the same time, the webcam-based surveillance turned out to offer major entertainment value as the biggest reality show in Russian history. The most popular polling station was a private home in Chechnya, where Internet users could follow a family, including the children, sitting around the table. Obviously no significant fraud could take place there, since this station had only a few registered voters. The Russian blogosphere was full of comic images that were taken on webcams such as observers falling asleep, a kissing couple, and an automatic rifle left on the committee table in a polling station in the Caucasus.

In many cases the motivation for surveillance had nothing to do with politics. People used the system to see how their old school looked, or watched their relatives and friends in other cities vote. Russian communication minister Igor Schegolev said the Webvybory "is a social video network that allows the country to see itself" and watch how Russian citizens live in other regions (RIA Novosti 2012d). A popular blogger Varlamov wrote in his Twitter feed: "Thanks to web-cameras people from Moscow discovered today the existence of the rest of the country."

In the summer of 2010, at the Tver Forum, President Medvedev said that the Internet contributes to rebuilding the territorial integrity of the country and argued that e-government allows for creating an undivided space within the borders of Russia. In some ways, the Webvybory project did contribute to statehood, by allowing a symbolic self-reflexivity of the state for its citizens. Thanks to the mediation of ICT, a fragmented physical territory was transformed into a more united space.

To conclude, the case of the Webvybory project goes beyond the imitation of transparency and illusion of accountability. The architecture of the system promised that the only result of it could be increased legitimacy. A system that in theory would be able to collect feedback and translate it into decision-making instead resulted in the construction of a façade of a system able get feedback and respond to it. The webcam project was not really created by the government to get more information about the election process. Rather it was an overly large sensor system constructed in a way that feedback could not be collected nor make an impact on the electoral process, while it functions to maintain and protect the status quo.

The Webvybory project has not led to a reconsideration of the election results. According to official results, Putin received 63.6% of votes, while some independent groups argued that the real degree of support just over 50% (Nichol 2012, 6).[9] At the same time, it should not be a surprise that while people went out into the streets to protest the election results, the official response was that the web cameras had made the elections fair and the most transparent in the world. Eventually, the Webvybory system was used not only to legitimize the results of elections, but also to delegitimize protests against the election results.

MOSCOW SNOWFALLS 2013 AND "PHOTOSHOP GOVERNANCE"

Another example of video surveillance as a digital Potemkin Village is found in an initiative in Moscow. In 2011, Moscow City Government launched the crowdsourcing platform "Our city: A portal for city governance" (http://gorod.mos.ru) in order to give citizens the ability to submit complaints about problems in city, as well as to express gratitude if something good has been done. According to the rules of the website, any complaint approved by moderator has to be responded within eight days by a relevant authority. In short order, the website received dozens thousands of complaints. Many of them apparently lead to solution of a problem brought to the attention of the city government. It would seem to be a positive innovation to city governance. Yet, some users questioned the efficiency of the website. Local media argued that the most active complainers were blocked by moderators and the website was accused of embellishing reality. Some users also argued that the platform had a suspicious number of "thank-you" messages posted to local authorities.

In winter of 2012–2013, due to the heavy snowfall, the city was almost paralyzed, and clearing the snow became major issue on the media agenda. One of the people who complained about situation through the website was a blogger and activist named Yuriy Ursu. Ursu submitted a message that said that the snow in front of his building hadn't been cleared for a long time. To prove the point he attached a photo of his snowbound building. A couple of days later day, the local authority of Orekhovo-Zuevo that was responsible for this neighborhood responded that the problem had been solved, the snow was cleared from his building, and that the local contractor responsible for the service was issued a fine. A photo with a cleaned path to the building was attached to this message.

When Ursu checked the attached photo he saw that it had been edited with Photoshop. He immediately went to take a new photo of the same location, clearly showing that the snow had been cleaned only in virtual reality. In the real world, the snow remained. When Ursu submitted a new complaint to the portal, it was blocked by a moderator. Ursu also wrote official letters to the mayor and local prosecutor office and posted the story and many updates on his personal blog. The blog post included detailed analysis of the image that proved that Photoshop was used in order to remove the snow (Ursu 2013).

Russian liberal media celebrated Moscow city government's "new strategy" for snow. It suggested that "Photoshop governance" should be used in order to solve a variety of problems, including traffic and lack of parking places. A few days later, Leonid Bogatyrev, the head of the Orekhovo-Zuevo district where the incident took place, resigned. According to official version, his resignation was voluntary. Moreover, another false response on crowdsourcing platform was identified through an internal investigation of Moscow government. A mayor of Moscow, Sergey Sobyanin, declared that there was a revolution in city management since every person who lives in the city is an inspector (or one would say a sensor) (Protzenko 2013).

In addition to human sensors, the Moscow government declared that the snow is monitored through a large network of nonhuman sensors. According to Artem Ermolaev, the head of IT department of the city government, the authorities use 87,000 cameras deployed all over the city and 53 human monitors to keep track of city business. The city conducts inspections that can lead to punishments where a local contractor fails to clear the snow in specific area.

Moreover, as a result of the "Photoshop scandal," the city government announced the formation of a special "feedback unit" that is to take photos of the places that were a subject to complaint. Once the problem has been remedied, a photo of the resolved issue will be posted online. According to Russian newspaper *Izvestia*, the officials want in this way to protect themselves from further "Photoshop scandals" (Basharova 2013).

"Clearing" the snow with Photoshop is a good example of digital Potemkin villages. Photoshop, in this case, is another substitution for action, a mere imitation of governance that conceals the degree of limited statehood. However, no less important is the fact that this practice was exposed and transformed into a scandal that forced the government to respond.

The way the scandal emerged demonstrates the power of the crowd to expose a fraud and attract attention not only to the problem, but also to the manipulation. The Internet user successfully employed a variety of means, including crowdsourcing platform, his personal blog, and official channels, in order to put the issue on the agenda.

While the efficiency of the Moscow government is still questionable, we can see that ICT leads to a change in the rules of the games around the accountability of authorities. Even if the technology was created to only imitate openness, transparency, and effective governance, it still eventually forced local authorities to adapt to a new information environment, one where the power of crowds wouldn't allow them to conduct simple manipulations. It also forces the officials to change the monitoring and control practices, as well as the organizational structure, in order to be able to deal with emerging surveillance power of the citizens.

At the same time, one can argue, the impact is limited since the government frames the problems in such a way, that only mid-level officials (e.g., heads of districts) and contractors held accountable, while the top leadership remains beyond the reach of accountability. From this perspective, ICT not only increases transparency and accountability but also frames accountability in a way that serves the interests of those who launched the system.

ANALYSIS: SENSOR POLARIZATION AND THE STATEHOOD BUBBLE

While statehood depends on the capacity of the state to collect and process information, ICT enables new strategies and methods to fulfill these tasks and, consequently, to increase the degree of statehood. It includes various technologies that allow deploying sensors or collecting information from existent human sensors, as well as applications for analyzing collected data and incorporating it into decision making.

However, what the case studies above demonstrate is that the new opportunities can be used in different ways and for different purposes. ICT can provide a toolbox for the imitation of transparency and accountability. It suggests a new means for the symbolic construction of statehood.

While ICT can increase statehood, in some political environments it leads to the opposite effect. For some political leaders, the symbolic power of ICT is more tempting than its functional capacities. Manipulation with ICT substitutes for action. A symbolic construction of statehood that relies on deployment of sensors and surveillance becomes a strategy to mask the state's inability to deliver basic public goods. The Russian webcam system was not created for monitoring reality, but for constructing reality.

In case these symbolic constructions are challenged by the counter-power of the citizens' mass self-communication, state-backed ICT systems can make an effort to restore the balance of power by limiting or harnessing the power of citizens, as well as distracting them from the problems. Citizen-based systems of sensors tend to provide more negative feedback that challenges the existent status quo and requires action to address social and political problems. State-sponsored systems of sensors are constructed in a way that provides positive feedback, with some with controlled negative feedback that focuses on specific institutional segments (e.g., regional bureaucracy) without challenging the top of the ruling power vertical. Consequently, the purpose of this system is to preserve the status quo (legitimize inaction) and avoid signals that require significant action.

Both systems are interrelated. While state-sponsored systems of sensors provide positive feedback with a controlled degree of negative information, citizen-based systems of sensors continue to collect and share a constant flow of negative feedback. However, traditional institutions ignore this feedback, since it challenges their political interests.

One the one hand, in the short term the deployment of sensors focused on the construction of symbolic statehood through the imitation of control and accountability can provide relative political stability. Surveillance systems designed to preserve the political status quo can temporarily improve state legitimacy. On the other hand, the constant flow of positive feedback creates an existential threat to any system. The state and its decisions become increasingly disconnected from reality.

Polarization of the two systems of sensors can lead to a point where dissonance can undermine the state's legitimacy and foment immediate socio-political unrest. The bubble of a symbolic statehood that relies on ICT-mediated construction can explode. It can lead not only to a wave of protests, but also the emergence of new modes of governance that provide an alternative to the inaction of the authorities.

Russian authorities have a rich and diverse e-government program. There is no doubt that development of e-government can contribute to the strengthening of statehood, as well as improve governmental services provided to citizens, increase transparency and accountability, and allow new forms of citizens' participation. However, these opportunities also provide new tools of manipulation. The case studies presented here have demonstrated that the manipulation is likely. However, ICT as a tool for the imitation of statehood and construction of legitimacy is not sustainable. Dysfunctional bureaucratic structures cannot be compensated for by the deployment of sensors, nor can decision making be replaced by observation. Such measures can postpone the crisis, but can also make the collapse more significant and inevitable.

In the fairytale "The Emperor's New Clothes," Hans Christian Andersen tells about two weavers who leave the Emperor naked after they promise him unique suite that won't be visible for stupid and incompetent people. The officials, the public, and the king himself afraid to confess that they can't see anything until the moment a child cries out, "But he isn't wearing anything at all!" ICT can provide invisible threads that enable weaving a new attire of statehood, but this only works until the Internet crowd exposes that the state is naked.

Notes

1. Most historians agree that the Potemkin villages are probably a myth.
2. Murray Edelman has noted that politics involves the specification of some social conditions as problems worthy of consideration by the polity (Edelman 1988).
3. Based on F. Husnoyarov (2010) on about monitoring and analysis of media and blogosphere in real time [RUS], eGov 2.0 conference 2010.
4. According to the "Freedom on the Net" report the Russian Internet is considered "partly free" (Kelly and Cook 2011).
5. According to a public opinion poll by the Levada Center, most of the citizens of Russia haven't changed their opinion about the government following wildfires; however, most Russians believed that the authorities were not able to provide appropriate response when the disaster started wildfires [Levada Center 2010]).
6. The cartoon, originally posted at www.yaplakal.com, can be found here: http://irevolution.net/2011/04/03/icts-limited-statehood/(Meier 2011b).
7. Based on interview that was conducted by the author (September 3, 2012).
8. "Falsifikatziya vyborov presidenta RF v Chechne. Yavka 99%," http://www.youtube.com/watch?v=jxf-nRTDvGQ.
9. For a statistical analysis of Russian elections results, please see Klimek, Yegorov, Hanel, and Thurner (2012).

4

E-government as a Means of Development in India

J. P. SINGH

Introduction

E-government expanded in India as the country leapfrogged from its limited landline-based infrastructure to its tremendous success with mobile telephony in the last decade. With 63 mobile and 7.5 Internet users per 100 population in 2010, the central and provincial governments in India are trying to leverage the information infrastructure and other resources to make expansive commitments toward provision of goods and services through electronic government (see Table 4.1).[1] For example, e-Sagu in Andhra Pradesh allows farmers to obtain information online from experts, Bhoomi in Karnataka enables easy access to land records, and recent graduates of high schools or college manage e-Seva information kiosks in Madhya Pradesh to provide services in rural areas. Meanwhile the national portal—india.gov.in—hosts over 5,000 government websites, including those for provincial and local governments. However, e-government in India, as one analyst notes, can be more about enhancing the "e" of technology rather than improving governance (Satyanarayana 2011, 1). E-government initiatives are often top-down and do not cater effectively to societal or business demands. They are also unsustainable financially and do not scale well. Despite this, there are success stories.

This essay evaluates the partially successful and the not so successful e-government initiatives in India to focus on the conditions for success and failure. Following the introduction, the term *e-governance* is employed to connote delivery of services in general, while *e-government* indicates such delivery from government units.[2] The next section provides the overall context for limited statehood and governance in India—the macro outline for understanding the environment within which e-government operates in India. The subsequent section examines India's relative success in the last decade with provision of an information infrastructure, the "backbone" for e-government and governance initiatives. The final two sections examine the operations of specific e-government and e-governance initiatives.

The key factors for the partial success of a few e-government initiatives include adequate telecommunication and human resources, societal and business demands, and well-placed champions within governments. Furthermore, e-government initiatives in India are most successful at the basic level—access to information and records, downloading government forms, and payment of utility bills—rather than providing for interactivity, dispute settlement, or a broader transformation in the relationship between government and the people.[3] To use Earl and Kimport's (2011) terms, analyzed in the introductory chapter, e-government in India is most successful in leveraging the information infrastructure for the affordance of a few services that come in bits or digitized forms. India's overall limited statehood stands in the way of moving any atoms or material resources. However, even the provision of bits reaches areas where state capacity was limited or inefficient, therefore contributing to state consolidation in micro ways.

Limited Statehood and Governance in India

Limited statehood in India comes with a paradox: The state is almost omnipresent in people's lives but circumscribed in its authority and legitimacy. In the immediate post-colonial era, the state carried enormous clout, but its mandate frittered away under limited resources and pluralistic pressures. At present, limited statehood in India can be noticed as much in the vast rural hinterlands out of government's reach as in the "proximate" urban spaces such as slums or the government's own departments, often incapacitated with internal fractures and external pressures.

Limited statehood in India resulted from unfulfilled post-colonial promises across a diverse and vast demography with rising pressures for governance. The post-colonial Indian state inherited a broad consensus regarding its role in economic development. During the 1950s, with Prime Minister Nehru at the helm, India came as close as ever to the notion of the consolidated state. By the 1970s, the Indian state found it hard to deliver on the promises made through a strategy of state-led domestic industrialization, which devolved into centralized control known as the *license-quota-permit-Raj* and reached only urban areas. The pressures on the state from agricultural farmers and private industry, often ignored in Indian politics, and the rising middle-income groups led to a breakdown in centralized control that allowed for market incentives. New forms of governance, such as empowering local governments, also emerged. Nevertheless, the myriad external pressures confront a rent-seeking state-machine that profits even from moves toward decentralization. The Indian government is one of the most corrupt in the world, and its biggest scandals have involved officials receiving bribes and payoffs while provisioning market licenses. These include high-profile cases involving telecommunication ministers in the last two decades. For example, the telecommunications minister Sukh Ram was indicted for corruption during telecommunication equipment sales in 1996 after Rs. 36 million in cash stuffed in suitcases was seized from his residence.

The internal fractures within the state point to its limitedness. At face value, the state possesses vast machinery—over 21 million government officials presiding over 1.3 billion people. In proportional terms, the limited state becomes apparent. As one recent analysis pointed out, there are only 1,622 government employees for every 100,000 people in India, as compared to 7,681 in the United States (*The Hindu* 2012). Of the 3.1 million federal or central government employees, nearly 45 percent are in state-run railways and, interestingly, 7.25 percent are in information and communication departments. Being a government official is a passport to having enormous power over large numbers of people, but a few cannot meet the demands of many. Politicians and bureaucracy are accustomed to being unresponsive to societal demands while, on the other hand, witnessing the clunky pluralism of the state resulting from India's democratic politics and the multi-party system. In the past, I have called the Indian state "dysfunctional," given the combination of internal incapacity and external pressures (J. P. Singh 1999). Comparatively, a state such as China or Singapore may be viewed as "catalytic" or relatively consolidated, in being internally well behaved and externally well situated to contain pressures (Singh 1999, chapters 3-4). State types are products of history, and thus the comparative statement is merely descriptive, not a value preference for one over another.

The task of governance is complicated for limited statehood: Prioritizing demands from areas it cannot reach is hard; containing internal divisions or external pressures further limit state capacity. These problems can spillover into e-government. It may be unclear to government which user groups and services should be prioritized. For example, given limited resources, should e-government focus on rural areas and agricultural information, or urban areas and interactive public service delivery? Second, even when prioritized, governance can devolve into inefficiencies and corruption—the business as usual in the Indian state—and many e-government plans may not be implemented or implementable.

The changing relationship of the government with the people, however, offers the most compelling clue toward improving governance in India. The term *sarkar* or government in Hindi, India's official language, historically carried connotations of an authority to be looked up to and obeyed, meeting the Weberian criterion of legitimacy or a consolidated state. The post-colonial state, including many leaders of the Indian nationalist movement, commanded moral authority in the public sphere of governance. It would not be far-fetched to say that *sarkar* now commands neither due obedience nor moral authority, meeting instead the conditions of limited statehood. However, within this changing ideology of *sarkar* may be located marginalized societal and business voices, at once impatient with India's limited statehood and demanding better governance. At an everyday level, these steps are barely noticeable, and India's lively mass media disseminate a daily dosage of government corruption and inefficiency. Over the long run, governance may be changing. For example, the halting steps India took toward the provision of an information infrastructure provide the first clue toward the ways in which better governance can emerge through limited statehood.

Provision of Information Infrastructure

E-governance requires an adequate information infrastructure. In India's case, the advent of mobile telephony in the last decade has made the difference—a leapfrogged infrastructure that expanded despite, rather than because of, the state's efforts. This followed intense pressures for telecommunications from middle-income and business groups since the 1980s. It took a while for telecommunication reform to get a hold: Indian telecommunication liberalization in the 1990s was driven by a state whose capacity and consensus frittered away over the last fifty years under the weight of pluralistic pressures and personalistic rule (such as under the so-called *Nehru-Gandhi dynasty*).

Limited statehood, as the introductory chapter notes, varies in its efforts to accommodate inputs into governance or effectively streamlining the outputs. Indian reform efforts in the 1980s were halting and nepotistic even though demands from businesses, urban residential users, and government administrations continued to grow. India was pushed further toward telecommunications liberalization after a severe fiscal and balance of payments crisis in 1991 that weakened the status quo constituencies in the country and empowered many businesses to demand liberalization. Specialized services, including cellular, were liberalized between 1991 and 1994, and basic telephone service was liberalized after the announcement of the National Telecommunications Policy in 1994. The 1994 policy announced ambitious goals for provision of telephones (20 million lines by 2000) and also liberalized the telecommunications sector further. The state owned monopoly, then called the Department of Telecommunications (DoT), could not be corporatized or privatized due to resistance from its 480,000 workers tacitly supported by 18 million employees in other state-owned enterprises. DoT was to compete with a private player in each of the twenty-one regions, known as Telecom Circles, but the complex licensing procedures, marred by government corruption and resistance from DoT, led to marginal service provision in only six of the twenty-one circles by 2000. The pro-business BJP party government announced a New Telecom Policy in 1999 (NTP 99), which tried to streamline the licensing process and free prospective operators of heavy license fee burdens through revenue-sharing arrangements. The operators were still shy of investment given lack of autonomous and transparent regulatory clout. In particular, foreign investment in telecommunication had slowed down to a trickle by 2000. NTP 99 also divided DoT into a policy-making body (named DoT) and a service provider, Department of Telecom Services (DTS). NTP 99 renewed plans for corporatization of DTS, and the corporation BSNL came into being in 2000, which at present has a customer share of nearly 100 million landline and mobile providers.

Each stage of the liberalization process in India was marked with awarding of contracts and licenses to those with most access to the state's decision-making processes along with many court battles and scandals. Limited statehood meant that groups found it hard to get their demands met from the state. While many groups with high demands for services (large businesses, exporters, urban users) continued to be denied services, the state also hedged between providing services to these groups and rural areas where more than two-thirds of Indian voters live but where the teledensity was only 0.4. All of India's 650,000 villages were to have connectivity by 1996, according to NTP 94, but by 2000 not even half that number had connectivity.

The phenomenal growth rate in mobile telephony (see Table 4.1) in the last decade followed not just liberalization of the Indian mobile market but also the separation of policy, regulatory, and dispute settlement functions in Indian telecommunications. The creation and sustenance of the regulatory authority, the Telecommunication Regulatory Authority of India (TRAI), was delayed with opposition from the DoT, which was loathe to give up its authority. From 1994 to 1997, the state hedged on TRAI creation, and even after it came into being, its decisions were publicly challenged by the DoT and not implemented. Because of the weak mandate given to TRAI, its willingness to play an aggressive role against the DoT/BSNL after 1997 was marred by judgments against its authority in the Indian courts. BJP moved toward strengthening TRAI authority in March 2000 and also created an independent Telecom Dispute Settlement and Appellate Authority (TDSAT) to arbitrate between operators and government. Despite the measures taken to create independent regulatory and dispute settlement authorities, politicians and government officials benefitted immensely from bribes. Telecommunications Minister Andimuthu Raja was charged in 2010 for a loss of $39 billion in revenues to the national treasury in 2008 after preferential 2G spectrum sales.

The context for infrastructural provision is important because it provides the backdrop for the e-governance efforts that began in the late-1990s. Interestingly, deregulation and infrastructural reform efforts work well in the case of limited statehood: the infrastructure offers an important instance of leapfrogging, even with a rent-seeking state appropriating revenues. Deregulation efforts also resulted in parallel state consolidation through design of regulatory and dispute settlement institutions. Most importantly, mobile phones now reach areas of limited statehood: 60 percent of India's urban population, or 240 million people,

Table 4.1 **Information Infrastructure in India**

Indicator Name	1990	1995	2000	2005	2010
Telephone lines (per 100 people)	0.58	1.24	3.08	4.40	2.87
Mobile cellular subscriptions (per 100 people)	0	0.008	0.34	7.91	61.42
Internet users (per 100 people)	0	0.026	0.53	2.39	7.5

Source: World Bank, World Development Indicators, World dataBank. Accessed August 2, 2012. http://databank.worldbank.org/ddp/home.do.

lives in slums; 65 percent of the country's total population, about 1.13 billion people, lives in rural areas in India's more than 600,000 villages (LC Singh 2009, xi).

Before the BJP government lost at the Parlimentary elections in 2004, it had run a stylish media campaign called "India Shining" that boasted of Indian growth rates in the post-1992 liberalization era. It was clear that India had only been shining for the 200 million high- and middle-income groups in urban areas. The urban poor and the rural populations had been ignored. While areas of limited statehood, the deregulation efforts at least readied them for future forms of e-governance provision, connecting them nominally to out-of-reach bureaucracies or getting prioritized for governance services through businesses and NGOs as described below.

Enter National e-governance

The history of e-governance initiatives in India must be understood within the context of an omnipresent but limited statehood or *sarkar* and the pluralist pressures the state faces to deliver on governance. In terms of omnipresence, we see the emergence of a techno-state, to use language building on Bruno Latour's (1987) analysis of the institutional context for technology, which tries to dominate in defining the meaning of electronic technology for people. In terms of pluralism, popular pressures begin to move the techno-state toward transparency and at the local level in the provision of governance services.

The central government in India dominates policy-planning; as a political system, India is often viewed as federal in form but unitary or centralized in spirit, even though provincial governments have grown in authority in the last decade. The story of National Informatics Centre (NIC) is instructive for the origins of the techno-state in e-governance. NIC was created in 1976 with $4.1 million United Nations Development Programme funding just as the central Indian government began to contemplate the potential of information technologies for government. One of its first networks was low-cost satellite VSAT-based NICNET, which connects 55 departments of the central government, with 35 provincial and 540 district headquarters. Not only was the initiative top-down, NICNET never achieved its purpose of providing an effective network for government interactions and decision-making. Nevertheless, it remains an early instance of state entrepreneurship in introducing an electronic culture, and many of the bureaucrats associated with NIC, including the founder N. Seshagiri, were champions of pushing the vision of an electronic culture in Indian government (Gautam 1996).

The next major step in e-governance came from the convening of National Conference in e-governance starting in 1997, which popularized the idea of e-government for provincial authorities and led to exchange of best practices. The Department of Information Technology in the central government has been a key sponsor. The sixteenthth conference in February 2013 focused on "Toward and Open Government" as its theme. The National Awards for e-Governance are also sponsored through these conferences.

Other steps in e-government also came from New Delhi, which often unveils new initiatives through its five-year planning exercises that set priorities and influence budget allocations. The Prime Minister's National Task Force on Information Technology and Software Development in 1998 recommended that all government departments should be required to prepare an IT plan and to allocate 1 to 3 percent of their budgets. This was impossible to implement and achieve.

The National E-Governance Action Plan was approved in 2006, which the Department of Information Technology summarizes as follows:

> The National e-Governance Plan (NeGP), takes a holistic view of e-Governance initiatives across the country, integrating them into a collective vision, a shared cause. Around this idea, a massive countrywide infrastructure reaching down to the remotest of villages is evolving, and large-scale digitization of records is taking place to enable easy, reliable access over the internet [sic]. The ultimate objective is to bring public services closer home to citizens, as articulated in the Vision Statement of NeGP. (DeitY 2012)

NeGP also entails NIC providing connectivity from the national to the local levels with the goal of bringing about decentralized administration and envisages government provision of services through electronic means. It would be difficult for a technological network to bring about decentralization by itself: Ironically, NIC succeeded in centralizing the access to all levels of Indian government through the national portal—india.gov.in. The site provides information on all levels of the Indian government. A few standard features of provincial websites include a feature to send complaints or e-mails to the chief inister, the de-facto elected executive authority in Indian provinces, and a listing of portals that provide informational or other services (utility payments, tickets for travel, downloading forms for government services). Below the state-level, the district and sub-district sites do not provide any useful or important information except for a handful of cases. For example, the icon labeled "e-governance" for my home district of Solan in Himachal Pradesh leads to a listing of all information technology equipment installed in offices of the district government (Solan 2012). A few provinces list the kinds of services that individuals can access at the local level, but most of them are not aggregated for access, leaving it to the user to figure out the services gateways among the many websites available on the portal. However, many of the websites do appear in many of the local languages such as Hindi, Gujarati, and Tamil. Central and provincial e-government budgets include expenditures for information intermediaries because of the policy imperative that citizens need an intermediary—a computer operator at information kiosks, for example—when accessing services.

Many bottom-up pressures have developed concurrently with the top-down e-government initiatives. Starting at the individual level, the Right to Information Act in 2005 empowered citizens to demand information from the government, which has to comply within 30 days. Until then, age-old British-era laws allowed government to work in relative opacity, but the act facilitates transparency with government "laws, policies, decisions, modes of public service delivery" that affect e-government (Karwal 2009, 67). Several corruption and bribery scandals have already been revealed with citizen and media use of the Right to Information Act. The government often touts the national portal as a response to this act.

Second, at the village level, the seventy-third amendment to the Indian constitution in 1992 directly empowered elected five-person village assemblies known as *panchayats*. The act also reserved seats for women and underprivileged castes and groups. There are 250,000 *panchayats* for 600,000 villages in India. In sheer numbers, that comes to 2.6 million elected officials at the village level out of a total of 3.3 million elected officials in the country (Aiyar 2008, 81). In practice, the seventy-third amendment has had mixed effects: Dominant groups manage to provide de-facto governance. For example, in many cases husbands govern instead of their wives who have been elected through the quotas for women. On the other hand, panchayats have seen increases in their budgets and relatedly village-level service delivery has at least begun to feature in government plans. Heller, Harilal, and Chaudhuri (2007) also provide a generally positive assessment of deepening democracy and participatory processes in the panchayats in their study of the Southern Indian province of Kerala.

Two things mentioned often in e-government plans are computerization of *panchayats* and the opening of information kiosks, at the village level, though the latter may not be related solely to Panchayats. The Ministry of Panchayati Raj in the central government has an ambitious e-panchayat program for all provinces, with generic software from NIC, which includes computerization and delivery of services such as birth and death certificates, bill payments, and issue of ration cards for subsidized food (which in India also serve as household or individual identity cards). The National e-Governance Plan (NeGP) in 2006 envisioned

100,000 community service centers or kiosks at the village level with budgets made available from the five-year plans. By 2011, in fact, 119,000 villages had Internet connectivity, though that does not mean they had information kiosks (Current Affairs and Analysis 2011). For example, the Western Indian state of Gujarat initiated the e-gram (gram in Hindi means village) project in 2003 and computerizing 13,753 panchayats (Sinha 2008) and other states have followed. The state also introduced another project, *Gyan Ganga* (meaning "knowledge Ganges"), that established information kiosks for service delivery but impact assessments listing tangible benefits to governance and services delivery are hard to find.[4]

Without impact assessments, it is difficult to evaluate the effectiveness of local level e-government initiatives. Comparatively in the two cases discussed above, the Right to Information Act responded to citizen pressures for transparency, while the e-panchayat initiatives seem to be pre-packaged and delivered with central planning. However, even in the latter case, the state seems to be responding to broad political currents such as those that led to the seventy-third amendment to the Indian Constitution.

Analyzing Quality of e-Governance Projects

This section analyzes three issues in quality of e-governance projects at the central and provincial levels to further develop some understanding of the underlying factors for success. These issues deal with top-down rollouts, types of services available and what they lack, and issues with scalability and sustainability. Many of these projects are often posited as partially successful. Empirically, the following sub-section starts with the projects of the techno-state, similar to those mentioned above, before moving to specific governance services and the problems associated with them.

TOP-DOWN ROLLOUTS

India is an example of e-government prioritization even with extremely low levels of connectivity until 2000, when the information infrastructure began to proliferate (see Table 4.1). NICNET and an educational network called ERNET were precedents and, to some extent, there existed awareness for e-government in the electronic connections among government units. By 2001, the government had a target of delivering 25 percent of the services through e-government (Haque 2002, 233). This target, like many others in five-year plans, would be hard to realize.

The earliest successful example at the national level of providing e-government may be railways in India. As noted earlier, the sector employs nearly 45 percent of the central government employees and commands enormous resources: The railway budget is presented to the government before the national budget and is a bellwether of things to follow. By 1982, Indian Railways started to move toward computerizing its freight and passenger reservation systems. By 1986, the Centre for Railway Information Systems (CRIS) was established and it now caters to 1.5 to 2 million passengers who travel daily on India's 2,500 trains (CRIS 2012). CRIS is not easy to use, but the long lines at India's railway stations have now disappeared. Similarly, nearly 60 percent of the payments for freight transactions are handled online now. Initially trade unions in railways opposed computerization but their opposition was overcome through slow negotiations and job assurances.[5]

Project champions and availability of suitable personnel also account for the success of top-down rollouts. Andhra Pradesh and Karnataka, with IT centers located in their capitals Hyderabad and Bangalore respectively, have also emerged as leaders in provision of governance.[6] Chandrababu Naidu, Chief Minister of AP from 1995 to 2004, earned the label of India's "laptop politician" and received the admiration of visitors such as US President Bill Clinton and UK Prime Minister Tony Blair for his e-government and other reform efforts. Andhra Pradesh consistently positions high in the National e-governance rankings (Gupta, Bhattacharya, and Agarwal 2009, 4; Tripathi 2007, 17). E-registration of deeds—for land, mortgages, gifts, and so on.—was introduced in the state in 1996 to facilitate over 1.2 registrations for 3 million people in the state annually in its 387 sub-registrar offices (Satyanarayana 2011, 241). Implemented through NIC, CARD (Computer Aided Registration of Deeds) was one of the first state-level e-government projects in India. It reduced the time for deeds from one to more days to 10 to 15 minutes. However, as Satyanarayana (2011, 247) notes, it was technologically driven, did not reduce corruption, and did not lead to parallel and necessary reforms in legal procedures. To employ this book's title, CARD leveraged atoms but not bits. Another project named e-Seva (seva means service) enabling a variety of transactions—including payment of utility bills, obtaining birth and death certificates, procuring driver's licenses—had most of its success around the state capital Hyderabad and was limited in integrating its various services.

Karnataka's most famous project is Bhoomi (meaning "Earth"), which was launched in 2002 and is a system of digitized land records, which affix property rights and also serve as collateral for government subsidies and bank loans. The project champion was a senior bureaucrat named Rajiv Chawla—from the elite Indian Civil Service—who mobilized the state and district level governments. More than 70 percent of the disputes in Indian courts are around land, and Bhoomi affected 6.7 million farmers in Karnataka through its 177 sub-district level kiosks or offices (Chawla 2009, 76–77). The land record system until then was monopolized through the often-corrupt village accountants called patwaris, approximately 9,000 in Karnataka alone. Now farmers obtain land records with a payment of 15 rupees (30 cents). However, farmers now incur travel costs for going to the kiosks at the sub-district level, and critics note that while dis-intermediating patwaris, it further centralizes administration in other bureaucracies (Prakash and De 2007).

The most visible, and equally controversial, e-governance initiative in India at present is the provision of unique identity (UID) twelve-digit cards using biometrics, which for the first time provide identity to Indians on a national basis. Earlier forms of identification included ration cards issued to procure subsidized food and driver's licenses. The central government launched the project in 2010 with outlays from the national Planning Commission, which are expected to be over $1 billion, though per capita expenditure would be less than $3 (*Economist* 2012). With participation from private sector technology firms such as Wipro, the central government's Unique Identification Authority, also provides cash incentives (about 50 cents) to local agents to issue cards. By July 2102, over 200 million cards had been issued, and the number is expected to be 600 million by 2014. Its purported benefits, apart from providing a national identity card, would include the ability of the government to identify individuals, especially wage labor, for cash payments through direct deposits rather than material benefits, which in the past were easily diverted (Bansal 2012). It would also facilitate transactions among individuals. However, without adequate data privacy protections, the cards increase the surveillance capacities of the Indian state. Misuse is also common: it is not hard to obtain these cards, and thus fraudulent cards have been issued to government contractors to collect revenues for non-existent labor, and there are also concerns that labor from neighboring countries can obtain these cards in India without adequate checks. Nevertheless, by the sheer volume of the enterprise, UIDs are a success story.

PROVIDING BITS, NOT ATOMS

Many of the weaknesses of e-governance projects have already been pointed out above and deal with the techno-centricity, the top-down implementation, and the provision of bits rather than atoms. This last point needs further specification.

Most of India's e-government projects are informational and lack complicated interactivity, integration across services, or far-fetched transformations between citizens and governors. As websites are not quite user-friendly, with some difficulty individuals can now make train or bus reservations, download forms for government services, and make utility payments. They can also obtain land records and registrations through services such as CARD and Bhoomi. The problems arise if any interactivity is needed for dispute settlement or "mutation"—the term often used among Bhoomi clients and officials. Digitization of records is not the same thing as resolving disputes, and Bhoomi does not seem to have reduced the number of disputes in court, only the time needed for obtaining land records. To take another example, many provincial state portals now feature a complaint box or e-mail icons for the Chief Minister. States themselves often tout statistics on how much e-mail the CM receives from citizens. They do not note how many e-mails were answered or how many disputes were resolved.

Broad conjectures regarding the transformation of governance services will need empirical validation to gauge the extent to which citizens feel empowered through e-governance. Ethnographies and surveys are necessary. At a minimal level of costs and time saved, we might conjecture that the answer would be positive. At the transformational level, the rising levels of India's middle income and educated groups—and 200 to 300 million is a huge number—can exert some real pressures for e-governance. Taking a position rooted in critical and cultural studies, Mazarella (2006, 281) notes that India's rhetoric on e-governance is mostly performative: "an ongoing attempt to bring old fashioned centralized power into alignment with a decentralized consumerist populist notion of empowerment. Indeed, the mark of e-governance was precisely this juxtaposition of a fetishized systems rationality with an affectively charged ideal of communicative immediacy." The article offers a close reading of the way online websites such as Tehelka have uncovered corruption scandals while the state continues its rhetoric of transparency through e-governance measures. The elephant in the room is that the government remains centralized, opaque, and corrupt. Grand claims like Mazarella's cannot be invalidated through data points—because they do not legitimize such methodologies. Nevertheless, the truth may be somewhere between fetishized performativity and optimal service provision.

SUSTENANCE AND SCALABILITY

Given the current momentum, e-government initiatives are likely to deepen. The caution, as Heeks (2008) points out, is that most initiatives are not financially compelling or scalable, especially in the ambitious community service centers or kiosks planned throughout the developing world. After initial donor or government funds are depleted, e-governance initiatives cannot sustain themselves.

It is instructive to compare two projects, one run with government financing and the other through private means. The Gyandoot project (meaning information diplomats in Hindi) in the state of Madhya Pradesh rolled out information kiosks throughout the state, which are run operated by recent high school and college graduates known as *soochaks* (information brokers in Hindi) who are intermediaries for providing access to government portals and other services. Sreekumar (2007) notes that the project and the soochaks are elite-controlled. Big famers, merchants, and economically advantaged users gain the most from Gyandoot services (12). Furthermore, the state of Madhya Pradesh does not have the kind of network and human resources that Hyderabad or Bangalore offer: Therefore, Gyandoot encounters ongoing technical and connectivity problems along with the difficulty of finding educated soochaks.

The e-Choupal project provides a contrast to the Gyandoot project. The agro-business division of the Indian firm ITC launched the project in 2000 and it now reaches 4 million farmers across 40,000 villages through 6,500 kiosks, in ten states including Madhya Pradesh, Andhra Pradesh, and Karnataka.[7] Local farmers called *sanchalaks* (information operators) run the kiosks. Interestingly, farmers were involved in designing the e-Choupal system, and the knowledge sharing that takes place is also farmer-driven. ITC also uses the website for its own marketing purposes and for providing access to businesses to sell equipment and services to farmers. However, e-Choupal has also cut out intermediaries in providing information exchanges especially about prices and marketplaces.

Conclusion

E-government in India provides neither a lamentable story of the inability of the state to provide services (see Chapters 3 and 7), nor a bombastic narrative of its success. The "in-betweenness" of the truth then helps to specify the kinds of services the limited Indian state is able to provide and the underlying conditions for the success of such e-governance initiatives, similar in logic to Siegle's analysis of Africa (see Chapter 5). In the words of this volume's introduction, the Indian state's e-government efforts are "patchy and poor."

First, instead of optimal provision of governance services, the Indian state is most successful at sustaining initiatives that can be leveraged with the current state of its information infrastructure, human resources, and the overall governance environment. Returning to Livingston and Walter-Drop's language, the Indian state is better at provisioning bits (information) rather than atoms (material collective goods)—online land records rather than offline judicial procedures. Relatedly, rudimentary services are most successful even in terms of the bits provided. Access to forms and records, simple bill payments, or purchase of travel reservations can be handled easily. However, services requiring higher levels of interactivity, especially with services personnel are not easily executed.

Second, some state consolidation and capacity building does take place, even if understood in terms of a techno-state that seeks to define the meaning of e-governance for people. Most of the initiatives for e-governance are top-down and, until recently, were planned in New Delhi. Agencies of the state such as the National Informatics Centre continue to play a central role in e-governance initiatives. But rudimentary e-governance services described above now reach many areas of limited statehood, such as India's urban slums and isolated rural geographies. To the extent that these projects work, a variety of causal factors may be isolated. They include reforms champions and location in regions that possess adequate information infrastructures and human resources.

Third, problems of limited statehood in general—state's lack of capacity in arbitrating plural pressures or reaching rural areas—also affect e-government. The biggest beneficiaries of e-government are the over 300-million middle-income groups, also best connected to government in general. The state struggles to reach the "other" one billion in rural areas and urban slums. This problem of course is not limited to India. According to some estimates, in the fastest growing urban areas in Amazonia, 80 percent of the population lives in slums on the edge of megacities. In Africa, there may be as many as 332 million slum-dwellers in sub-Saharan Africa by 2015 (Davis 2006, 17–19).

In India, ideas for running community service centers, while mostly unsustainable in their implementation, respond to such pressures. Alternatives might include incentives for private firms or individuals to provide financially sustainable services at the local level. E-Choupal is an example, as also the hundreds and thousands of privately run information kiosks in Indian villages that make revenues from providing access to government services but also package photocopying, facsimile, and computer services. Another successful example is the cash incentives for local agents to issue Universal Identity cards (UIDs) along with partnerships with private firms using biometric technology. Each of these successes has a drawback: e-Choupal is critiqued for its commercialization, UIDs for surveillance and fraud.

Fourth, e-governance in India must be understood within the broad context of on-going transformations in Indian governance. These include the increasing power of provincial governments and the devolution of power to village level Panchayats. Without detailed studies, it is hard to gauge the effectiveness of e-governance in terms of its transformative impact, but the initiatives provide some evidence for the claim that limited states can, under specific circumstances, provide forms of governance that were impossible two decades ago.

Notes

1. Geographically, India is divided into twenty-eight states and seven federally administered "Union Territories" collectively referred to as *provinces* in this chapter. The federal government is known as *central government* in India and this term is employed here.
2. An alternative academic convention lists e-government as connections among government units.
3. See Guida and Crow (2009) and Heeks (2008) for stages of provision of services and the relationship between the governors and the governed.
4. A government informational video, albeit in Gujarati language, describing the e-gram initiative can be found at http://www.youtube.com/watch?v=nWeztbn-usQ.
5. Banks in India followed a similar path. Reserve Bank of India's Rangarajan Committee Report in 1986 recommended computerization but this did not begin to happen until the late 1990s. Apart from trade unions, India also lacked an adequate information infrastructure.
6. Both states, interestingly, also feature strong regional parties, which goes against the domination of national parties in India. This gives these states additional bargaining leverage with New Delhi through coalitional politics or in their negotiations over divisions of resources and revenues with the center. The growing strength of regional parties is also credited with breaking New Delhi's monopoly in the seemingly unitary system and paving way for federalism.
7. Data from "About e-Choupal" at EChoupal.com.

5

ICT and Accountability in Areas of Limited Statehood

JOSEPH SIEGLE

The Value of Accountability

Endowed with large tracts of fertile arable land and reserves of oil and diamonds that generate over 90 percent of government revenues a year, Angola is seemingly well positioned to improve living conditions for its roughly 18 million citizens following the country's long civil war, which ended in 2002. Indeed, with annual economic growth since then averaging around 10 percent, Angola's per capita income is in the top quartile of sub-Saharan African countries. Yet, 60 percent of Angolans still live in extreme poverty, subsisting on less than $1.70 per day. Infant mortality rates are nearly one out of ten, only a third of age-eligible children attend secondary school, and cereal yields are, on average, just 600 kg/hectare.[1] On each of these indicators, Angola scores in the bottom quartile of performance within sub-Saharan Africa, the world's poorest continent. In contrast, family members of President José Eduardo do Santos, who has been in power since 1979, senior party members, government officials, and military leaders have become fabulously wealthy.

The disconnect between Angola's revenues and socio-economic performance is closely linked to its governance practices. The state-owned oil company, Sonangol, has frequently been criticized for opaque management and plays conflicting roles as concessionaire, operator, and regulator (Marques 2010; Warner 2013). Sonangol reports directly to the Office of the President with oil revenues bypassing the Ministry of Finance and the Central Bank. A KPMG audit sponsored by Human Rights Watch found that Sonangol could not account for over $4 billion in revenues over a five-year period (HRW 2004). In some years a third of Angola's state income is unaccounted for. Similar issues plague the diamond sector where licenses are granted to companies run by political insiders and high-level military officials (PAC 2007). Concerned by the Arab Spring protests of 2011, the Angolan government instituted new restrictions on the Internet (even though the penetration rate was a meager 12 percent) that allow the government greater access to users' personal data. In essence, Angolan leaders largely govern with impunity.

Angola's neighbor, Botswana, is also well endowed with natural resources. It is the world's leading diamond producer, generating 50 percent of government revenues from the mining industry. Botswana has limited arable land with most of its territory comprised of the Kalahari Desert. Botswana's natural resource revenues also place it in the top quartile of per capita incomes in Africa. However, unlike Angola, this natural resource affluence is matched by its performance on social indicators. Infant mortality rates are a third of those in Angola. Over 80 percent of children attend secondary school. Nearly all citizens have access to safe drinking water (The World Bank 2012). Each of these measures is in the top quartile of African states.

Botswana does not impose any restrictions on Internet use and has one of the highest mobile phone penetration rates in Africa at 164% as of the end of 2012. Transparency International regularly ranks Botswana as among the least corrupt nation-states in Africa. Mining revenue is treated as a national resource and directed to the Central Bank. These revenues are then allocated to government ministries according to established national development plans, fostering broad-based economic development. Botswana maintains stable macroeconomic policies including very limited external debt and low inflation. The divergence in social performance seen between Angola and Botswana is illustrative of governance patterns globally (Halperin, Siegle, and Weinstein 2010; Kaufmann, Kraay, and Mastruzzi 2006). States with relatively stronger structures of accountability[2] tend to realize superior and more consistent socioeconomic performance.

This chapter examines why and how the emergence of information and communications technology (ICT) can contribute to building state accountability structures in areas of limited statehood (ALS) while improving governance performance. In this way, this essay provides a conceptual link between the earlier chapters of the volume with their focus on the impact of ICT on *statehood* and the emphasis of subsequent chapters on ICT's implications for *governance performance*. The chapter starts with a framework by which accountability processes shape incentives and parameters for states in ALS. It then examines some of the primary channels through which ICT is changing accountability processes in ALS. Recognizing that the emergence of ICT does not automatically result in improved governance, the chapter concludes by identifying key conditions that constrain and enhance the ICT and accountability relationship. Key findings that emerge include the indispensability of nonstate actors for advancing accountability in ALS, the vital role of external organizations and states in ensuring there are consequences for repressive or corrupt patterns of governance, and the need for stronger protections of journalists and watchdog groups since these actors are more than private citizens but representatives of the broader society and international community seeking independent information.

Accountability in Areas of Limited Statehood

Accountability mechanisms are means by which public officials are obliged to abide by the rule of law. They provide incentives to be responsive to the priorities of the general public and foster transparency and fairness of state institutions—as well as stipulate sanctions for abuses of power (Siegle 2001; The World Bank 2011). Accountability is thus a broader concept than establishing controls on corruption. While accountability does not preclude abuses of power, it ensures there are established channels for corrective action. In short, accountability is the antithesis of impunity.

To be meaningful, accountability must extend beyond de jure statutes or declarations to encompass genuine checks and balances. Thus, accountability not only involves the seating of a legislature but also entails elected representatives holding credible hearings and exerting a counter-balance on the priorities of the executive branch. Similarly, the judiciary must be able to function apolitically when the executive or legislative branches are deemed to be acting outside the law. Accountability in practice takes many forms beyond power-sharing between branches of government, however. Audits of public expenditures by an Inspector General's office, reporting by civil society watchdogs, independent inquiries, Ombudsman offices, anticorruption commissions, Central Banks, independent election commissions, regulatory bodies, accreditation institutes, and professional societies, are among the many other possibilities for accountability to be effected. Meaningful accountability must also have teeth, resulting in changes in behavior as a result of oversight, such as the establishment of new building codes, more transparent contracting procedures, fines for violating regulations, resignations of senior officials, the electoral defeat of incumbent politicians, and prosecution of political and security sector leaders responsible for human rights violations, among others.

The multiple mechanisms by which checks and balances are created reflect what can be conceived of as a "web" or "layers of accountability" (see Figure 5.1). Since risks of the abuse of power in ALS typically emanate from the executive branch, accountability is thus often about establishing effective counterweights to the monopolization of executive power. These include state institutions such as the legislature, judiciary, merit-based civil service, and local government (represented as the inner ring of accountability in Figure 5.1). These state institutions are reinforced and complemented by another layer of nonstate mechanisms, including civil society, the media, the private sector, traditional authorities, and external actors that aim to balance executive power through transparency, oversight, awareness-raising, and mobilizing public support for effective governance. No single dimension is sufficient or predominant, though all are interconnected. Nor is there a one-size-fits-all configuration of accountability that is "right" for every society. Rather it is the redundancy of accountability mechanisms that

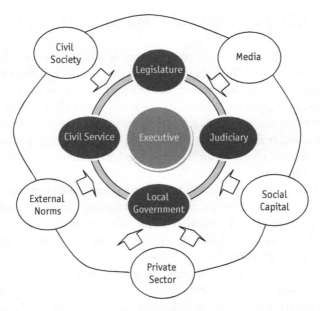

Figure 5.1 Webs of Public Accountability. Layers of both state and nonstate factors contribute to the density of accountability in a society.

provides a system's strength. Societies with more dense webs of accountability are more effective at constraining or correcting abuses of public power.

ALS rely to a relatively greater extent on their nonstate facets of accountability. State-based accountability institutions in ALS tend to be under-capacitized and politically beholden to the executive branch. They also take time to establish– at least a decade and usually longer—given that they must often overcome entrenched patronage networks, arbitrary applications of the rule of law, and self-serving leadership norms (Barkan, Mattes, Mozaffar, and Smiddy 2010; Siegle 2007). As a result, nonstate actors play an indispensable role in advancing accountability in the early years of a transition process and in sustaining momentum for these reforms until state-based accountability structures can gain traction (Siegle 2012a). Advancing accountability, therefore, is not a one-time, intensive push but requires a sustained effort.

While there are various configurations of accountability, an important common denominator is that they all depend on access to independent information. Information is the lifeblood of accountability. Parliaments cannot assert effective oversight of the executive branch without independent information and analysis. Judges cannot be held accountable unless their decisions can be reviewed based on the transparent documentation of evidence. A public dialogue over societal priorities cannot take place unless independent voices with alternate choices have space to express their views. The degree to which private sector is independent of political influences requires access to records tracking the granting of business licenses, property, and credit. Likewise, investigative journalism and watchdog groups, so critical to exposing corruption and other abuses of power, cannot survive unless there is a degree of access to information, basic protections for journalists, and the ability to disseminate information. Not surprisingly, access to various forms of media and ICT are significantly greater in states with stronger accountability.

The primacy of access to information for accountability highlights the collective action framework that applies to much of the process of strengthening accountability (Olson 1965). Patronage or abuses of power that benefit a politically connected minority at the expense of the majority in a society persist because insiders are relatively few, well informed, relatively easy to organize, and clearly aware of the benefits from their cooperation. By controlling the media and information flows, this minority is able to further amplify their influence by controlling the narrative or frame by which the rest of the society interprets events (Castells 2007; Scott 1998).

The majority typically faces an uphill challenge in overcoming their disadvantage because they are physically dispersed, face obstacles to information dissemination, start from low levels of awareness of the benefits that would accrue from a more equitable distribution of public resources, and therefore are difficult to organize to represent their interests. In other words, exclusive political arrangements persist because of weak accountability. Recognizing this, those benefitting from these arrangements are usually actively resistant to subjecting themselves to accountability, at times to the point of violence. Not only would accountability processes likely result in the loss of their source of self-enrichment or influence, it would also make them highly vulnerable to losing power altogether.

How ICT is Changing Accountability in ALS

Given the centrality of information to accountability and good governance, the explosion of ICT in ALS is of historic importance. For the first time, individuals even in remote areas are able to receive and communicate information in real time, usually via cell phones and SMS given their greater affordability, thereby connecting them to their compatriots and with the rest of the world (Livingston 2011). This is a major departure from previous eras. The ready access these individuals now have to multiple opinions versus the dominant narrative that governments have been able to maintain is necessarily changing state-society relations. Governments simply cannot control the message the way they have in the past. Instead there are now "competing frames" of the state's engagement with societal priorities (Scott 1998). Asmolov makes this point in his analysis of the Russian government's inability to paper over the severity of the 2010 wildfires and their affect on mortality rates in Moscow (see Chapter 7).

Not only does the expansion of ICT give individuals greater ability to communicate, but the velocity and reach of information has also accelerated dramatically. Information can be transmitted from a single individual to thousands, even millions of others simultaneously. This has created new ties for communities in remote locations including means for alerting the outside world in times of insecurity (see Chapter 10). The reduction in costs of information and organization, historically two major advantages of exclusive governance networks, is resulting in a rebalancing of the collective action equation (Livingston 2011). As Sharath Srinivasan describes in Chapter 6, on Frontline SMS, the horizontal linkages within a society that are established through the accessibility of ICT are contributing to a reshaping of state-society relations from their historical hierarchal structure toward stronger mechanisms of "co-governance" involving a combination of associations, municipal authorities, civil servants, development organizations, merchants, and religious leaders. Heightened access to information among the majority, then, offers the opportunity to better inform and educate citizens of what is at stake from ongoing government policies and priorities—and what citizens can do to better promote their own interests. Following are several key channels by which ICT is changing the accountability equation:

Enhanced Policy Dialogue. Greater access to information means that there is a stronger likelihood that independent perspectives can be articulated and considered in the policy dialogue. While a government may continue to press for its preferred policy course, it can no longer ignore other perspectives. Instead it must respond to unwelcome information and address proposals calling for alternative priorities or means of achieving an agreed-upon goal. In addition to making the policy process more participatory and widening the number of stakeholders, more information and analysis at the front end of a decision-making process reduces the likelihood of calamitous outcomes because key assumptions went unchallenged.

An example of how greater participation enhances the interests of the general population can be seen in Mozambique where the online newspaper @Verdade has published investigative reports on the poor service delivery of the state utility provider (Baldwin 2010). @Verdade has followed up with solicitations from its readers on ways to improve the utility's service provision in Mozambique. This has generated a raft of suggestions and sparked a broader public dialogue on standards of service delivery, oversight, and means of improving the quality and accessibility of services. Using the framework of Figure 5.1, this shows how ICT strengthens the avenues by which the media and civil society can contribute to the policy dialogue—affecting the choices made by the executive, legislative, and local government actors.

While ICT is contributing to more dialogue and accountability, the growing accessibility of ICT in the hands of the general population does not necessarily mean a more confrontational relationship with the state. Readers of @Verdade are 10 percent more likely to vote than others in Mozambique, and this willingness to participate has grown since they started reading the paper. Similarly, surveys in the Democratic Republic of the Congo and the Central African Republic show that citizens who use ICT tools to follow government actions have a greater appreciation for the challenges faced by government leaders than those who are not as engaged. Moreover, ICT users are more likely to approach a government official with a concern or priority than they were previously (Katz-Lavigne 2011). These examples suggest that ICT may help build the connections between government and citizens in ALS. They may also contribute to strengthening citizens' voice— and "demand" for higher standards of services from their governments.

ICT Helps Reduce Corruption and Abuses of Power. Corruption, by its nature, persists because of opacity. If citizens were aware of which public officials were misusing state resources, there would be much greater pressure to take corrective action. The greater ability to communicate and connect citizens via ICT is contributing to greater transparency and therefore facilitating the exposure of corruption. To start, ICT, particularly the Internet, greatly facilitates public access to government budgets and expenditures. This enables watchdog groups to conduct the analysis and forensic accounting required to trace public revenues and identify when they have been diverted for non-approved purposes. Some local governments have adopted budget-tracking tools that allow citizens to monitor the level of revenues and uses public resources to provide goods and services.

ICT, similarly, facilitates the oversight of procurement practices, where a significant volume of corruption occurs, by fostering the analysis of competing bids, and the relationships between winning contractors and government officials. This is represented in Figure 5.1 by the strengthened oversight capacity of the procurement process made possible by ICT realized by private sector actors, civil society, and media. Along these lines, the Internet also connects citizens in one country with individuals and institutions around the globe working on similar issues. In addition to accelerating the adoption of best practices, this empowers citizens' ability to trace public officials' ill-gotten assets to global financial centers or offshore accounts where they are stored.

ICT also facilitates the collective compilation of corruption "event mapping" that documents the location and type of bribes that citizens may be required to pay police or other government officials to obtain licenses or other clearances. Examples of this are Ipaidabribe.com and stopthebribes.com. ICT, thus, transforms what is a solitary indignity and exploitative experience into a shared recognition that many others have encountered similar circumstances. This experience is empowering to victims and the society at large—diminishing their sense of helplessness—and providing them a tool by which to take initiative in redressing their grievance.

ICT's role in controlling corruption also directly contributes to state building. Experience from efforts to reform the judiciary in Indonesia, for example, has found that requiring judges to justify their rulings in writing dramatically improves the impartiality of the court system. Judges realize that once their rulings are recorded, and therefore subject to review, they are more circumspect in their judgments. Accordingly, something as seemingly simple as establishing records can significantly reduce the arbitrariness of the judicial process. ICT has the potential to amplify these effects by capturing and expanding the capacity for remote public purview over the judicial sector. As judges realize their behavior and decisions will be scrutinized, they have incentives to act more accountably.

By reducing corruption, ICT is also improving development effectiveness. One popular mechanism promoted by the World Bank Institute is CheckMySchool. org. This website (accessible from SMS and social networking platforms) allows all participating communities to review issues reported with their schools and post other concerns they may have. These anonymous reporting tools provide local community organizations, parents' groups, and other stakeholders patterns of comments through which they can proactively and constructively engage school authorities in an effort to resolve shortcomings (CheckMySchool 2012). This online oversight mechanism builds on experience showing that when local communities are made aware of the resources designated for their local school district, they are likely to be much more assertive in demanding an accounting of what percentage of those resources reached the local level and how they were used.

Enhances Legitimacy. ICT is having a fundamental impact on the growing number of elections that are taking place in the Global South, including ALS. Mobile phones, SMS, and Internet communications are allowing real-time election-monitoring by independent groups as never before. This has proven vital for the parallel vote counts that election-monitoring organizations have found to be an effective tool to preempt government candidates from claiming victories with unrealistic margins. Instead, exit surveys of voters can be communicated to a central repository and district by district tallies can be kept comparing candidate vote totals with numbers of registered voters and pre-election surveys. This allows immediate challenges to be raised when official tallies deviate markedly from the parallel counts.

Video capabilities built into most mobile phones and other handheld devices, furthermore, have created millions of mobile observation posts monitoring electoral misdeeds. Those engaged in or attempting to rig an election are under far greater surveillance than they ever were in a pre-ICT world. By capturing electoral abuses that can then be uploaded and quickly disseminated to citizens across a nation and viewers globally, this technology represents an unprecedented accountability tool. Vote-rigging and manipulation are much harder to conceal.

Indeed, it was the mobile phone images of unsuspecting electoral workers stuffing ballots in favor of Russian President Vladimir Putin's United Russia party during legislative elections in December 2011 that caused great embarrassment for the Russian leadership (White and Barry 2011). The episode went viral in Russia and beyond, mobilizing massive popular protests and badly damaging Putin's credibility and political capital.

The growing presence of mobile phones has been cited as a reason why Nigeria's April 2011 presidential election went as smoothly as it did (Asuni and Farris 2011). One ruling party official acknowledged that even if they had wanted to steal the election, they were not sure who might be looking over their shoulder with a cell phone, taking a picture or writing a SMS. In short, incumbent regimes are being forced into higher standards of accountability, often against their will. ICT is thus contributing to stronger state electoral management bodies, reflected in Figure 5.1 by the exchanges between media and civil society actors and the judicial, civil service, and local government officials responsible for organizing elections.

ICT is also fostering greater popular participation in the electoral process. Facebook, Twitter, and e-mail messages have become staples in electoral campaigns even in developing nations. This is providing another means for candidates to reach and directly communicate with citizens in ALS, establishing a relationship they can define outside of traditional media filters. In Nigeria, President Goodluck Jonathan has used Facebook to solicit feedback, conduct surveys, announce initiatives, and connect with ordinary Nigerians. His postings have elicited tens of thousands of comments (Akintayo 2011).

An outcome of the expanded role of ICT in electoral campaigns is that victorious candidates emerge with far greater levels of legitimacy than is the case in opaque systems. In other words, ICT is helping widen the legitimacy gap between leaders who have genuinely been bestowed power from their compatriots versus those whose authority is self-declared. Greater legitimacy contributes to stability and enables leaders to make difficult choices with the support of the population contributing to more accountable governments' superior performance.

Responsiveness to Humanitarian Crises. More open societies have long been recognized for better mitigating and responding to natural disasters and other crises than those where information flow is limited (Cuny 1983). In general there are several links to this chain. First, in more information-rich environments, media play a critical role as early warning signals when a humanitarian emergency, often in an outlying region from the capital city is unfolding. As a result, awareness of the disaster is realized sooner and more broadly than in closed contexts where news of a disaster can be suppressed. ICT accelerates this signaling loop (traversing the nonstate accountability ring of Figure 5.1, thereby accentuating pressure on the state-based accountability bodies).

Second, with broad public awareness comes immense pressure on a government to act to ameliorate the suffering. Democratic leaders need to maintain popular support if they hope to win reelection and thus have reinforcing incentives to be responsive. Democratic governance also relies on a degree of trust between citizens and their leaders. Failure to be responsive and be perceived as responsive can dramatically undercut the credibility of a government and thus its ability to govern.

In autocracies, the initial impulse is often to suppress news of a crisis. Perhaps the most famous example of this was during the great Ethiopian famine of 1984–1985 when the repressive government of Mengistu Haile Mariam was able to ignore and keep the tragedy out of national and international media for months, coinciding as it did with the ten-year anniversary celebrations of the regime's time in power. It was only when a BBC video team, working with NGOs, was able to secret out images of the suffering was the international consciousness awakened. Subsequent international pressure led to a massive assistance effort.

Once the public becomes aware of a crisis, autocratic leaders also face pressure to act. While not freely elected, these leaders govern by maintaining the veneer of popular support and perceived performance competence. If these perceptions are punctured, the popular backlash could become destabilizing for the ruling authorities. This explains the response of the Russian government to the wildfires of 2010 (see Chapter 7). After initially claiming the situation was under control, the government was compelled to act once phone, video, and text messages from the public refuted these assertions.

A third key link in the governance response to humanitarian crises that is shaped by information access is demand for post-crisis action. A common demand is for independent investigations into why affected communities were vulnerable, why there were insufficient mitigative measures, and why the response was ineffective. On this, there is often marked divergence between more open and closed governance systems—largely due to the ability of nonstate actors and media to sustain attention and pressure. With ICT, this effect is amplified. This high-profile scrutiny propels the political process in democracies to take action to prepare more effectively for future humanitarian crises. Investments for prevention and mitigation are thus made (e.g., new building codes, evacuation procedures, etc.). Nobel Laureate Amartya Sen's famous observation that there has never been a major famine in a democracy with a free press, thus, is grounded on the reality of accountability processes.

Protecting Human Rights. Greater access to ICT-generated information has similarly elevated international public awareness of systematic human rights violations, often in real time, accelerating the scrutiny and pressure facing violators. Historically, many gross human rights violations were conducted in obscurity and only became widely known internationally, if ever, months or years later. Such was the case, for example in Hafez al-Assad's massacre of 40,000 people and razing of the town of Homs, Syria, in 1982 following protests there for greater liberties. There are, unfortunately, many other such illustrations. The temporal lag made international efforts to prevent or mitigate such human rights violations largely moot. Any attempt to impose penalties had to be applied retroactively.

Human rights violations certainly continue in the ICT era. However, they are much more likely to be recorded, uploaded to the Internet, and circulated globally within days of the transgressions. This, then, removes a key impediment to international collective action—ambiguity as to what is actually going on. While the ability to forge international consensus for action in these instances remains hamstrung by geostrategic politics as seen at the United Nations Security Council, this heightened level of awareness has put the perpetuating regimes under a much brighter spotlight than in the pre-ICT era. As a point of comparison, when Syrian President Bashar al-Assad, the son of the previous repressive leader, launched a violent campaign of repression against peaceful protesters demanding democratization in 2011, these killings were captured on video and transmitted globally. This quickly led to widespread international condemnation, sanctions, and isolation of the Assad regime. Muzammil M. Hussain and Philip N. Howard's chapter on ICT and the Arab Spring (Chapter 2) further unpacks the varied influences that ICT had in the respective transition experiences in the Arab world starting in 2011.

In Sudan, the regime of Omar al-Bashir has sponsored militias and deployed attack aircraft to kill, intimidate, and uproot civilian populations in the Darfur region and the South of the country since 1989. This was largely undertaken with complete impunity, as these regions of Sudan are among the most impoverished and inaccessible in the world. With the advent of ICT, however, this government has also been under greater scrutiny. This is exemplified by the launching of the Sentinel satellite by the NGO, Enough, in association with American actor, George Clooney, to monitor Sudanese troop and militia movements for atrocities. Clooney captures the objective succinctly, "We are just going to keep the pressure on. Turning the lights on doesn't make anything [atrocities] stop. But it makes it harder, and that's our job" (SSP 2012). This heightened awareness has denied the regime one of its most commonly employed tactics of obfuscating realities on the ground so as to confound consensus and decisive action on the part of the international community.

ICT: Vital but Not Sufficient

This chapter has argued that by accelerating the flow of information, greatly enabling awareness-raising and networking among ordinary citizens, ICT is vividly changing the accountability relationship between the state and the citizenry. Such real-time access to information by communities via ICT tools empowers ordinary citizens, even in remote areas with limited state presence that did not exist in the pre-ICT era. This establishes both a reputational and legal constraint on states that was not as readily available in the pre-ICT era.

Still, ICT is not a panacea. Some ALS that have gained broad access to ICT tools, continue to suffer from weak accountability. Kenya's experience in the Niarobi slums, described in Primož Kovačič and Jamie Lundine's chapter (Chapter 8), provides an illustration. Even with the mapping of these heretofore "invisible" areas and the awareness-raising of the desperate conditions in which individuals live in these communities, there has not been a surge in government attention, resources, and services. This highlights several important conditions necessary for ICT to have an impact on accountability.

First is that accountability is not self-enforcing. While enhancing access to information is vital, it is not sufficient to effect change. In other words, ICT is but a tool. The effectiveness of this tool depends on reformers, typically civil society organizations, that can use the richer information environment generated by ICT (often in conjunction with traditional media and outreach campaigns) to organize communities, put pressure on governments for responsiveness, and press for change. Civil society groups, or reformist elements within the state, then, are the essential organizational building blocks needed to focus and mobilize the interests of ordinary citizens so that they realize a fairer distribution of public goods and services. ICT can be highly empowering to these groups. However, if these citizen networks are feeble or do not exist, then the awareness-raising possible from ICT will have negligible effect. This is one of the telling findings from a study of Ushahidi launches that are sustained over time discussed in Peter Meier's chapter on event-mapping. The preparation and organizational structure to support and use the information generated from the event-mapping exercise are vital to its continued use and ultimate public impact. This is consistent with the emphasis on planning and civil society networking found in successful nonviolent campaigns to remove autocratic leaders (Karatnycky and Ackerman 2005). In the end, accountability is about overcoming collective action challenges. ICT can be vitally helpful in that regard but must be operationalized. Kibera has lacked such effective civil society actors to use the greater information available and hold corrupt politicians accountable.

Insights from India provide another explanation for the muted accountability impact in certain contexts with access to ICT. With 1.2 billion people and 640 districts, India has long been recognized for its variance in governance capacities within a single state. However, as described in the chapter by J. P. Singh (Chapter 4), even in certain districts where ICT has become prevalent, better governance and accountability have not always followed. While relatively weak civil society organizations partly explain the disconnect, it also reflects the low costs for local politicians who fail to deliver improved public services. These politicians inhabit "safe" seats and therefore win reelection regardless of the governance performance in their local jurisdiction. Often the dominant party represents a local ethnic or religious majority of the population and therefore faces little real competition, even if local state policies are perceived as unfair. At times, local politicians operate in a form of client-patron relationship where they provide benefits to clients in the form of money, contracts, or rent-seeking opportunities in exchange for electoral support. The result is a network of individuals accruing personal benefits, while public goods and services remain sparse. In short, ICT cannot overcome, on its own, noncompetitive political contexts where politicians face few incentives to perform in the public interest. Much like in an autocratic governance setting, the absence of political incentives for reform stymies the creation and strengthening of state-based forms of accountability. The burden for mobilizing accountability processes and norms, therefore, falls to nonstate actors. The difference from an autocratic setting, however, is that in India freedoms of speech, media, and association have been established. Therefore, reformist groups have the space to begin the awareness-raising and mobilization process to realize more oversight and responsiveness. Accordingly, rather than classifying these contexts as places where ICT has "failed" to deliver better accountability and governance, it may be more appropriate to characterize the process as one of iterative progress—with a steep slope to climb.

Russia represents a third strand of how the expansion of ICT does not necessarily translate into improved accountability. Rather than adapt to the transparency and oversight required of a more open society or try to block access to potentially threatening information transmitted via ICT as China has done with its Great Firewall, Russia has opted to publicly embrace access to ICT while attempting to manipulate the messages conveyed so as to ensure the image of state effectiveness is maintained. An example of this is the Russian government's decision to install web cameras at all 91,000 polling sites ahead of the 2011 parliamentary elections, ostensibly to provide assurance of the transparency of the electoral process. The video images from these cameras appeared to show a very normal, orderly, and well-managed process. Upon inspection of the video feeds, however, a Russian civil society group found numerous cases of repeating images (see Chapter 3). In other instances, the same individuals on the video were seen voting multiple times. In other words, the government had tried to stage the images to convey its intended narrative. The discovery of the misrepresentation, however, only further tarnished the legitimacy of the government and eroded public trust. Being unable to fully control the information narrative despite its best efforts, the Russian government has resorted to further restrictions on civil society, the media, and their international supporters. In brief, governments resistant to oversight will continue to seek ways to evade this scrutiny. With the increasingly sophisticated monitoring tools in the hands of ordinary citizens, however, authorities must go to greater lengths to do so.

In sum, the emergence of ICT is not synonymous with greater accountability. Other steps in the process are required, not least of which is the emergence of civil society organizations that can sustain a reform campaign over the extended period that genuine change usually requires. Government officials in both democratic and autocratic systems will attempt to resist such oversight, though in different ways and to varying degrees. Such responses are to be expected and are consistent with resistance to accountability measures historically. The growth of ICT does fundamentally alter the collective action equation, however, by empowering ordinary citizens in their ability to access information and organize themselves with unprecedented efficiency and savings. The concrete potential of this new set of tools can be appreciated by the seriousness with which autocratic states have moved to try and limit the accountability impacts of ICT.

Implications for Enhancing ICT's Accountability Potential in ALS

ICT's emerging effect on accountability in ALS highlights several priorities for reformers aiming to maximize the beneficial effects on governance. A first priority is to strengthen and support civil society actors that can use ICT to realize genuine institutional reform. Investments in ICT technologies and capacities alone are insufficient. Rather, civil society organizations provide the ground forces that are needed to generate independent information, analyze and interpret the information that is available so that it is meaningful to a general audience, scrutinize public budgets and functions, provide viable policy alternatives, educate the public, and build grassroots support for reform that can be sustained over time, among other functions. Beyond civil society, nonstate actors more generally, especially the media and traditional authorities, are needed to promote a culture of accountability. This is particularly the case in ALS where formal state institutions of accountability are likely to be weak, oriented toward an established system of protecting entrenched interests, and take a decade or more of sustained effort to build into credible structures of accountability.

Experience from ALS also underscores the importance of external actors in reinforcing norms of accountability, thereby limiting avenues for corruption and moderating abuses of power. While the lines between domestic and international may have become increasingly blurred with regards to information, this is not the case in terms of vulnerability to intimidation and violence. Therefore, international engagement is vital for providing "voice" to human rights concerns in states where there is limited domestic space for political competition or civil society oversight. And international attention matters. Regardless of how impervious a regime may seem to international pressure, these states go to great lengths to demonstrate that they are adhering to global human rights standards. International actors can advance accountability in these states by using enhanced information tools to monitor events on the ground and forge broader coalitions of reform-minded states in dealing with leaders and states that habitually violate established human rights standards.

Establishing norms supporting the free flow of information needed to create a culture of accountability requires protecting the journalists and civil society actors who generate and disseminate independent information. These individuals fulfill a critical role in fostering a public dialogue that benefits the entire society. Recognizing this unique role, strong measures must be established to safeguard journalists, bloggers, and civil society actors. Violence and intimidation against these individuals is not an ordinary crime but a crime against the entire society. Indeed, they are targeted not as ordinary citizens but because of the irreplaceable role they play in informing the general population. Intimidation against individuals who are information hubs, however, is often harsh. Approximately seventy-five journalists are killed around the world every year (CPJ 2012). Ninety percent of these murders go unsolved. Many are never even investigated (Mijatovic 2012). Legislatures and civil society reformers should, therefore, prioritize the creation of strong domestic laws that safeguard protections for journalists, bloggers, and civil rights actors in the conduct of their roles (see Siegle 2012b). Removing the cloak of impunity for attacks against journalists and bloggers is a major step in enhancing the accountability potential that can result from the spread of ICT.

Conclusion

By amplifying the accessibility of information and facilitating the horizontal linkages in a society that help ordinary citizens to communicate and coordinate, ICT is a vitally important tool for strengthening accountability in ALS. Accountability is not self-enforcing, however. Rather it requires the sustained engagement of networks of reformers to overcome the entrenched institutionalized interests that typically have benefitted from an exclusive governing structure at the expense of the broader public. In ALS—contexts with weak state structures—nonstate actors have an indispensable role to play in advancing accountability. Accountability, moreover, is not achieved in a single act but by establishing layers of state and nonstate processes that can better ensure fairness in the use of public resources and controls against the abuse of power. While accountability does not guarantee such abuses will not occur, it does provide mechanisms for remediation. Advancing ICT's positive impact in ALS, therefore, is not just a matter of promoting technological advancement but recognizing that ICT is part of a broader governance process that must be integrated with strategies enhancing space for civil society, the media, and popular participation.

Notes

1. Based on the World Bank's World Development Indicators 2012.
2. Accountability is instrumentalized as a fifty-point scale with equal weightings of five different institutional measures: checks on the chief executive, independence of the civil service, autonomy of the private sector, independence of the judiciary, and freedom of the press (see Siegle 2001).

Part Two

SUBSTITUTION: ICT AS A TOOL FOR NONSTATE GOVERNANCE

6

FrontlineSMS, Mobile-for-Development, and the "Long Tail" of Governance[1]

SHARATH SRINIVASAN

Introduction

This chapter examines the governance implications of deployments of FrontlineSMS, a free and open source software tool that enables users with a basic computer and a mobile phone or GSM modem to deploy a text-messaging system for distributed communication at scale. FrontlineSMS is one of the most innovative Mobile-for-Development (M4D) tools to emerge in the past decade, and a diverse range of actors operating in over seventy countries uses it. By analyzing data on FrontlineSMS use, this chapter helps to address a common knowledge gap in academic assessments of the significance of such "last mile" ICT innovations in areas of limited statehood. While anecdotal accounts are plentiful, developing a robust understanding of the parameters of governance effects of these technologies is difficult owing to the diffuse, heterogeneous, and user-driven nature of their application.

There are some dominant, though not exclusive, typologies of FrontlineSMS deployments with governance outcomes in areas of limited statehood. There are key differences between deployments in which information is the public good, such as agricultural market prices, and those in which information flows enhance delivery of material public goods and services, such as coordinating more rapid and effective health services through community health volunteer networks. These are not, of course, binary conditions, but rather arrayed along a continuum. The ability of governance actors—whether state or nonstate, local, national, or international—to deliver many essential governance outcomes still relies on material factors that new digital communication tools alone cannot surmount. To use Livingston and Walter-Drop's language in the introductory chapter, digital technology can transmit bits (information), but it cannot deliver atoms (needed material goods). Innovative ICT tools such as FrontlineSMS can enhance governance outcomes in areas of limited statehood by expanding and strengthening informational flows and thus the supply and demand logics of responsive governance provision by diverse kinds of actors. The probability of efficiently delivered goods is increased by the now more readily available awareness of what is needed, where it is needed, and how quickly it is needed. More effective informational flows also amplify the voice of constituents in shaping the meaning and prioritization of public goods and thus strengthen the accountability of governance actors. Most sustained and effective deployments of FrontlineSMS are by organizations, not individuals or communities, and it is thus more appropriate to talk of more effective co-governance rather than self-governance.

In elaborating these arguments, this chapter adapts Chris Anderson's explanation of web-based "long tail" retail economies (Anderson 2006) to propose how applications of FrontlineSMS might sustain governance effects in areas of limited statehood. It also takes up Jonathan Donner's injunction to empirically evaluate a core tension in how M4D is conceptualized, between a user-choice ideal that might foster grassroots self-governance, and an "embedded directionality" critique that insists upon analyzing the recursive relationship between the technology, the actors intervening with it, and the relevant social context (Donner 2010).

The chapter proceeds as follows. The first section introduces conceptual and theoretical heuristics that inform a critical analysis of the governance affects of M4D innovations, such as FrontlineSMS. The second section charts the rapid rise to prominence of FrontlineSMS, exploring the tension between a low-cost, low-tech, grassroots, user-choice ideal and the fact that sustained impactful use often relies upon product offerings and user types that are more easily institutionalized and monetized. The fourth section analyzes two datasets—information provided by those who downloaded the software and the results from user surveys conducted by FrontlineSMS—to probe the profile of FrontlineSMS users and uses. The last section draws upon the previous section to propose some dominant typologies of FrontlineSMS use that has governance effects.

The chapter concludes that FrontlineSMS is most often deployed as a tool in complex, sometimes crowded, co-governance spaces populated by multiple actors besides state institutions aiming to achieve an array of governance outcomes particular to their own objectives. Whether these diverse nonstate actors are better than the state for achieving governance outcomes is a normative and evaluative question. What is clear, however, is that tools such as FrontlineSMS help these actors, working with the constituents they serve, to more effectively complement *and* challenge the state's privileged position as the presumed primary governance provider.

ICT and the "Long Tail" of Governance

The governance deficit in areas of limited statehood results as much from objective conditions constraining centralized coordination of public goods and services delivery that meets principal-agent accountabilities as from failures of political will or responsibility. The same structural features that often limit the state's effectiveness—population instability or low density, hard-to-reach communities, limited surplus production, weak infrastructure, and constrained resources—also make governance difficult. In underserved areas, information and communication obstacles historically converged with these fiscal, infrastructural, or technical obstacles to undermine effective centralized governance provision.

Now, M4D and ICT-for-Development (ICT4D) innovations are charting diverse trajectories where a range of localized governance-style outcomes built upon new hybrid digital information ecologies are more viable in spite of the limited state. Areas of limited statehood are often still areas of limited Internet penetration. Yet ICT innovations that harness mobile telephony are generating effects in these contexts that meaningfully relate to core "Web 2.0" ideas and inspirations, such as enabling "user-generated content"; facilitating crowdsourcing and harnessing the "wisdom of crowds" (O'Reilly 2005; Surowiecki 2004); user-based tailoring of content and tool development based around an "architecture of participation" (Attwell and Elferink 2007; O'Reilly 2003); network effects (Benkler 2006); the Internet's "key affordances" for social activism (Earl and Kimport 2011), and, discussed in more detail here, how it opens up "long tail" economies (Anderson 2006a).

Successful innovations help to overturn information scarcity and communication intermittence and allow for new opportunities of social coordination to enhance public goods outcomes. Short message service (SMS), a nearly ubiquitous feature of mobile handsets, is proving uniquely powerful. Its core features of asynchronous communication, ease of replication, relative anonymity, comparability, and storability, lend it essential digital data functionalities for coordinated action unattainable with voice. FrontlineSMS is only one of many SMS communications management tools in this space. Others include SMSSync, a Google Android application written by the team behind the crowdmapping platform, Ushahidi, that replaces the computer as the intermediary and runs the SMS gateway program on the phone itself, Telerivet, a venture-capital backed commercial SMS gateway product that uses Android phones and web-based portals, and RapidSMS, a web-based (rather than desktop/laptop based) bulk-messaging tool developed by UNICEF's Innovations and Development team in 2008.

Innovative users of such M4D tools conducting governance-related work do not see "like a state" to centrally deploy information and communication technologies to pursue comprehensive scale and institutionalization from "above," as James Scott (1998) analyzed, but instead support the achievement of localized solutions from the "bottom-up." The innovations themselves require a level of local appropriateness that often eschews technological wizardry in favor of suitability, adaptability, and ease of use.

Ken Banks, the developer of FrontlineSMS, has borrowed and adapted Anderson's popular Web 2.0 idea to explain this in terms of "social mobile and the 'long tail'" and the need for "last mile technologies" (Banks 2008; see also, Banks 2009a; 2009b; 2009d). In his seminal analysis, Chris Anderson coined the "long tail" to capture how the Internet is fostering rich diversity and niche pref-erences in social and cultural life, and rendering them economically viable tar-gets for savvy end-user focused Web 2.0 businesses. The space-constrained and cost-heavy centralized music retail outlet could not viably cater to niche hard-to-reach markets until Internet-based retailers changed the economics of chasing margins in the "long tail" (Anderson 2006).

In the social mobile or M4D space, the FrontlineSMS team argues that the long tail captures the important inverse relationship between "between highly complex, expensive technologies and the likelihood that a broad range of organi-zations will be able to use them. The standard of replicability can be quite difficult to attain, especially when targeting grassroots organizations in under resourced or 'last mile' environments" (Banks, McDonald, and Scialom 2011, 10). Instead, FrontlineSMS takes a leaf from David Edgerton's book, *The Shock of the Old* (Edgerton 2006), which argues for more focus on technology-in-use and less on technology-as-invention and doffs its hat to a long lineage of development think-ing advocating small-scale "appropriate technology" (Schumacher 1973). Leading commentators on innovation and social change, such as MIT's Ethan Zuckerman, laud FrontlineSMS for "not being shiny at all."[2]

We can push the usefulness of the "long tail" concept further. The break-through in the supply-demand equation that Anderson analyzed in relation to the Internet-based music industry also resonates with M4D and governance in areas of limited statehood. Where resource-strapped centralized authorities might consider it uneconomical and politically unnecessary to improve governance out-comes among remote and/or marginal populations, FrontlineSMS and similar "low-tech" ICT-enabled mobile telephony platforms for distributed interaction potentially recalibrate demand and supply logics, and thus the political economy, of informational flows that underpin governance.

Such platforms can change the demand side by amplifying and aggregating the voice—and thus possibilities for recognition—of least-served constituencies, and by raising their realistic expectations of meaningfully tailored information/content delivery. They can change the supply side in two ways: First, they enable increasingly user-shaped governance outcomes, especially where the public good and governance outcome is informational in nature; and second, they provide new affordances to governance actors, sometimes state authorities but most often nonstate actors (local and international), to organize their work with effi-cient cost-saving modalities that better approximate the level of institutionalized coordination attributed to governance. The net effect is to make it more viable *as well as more politically necessary* to serve areas of limited statehood.

However, given that most deployments of M4D innovations are by organiza-tions of one kind or another, there are limitations in seeing such platforms as sim-ply enabling citizen "collective action" or community "self-governance." Optimists hold out that ICT innovations are a "disruptive technology" for development, a possible "game-changer" that heralds Development 2.0 by disintermediating flows of development assistance and de-institutionalizing, networking, and local-izing developmental agency (Heeks 2010; Thompson 2008). The best ICT innova-tions certainly can and do achieve some of this, but with evident limits. Here, Donner (2010) has proposed that M4D embodies a tension between its "dual heritages" or two "interpretive frames": the "user choice" frame applied initially to the impact of landline telephony on people's lives and the "embedded direc-tionality" frame attributed to studies of socio-technical systems and development informatics that suggests a recursive relationship between technology, directed application by actors deploying the technology, and social context.

Neither frame exclusively captures the essence of M4D processes. While the "user choice" frame holds out promise for local agency and "horizontal" collective action, M4D innovators and their intended users operate within an "embedded directionality" frame of being "4 development," and adapt it to their own ends. There is an implied "spirit of the feature set" of M4D tools (Donner 2010, 4)—the "official line which the technology present to people regarding how to act when using the system... supplying a normative frame with regard to the behaviors that are appropriate within the context of the technology" (DeSanctis and Poole 1994, 126)—that, while facilitative and user-choice focused, structures and is struc-tured by the context of application.

There is also a fundamental challenge in tracking actual achievements with assumed causal logics of "long tail" M4D. Where highly visible and publicized top-down solutions to the Digital Divide and the Information Society's "Fourth World" (Castells 1996; 1997; 1998)—such as telecenters (Heeks 2002)—were seen to be based on flawed assumptions, innovations such as FrontlineSMS exemplify technological innovations that embody Richard Heek's manifesto for ICT4D 2.0, namely to focus on technologies in use, on local application and inno-vation and on scaling existing successes (Heeks 2008). Yet Donner rightly points out that much more empirical knowledge needs to be gathered on M4D inno-vations of this kind to assess whether they are not simply, often inadvertently, "fractals" (smaller-scale replications) of the asymmetrical structural effects of the Information Society that Castell's identified in his seminal work. Here, the analy-sis of FrontlineSMS use in the remainder of this chapter affords us some valuable insights.

FrontlineSMS: Grassroots M4D Innovation and the Challenges of Success

This section introduces FrontlineSMS and then considers what the story of its rapid rise to prominence can tell us about the potential for ICT-based innovations to be deployed in sustained and institutionalized ways with sufficient scale such that they might support governance outcomes.

FrontlineSMS is a freely available and open source software tool that enables users with only a mobile phone or GSM modem and basic computer to deploy a text messaging system for two-way communication at scale. It harnesses the phenomenal growth of mobile phone penetration to enhance the work of diverse actors, from grassroots organizations and local nonprofits to international NGOs and academic researchers, helping them to connect more easily with their staff, partners and target audiences.

In June 2012, the team behind FrontlineSMS launched Version 2 of their flagship software tool in Nairobi, London, and Washington, DC, to a captive audience of existing users and supporters with considerable fanfare and publicity. This was a far cry from its humble origins in early 2005, when inventor Ken Banks needed a mere US$15,000 to develop a low-cost text-messaging system for charitable organizations working in conservation and development. Self-taught, he wrote the original code in five weeks on a kitchen table in a farmhouse in Finland. This was a "last mile" solution that began with "last mile" means.

In the intervening years, the tool (albeit significantly reworked in 2008 and made open source) had been downloaded over 25,000 times in over seventy countries, the vast majority within regions constituting the "Global South" (see Figure 6.1). The FrontlineSMS team champion "mobile for social change" and M4D, and FrontlineSMS applications have been wide-ranging in this regard, including election-monitoring in Nigeria, Burundi, and the Philippines; interactive agricultural radio programming in Kenya; coordination of district health outreach in Malawi; delivering HIV/AIDS awareness and support information in Uganda and India; monitoring human rights abuses in Egypt; monitoring and response on domestic violence in Benin; disaster response in Haiti, Pakistan, and the Horn of Africa; and citizen reporting of corporate malpractice in Indonesia.

FrontlineSMS does not require an Internet connection and, when used with a laptop, can be portable and operate soundly where electricity is intermittent. For many of its users, it is simply useful. They download and install the software (one moment where an Internet connection is handy), connect a GSM modem or mobile phone with active SIM card to their computer, and use the software interface to send and receive messages to and from one or many phone users; build and tailor contacts databases; target and schedule regular communications; archive, search, and analyze message data; and utilize additional task or sector specific functionality or build it for themselves and share it with the FrontlineSMS user community. The team behind the software has also developed tailored versions in key sectors, including FrontlineSMS:Medic,[3] FrontlineSMS:Credit, FrontlineSMS:Legal, FrontlineSMS:Learn, and FrontlineSMS:Radio.[4]

The duality of frames that Donner suggested is evident in how the FrontlineSMS team conceive of their raison d'être. The "About Us" page on their website draws on both frames (FrontlineSMS 2012). First, there is a stated belief in "giving *people ownership* of the tools they need to change their world *for the better*. Our textable \o/ logo represents a person with their arms outstretched—a manifestation of our mission to *empower people* to use their own ingenuity to craft solutions and create *positive change in their own communities* using mobile technology." There is a clear privileging of user-choice, yet, operationally, the target users are organizations: the tool "helps *organizations* across the world to overcome communication barriers they face" (FrontlineSMS 2012). The tensions between user choice, scale, institutionalization, and embedded normative frames also appear in Banks's posts on "social mobile's long tail":

> The default position for many people working in ICT4D is to build centralized solutions to local problems—things that "integrate" and "scale." With little local ownership and engagement, many of these top-down approaches fail to appreciate the culture of technology and its users.... Users... want to have their own system, something which works with them to solve their problem. (Banks 2009a; see also, Banks 2009b; 2008)

The imagined user here is an intervener of sorts, albeit a local one, within the frame of what M4D and ICT4D aims to achieve. As such, intended users minimally share with FrontlineSMS an ideal of positive developmental change, with the team privileging "small organizations that meet the challenges of their underserved communities. We at FrontlineSMS not only admit, but celebrate, that it is this incredible group of people who continue to drive both the development and innovation around M4D" (Banks, McDonald, and Scialom 2011, 12).

Such an appreciation of the tensions, healthy though they might be, in how the use of FrontlineSMS is imagined by its creators undergirds the empirical interrogation in this chapter of FrontlineSMS user data in terms of which type and size of actor (ranging from individuals and local and small grassroots organizations to international organizations); operating in which geographic locations (region and country level, but also rural and urban) and in which governance sectors (from community work, health, education and agriculture to media, activism and research); and deploying the tool to achieve which kinds of work efficiencies (communicating with staff, sourcing and then using crowd information, providing informational goods and services to constituents, etc.), tends to predominate, or be underrepresented, in the use of FrontlineSMS to date.

Organizationally, the FrontlineSMS team grew rapidly from just Ken Banks on his own to five in 2010 and seventeen in 2012, the majority of them now based in Nairobi, Kenya. Initial supporters had shelled out a trifling $15,000 in 2005 to get the first version built. By 2010, FrontlineSMS had attracted over $1,000,000 in funding from the likes of the MacArthur Foundation, the Hewlett Foundation, the Open Society Initiative, the Rockefeller Foundation, and the Omidyar Network, to enhance the tool and support or users, expand its reach, and sustain the organization's future. The innovativeness and value of the tool was widely recognized, and between 2009 and 2011, FrontlineSMS received a Silicon Valley Tech Award,[5] the

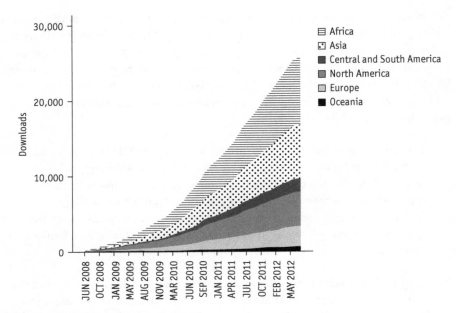

Figure 6.1 FrontlineSMS downloads.[12]

Curry Stone Design Award for social design pioneers (see Curry Stone 2013), a finalist prize in the Buckminster Fuller Challenge for socially responsible design (see Buckminster Fuller 2013), and the Tides Foundation's Pizzigati Prize for software in the public interest (see Tides 2013). Banks in turn was honored as a Reuters Digital Vision Fellow at Stanford University, as a PopTech! Social Innovation Fellow, as an Ashoka Fellow, and as a National Geographic Emerging Explorer.

The rapid and successful development of FrontlineSMS and the organization behind it tells an important story about ICT innovation that fosters enhanced governance outcomes in M4D's "long tail." Such innovations are often borne of smallness, cheapness, low-tech contextual appropriateness, adaptability, and ease of use. The features enable users *themselves* (and not the technology alone) to rapidly drive adoption, adaption, and outcomes in multiple global localities and within short time horizons. Yet these same logics attract excitement at other levels for their scalable potential as "killer apps" for social development in underserved and hard to reach areas writ-large. There was thus a challenge to reconcile the ethos of the initial innovation with the opportunities, and burdens, of success. Banks, a self-described "reluctant innovator" (see Banks 2012), had no intention to create and sustain an organization around him buttressed by reliable revenue streams. Yet leaving FrontlineSMS to a wiki-style open source future was unworkable. In 2011 and 2012, Banks stepped back from day-to-day operations, handing over to a team to take the organization forward.

With FrontlineSMS Version 2, and with a Cloud-based version proposed for 2013 or 2014, the team focused their efforts on introducing users to more complex features. FrontlineSMS has also sought to attract and, crucially, retain larger NGO and for-profit users who might make a subscription model workable and thus help ensure the organization's sustainability. These types of users often require different features and functionalities, such as higher-volume, more configurable, and web-based services. In sum, although the story starts with the genius of reluctance, and with simplicity, locality, and cheapness, it becomes one of organizational strategy, technical complexity (with a user-friendly interface), local and global audiences, and financial sustainability.

As discussed below, a similar "institutional" effect applies to many users of the tool seeking to achieve and sustain governance outcomes: beyond initial ad hoc successes, advances in the flow of bits often need atoms (human and physical) to be of enduring use, and this often involves inputs by actors and interests beyond the beneficiary community who are capable of institutionalizing modes and modalities of governance-related activities.

The FrontlineSMS downloads data, introduced above, tell us little about actual situated use and outcomes, about local contestations over control and use of informational flows, and, in sum, about whether M4D tools can really be "weapons of the weak" (or at least those credibly working with and for them) to achieve self-defined emancipatory social change, or are instead put to the service of holders of relative power (local or international, state or nonstate, charitable or for-profit) with directed and instrumental objectives that might reinforce inequities and dependencies. The very "legibility" (Scott 1998) that states seek to have of their citizens through systematic knowledge is what proponents of user-focused, free, and open-source "bottom-up" solutions emphatically criticize, yet this also saddles them very limited knowledge on actual use and outcomes.

Salient here is the long tradition in the development studies literature of critiquing the extent of local beneficiary ownership and agency in defining problems and pursuing solutions. Just because it is not the limited—and too often predatory or partisan—state that is acting, does not mean that the nonstate actors are better able or intentioned. Nor is "participation" automatically a source of empowerment where it is instrumentalized to legitimate pre-decided objectives of interveners (Cooke and Kothari 2001). The abstract "user choice" qualities of M4D innovations might be too easily overdetermined without the empirical analysis to question actual intentions, processes, and outcomes. Considerable faith is also placed in the "spirit of feature set" of the M4D innovation and trust in the spirituality of the "4D" tool user. The following analysis points to such ambivalences, while demonstrating some of the most significant governance contexts and outcomes of FrontlineSMS deployment.

Deployments of FrontlineSMS: Who, What, Where, and How?

This section probes further into the data on Frontline's downloads and into results of two FrontlineSMS administered user surveys. This enables a sharper picture of FrontlineSMS use and its implications for substituted governance.

The download data analyzed gives us only a broad brush, and clearly imperfect, picture of FrontlineSMS use. However, we can see some trends from the aggregate information, such as the growing dominance of users from Africa and Asia, who account for 34.8 percent and 27.7 percent of total downloads, respectively. Within Africa, 47.8 percent of users came from just four countries: Kenya (25.7 percent), Nigeria (8.6 percent), Uganda (7.6 percent), and Ghana (5.9 percent). Within Asia, India (24.4 percent), Philippines (16.6 percent), Indonesia (14.9 percent), and Pakistan (8.9 percent) accounted for 64.8 percent of the region's downloads. All eight countries are characterized by a combination of certain structural features relative to the rest of their region, including: (1) liberalized telecommunications sectors; (2) strong civil society sectors; and (3) areas of limited statehood, in terms of sectoral and socio-geographic state presence in governance. Word-of-mouth and network effects are likely important for how actors come to know about the software.

We can also glean from the information contributed by those who downloaded the software that their dominant fields of operation correspond with certain core governance sectors. Education (19.9 percent) and health (13.8 percent) dominate, with agriculture significant in Africa and Asia, but less so elsewhere, and economic development less significant amongst users in Asia. This can be compared with richer data from surveyed users.

A second dataset with two rounds of a web-survey administered to the FrontlineSMS community enables sharper analysis. The first round of the survey was conducted between November 2010 and January 2011 and the second round between December 2011 and March 2012.[6] The invitation to participate was made through an open call via FrontlineSMS website, Twitter, Facebook, and the FrontlineSMS Ning forum and newsletter, and a prize-draw was held from the pool of respondents.

This dataset contains a total of 304 unique responses to a range of questions relating to user profile (country, actor type, sector(s) of work), use of the software tool, and use of FrontlineSMS user support resources.[7] Thus, while the more comprehensive downloads dataset reveals little about actual use of the tool, the more limited survey data, albeit not a random sample (and certainly not representative), helps us to probe the use of FrontlineSMS on governance-related activity. The strong alignment in regional distribution of survey respondents with downloaders (see Table 6.1, below), gives some confidence that conclusions drawn from the survey data are indicative of the wider population of users/downloaders.[8]

Table 6.1 **Regional Comparison of Downloads and Survey Datasets**

Region	Percent of survey responses (n = 304)	Percent of downloaders (n = 25,677)
Africa	35.5	34.8
Asia	25.3	27.7
Central and South America	5.9	8.8
North America	20.1	15.7
Europe	11.2	10.6
Oceania	2.0	2.3
Total	**100**	**100**

Overall, the survey shows dominant sectors of FrontlineSMS use are health and education, followed by activism, campaigning and elections, emergency and crisis response, and agriculture. However, there is considerable regional variation (see Figure 6.2). This is examined below.

The majority of organizations sampled based in Africa (73.8 percent), Asia (81.6 percent), and Central and South America (88.9 percent) operate in their own country. On the contrary, North America– and Europe-based organizations operate mostly in developing countries in Africa, Asia, and South America (61 percent and 56.3 percent respectively). Thus, we can credibly propose that although "emergency response" was a significant sector for users based in North America, this is because many humanitarian organizations operating internationally are headquartered there. This confirms that FrontlineSMS is an ICT tool mostly deployed in areas (geographic, sectoral, and temporal) of limited statehood.

Given that downloading the software is free and relatively easy, the first reality-check that the survey allows for concerns active use of FrontlineSMS. While 77.6 percent of respondents in sixty-seven countries were either testing (37.2 percent), actively using (32.2 percent) or had previously used (8.2 percent) the software, 18.1 percent had chosen another tool (3 percent) or never deployed (15.1 percent) the tool at all. Respondents based in Europe and North America accounted for close to half of the latter cases, 32.4 percent and 26.2 percent of each region's respondents respectively. The European and North American cases of downloading but never using FrontlineSMS were especially in the sectors of activism/campaigning/election monitoring and human rights, dominated by national and international nonprofit organizations.

By contrast, the take-up rate (aggregating categories of "prior use," "currently testing," and "active use") is much higher in Central and Southern America (88.9 percent), Asia (85.7 percent), and Africa (83.3 percent). A full two-thirds (66.1 percent) of users surveyed who are actively using the tool are in Africa and

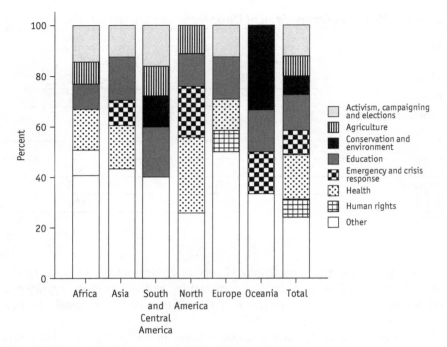

Figure 6.2 FrontlineSMS users' major sectors of operation by region.

Asia. With sectors of work, the proportion of active users is highest in health and education, which in turn are dominated by local or national nonprofit organizations and academic/research users operating in these two regions. Just as its creators would hope to see, take-up of FrontlineSMS appears not to be a function of technological capability but rather of appropriateness and usefulness in "last mile" contexts.

An analysis of governance substitution requires attention be paid to the type of actors working to institutionalize social coordination in particular sectors to achieve public goods outcomes. Aligning with the ethos of FrontlineSMS, local or national nonprofit/NGOs (38.2 percent) dominate the types of organizations using the tool. Interestingly, the next significant "type" of organization is not international organizations (such as UN agencies) (6.6 percent) or international NGOs (7.3 percent), but rather "academic/research" organizations (17.6 percent), followed by "for-profit" organizations (14.3 percent). In terms of regional skews from the survey data, Africa accounts for over half of the locations where international organizations (55 percent) or international NGOs (54.5 percent) are using FrontlineSMS, and North America accounts for nearly a third (28.3 percent) of where academic/research organizations using FrontlineSMS are located, though often working internationally.

While the survey indicates that all sectors are dominated by local or national nonprofit/NGOs, some particular skews are noteworthy and emphasize the heterogeneity of "4 development" actors. Nearly half (47.1 percent) of surveyed organizations in 2011 and 2012 employing FrontlineSMS for activism/campaigning were local or national organizations. In traditionally "core" governance sectors of agriculture, health, and education, academic/research organizations are more prominent than they are in other sectors. For-profit organizations are also prominent in agriculture, conservation/environment, and emergency response work, as well as in more obvious sectors such as microfinance. In elections monitoring, human rights, and media work, international organizations and international NGOs are more prominent than in other sectors.

The user survey data also illuminates the nature of FrontlineSMS use. By far the main use is to send (and receive) messages to small groups and individuals and to send bulk messages. In Africa and Asia, FrontlineSMS is also used for data collection (over 40 percent of users) mainly in health, education, and activism/campaigning/elections monitoring. Here, the interoperable qualities of FrontlineSMS make it a useful SMS aggregator in support of other ICT tools, notably the crowdmapping platform Ushahidi. Nearly a quarter of surveyed FrontlineSMS users integrated FrontlineSMS with Ushahidi in their work, mostly in the sectors of health, agriculture and emergency response. A disproportionate number (36 percent) of such users are based in North America, again often working in the developing world. For these actors working in these sectors, flows of information supported by FrontlineSMS populate interactive Google Maps to give nonstate actors the kind of aggregated legibility of human geography historically attainable only by centralized authorities.

Related to crowdsourcing uses, over a third of organizations use FrontlineSMS to communicate with the "general public" (37.9 percent) and this assumes more relevance in Asia (57.6 percent of organizations in that region) distributed across a wide range of sectors. Internationally, communications with the "general public" assume higher relevance in human rights (71.4 percent) and media sectors (66.7 percent).

Yet the data reinforces the embedded directionality of ICT tool deployment over a more user-choice-focused idealization of public collective action: rather than the general public, users surveyed mostly target their SMS communications at predetermined audiences (50.5 percent of users communicate with "project participants/beneficiaries" and 50.5 percent communicate with "staff and volunteers").[9] In Africa and South and Central America "project participants and beneficiaries" are a strong focus of SMS communications (respectively, 56.7 percent and 66.7 percent of organizations sampled) whereas most users based in North America and Europe, use FrontlineSMS to communicate with "staff and volunteers" (78.9 percent and 55.6 percent respectively).

The survey data thus provide a complex and nuanced insight into how FrontlineSMS appears to be used. The dataset is too limited to test multivariate hypotheses in any predictive manner, but it does allow us to suggest some dominant typologies of when and how FrontlineSMS is enhancing governance substitution by nonstate actors. These are developed below, together with some illustrative cases.

FrontlineSMS and Governance: Dominant Typologies and Illustrative Cases

This section advances three dominant, but by no means exhaustive, typologies of governance effects of FrontlineSMS use and some illustrative cases. The aim here is to help delimit the territory of actual versus idealized potentialities for governance substitution by nonstate actors using ICT.

In world regions where limited statehood is more common, local or national organizations working in sector areas where information-based services are significant (even if alongside delivering material public goods) or where communication with intended beneficiaries or workers enhances governance-related outcomes are more likely to deploy FrontlineSMS productively. A first dominant typology of FrontlineSMS governance-related use is thus local or national non-profit organizations working in a focused number of African and Asian countries in sectors where better informational flows (1) are intrinsic to a governance activity; or (2) help these organizations to facilitate more optimal delivery of public goods or services.

The use of FrontlineSMS in the agricultural sector is a good example. The *Organic Farmer*, a Kenyan for-profit print magazine on ecologically friendly farming practices for small-scale farmers, also sponsors radio programs and now uses FrontlineSMS to interact with rural audiences separated by vast distances. By helping to transform radio broadcasts into a dialogue between farmers and experts, radio producers can respond to listener questions, build listener databases and profiles, better tailor content, and send program reminders. In Côte d'Ivoire, the local office RONGEAD, a European NGO, uses FrontlineSMS to support small-scale cashew producers to gain better access to markets. RONGEAD use FrontlineSMS to send 3,000 SMSs every week with updated market price information and to share knowledge across a network of thousands of producers that improves market understanding and decision-making.

Election-monitoring is another sector in which local networks and organizations are using FrontlineSMS and similar systems to mobilize and coordinate citizen action and to aggregate information that generates public goods, primarily evidence in the public domain that supports accountability. In April 2007, one of the first FrontlineSMS deployments to capture global media attention (BBC 2007) was by the Network of Mobile Election Monitors of Nigeria (NMEM), created by a Nigerian nonprofit group, the Human Emancipation Lead Project

(HELP) foundation. Their aim for the presidential elections was to augment formal monitoring efforts but also to engage Nigerians as evaluators in the election process. Registered NMEM associates and recruited volunteers throughout Nigeria's thirty-six states, all coordinated through FrontlineSMS, sent over 10,000 text messages on the day of the election. The cross-checked data was used to provide an alternative perspective on the conduct of the elections and whether they adhered to electoral policy. Since then SMS-based election monitoring has grown rapidly, and reappeared in Nigeria for the 2011 presidential elections, when a group of Nigerian grassroots organizations and agencies formed ReclaimNaija (see ReclaimNaija 2013),[10] to gather incidence reports using FrontlineSMS and map them online using Ushahidi. Importantly, though, both initiatives were reactive and temporally limited, and driven by loose networks. Their salience for sustained governance outcomes may therefore be limited.

Before the Arab Spring, many ICT-based social innovations in Egypt focused on everyday governance issues. One of these was HarassMap, launched in late 2010.[11] HarassMap used FrontlineSMS to capture messages sent by victims of harassment, including their street location, which was mapped online using Ushahidi. HarassMap organized volunteers to visit hotspot areas and raise awareness of the risks there as well as the HarassMap service and to help coordinate community action. HarassMap volunteers run community-based events, with the purpose of openly discussing the issue of intimidating behavior in the area. The evidence gathered also allows the organization to advocate and lobby towards authorities. We thus see a combination of ICT-supported self-governance and collective action with evidence-based activism aimed at formal governance providers.

Another example of FrontlineSMS-Ushahidi integration is the Stop Stockouts campaign in Uganda, Kenya, and Zambia, which aims to increase access to essential medicines in local health centers and pharmacies. The campaign is an initiative of Health Action International (HAI) Africa, part of a global network organization, with support from Oxfam GB and the Open Society Initiative. However, its key implementation partners in country are national or local nongovernmental organizations (see Stop Stock-Outs 2013). The overriding focus is lobby governments to improve policy and practice in fulfilling obligations for the sustained supply of these medicines. FrontlineSMS captures and aggregates messages sent by researchers and members of the public on stockouts during "pill check weeks," which is then mapped using Ushahidi. The Stop Stockouts campaign team, often working with the media, uses the evidence gathered to advocate to policy-makers and to hold them to account. The tool also enables organizational communications between a range of local network members to enhance coordination of campaigning activity.

A common characteristic for most of the actors and examples in this first typology is that there is either no clear path for them to sustain activities and institutionalize the modes of coordination or public goods and service provision, or, in the case of activism-based initiatives, it is not clear that they aim to do so.

Initiatives, individuals, organizations, and networks come and go, as is common in the broad space of civil society. Governance outcomes occur at an aggregate level only amidst somewhat ad hoc and unpredictable developments at a lower scale.

The survey data suggested that for activists and campaigners based in Europe and North America the affordances FrontlineSMS offers in sectors such as human rights and media are valuable, but the take-up rate is lower, perhaps because they are outweighed by opportunities to leverage social media and other web-based platforms. However, for researchers based in the North, FrontlineSMS offers an effective platform for communications and data collection in core governance sectors such as health and education. These researchers are most often working collaboratively with governance providers in the South.

A second dominant typology of governance-related FrontlineSMS use is thus a "northern" academic or research institution working in the Global South in key socio-economic sectors such as health and agriculture as well as in political governance (such as voter education campaigns or community security monitoring.) The unique aspect of governance substitution here is one of collaborative co-governance between different actors operating at different scales. ICT allows relatively more technology-literate external actors to be useful (and powerful) in enabling information flows and knowledge production that can inform governance action.

One example is Georgetown University's Institute for Reproductive Health (IRH), which in 2010 and 2011 used FrontlineSMS to provide a rapid prototype of a new mobile health (mHealth) service in India. The pilot was part of a five-year multi-country United States Agency for International Development (USAID) funded Fertility Awareness-Based Methods (FAM) project. This service—called CycleTel™—provided women with accessible reproductive health information through SMS, based on the Standard Days Method® (SDM) of family planning. After the successful proof-of-concept and initial testing phases using FrontlineSMS, IRH turned to specialist technology developers for a more tailored solution.

Other initiatives by northern-based applied researchers focus on organizational efficiencies that enhance governance capacity and reach. FrontlineSMS:Medic, the first "sister project" of FrontlineSMS, began as a pilot in Malawi by North American undergraduate students. Focusing on communication challenges for rural healthcare in the developing world, their "m-Health" pilot at St. Gabriel's Hospital in Malawi aimed at eliminating costs in the work of community health workers (CHWs). A group of seventy-five CHWs were supplied with phones and trained to use FrontlineSMS for activities including patient adherence reporting, appointment reminders, and physician queries. During the pilot, the hospital saved approximately 2,048 worker hours and $2,750, and doubled the capacity of its tuberculosis treatment program (Mahmud, Rodriguez, and Nesbit 2010). Medic Mobile now operates in a range of countries, deploying various open-source tools including FrontlineSMS to enhance patient care in different ways, often working with health authorities.

Similarly, during 2009 and 2010 students from the University of Southern California partnered with the governmental Karnataka Health Promotion Trust (KHPT) and a local NGO, Bhoruka Charitable Trust (BCT), in India on a HIV information project aimed at promoting health and livelihoods among female sex workers. The effort successfully focused on cheaper and more effective communications across a rural network of volunteers and workers. FrontlineSMS was also used by Columbia University researchers in the Voix des Kivus crowdseeding project (see Chapter 10) and in a collaborative project with the Ugandan parliament and the US-based NGO, National Democratic Institute, experimenting on constituent access to political communication with parliamentary representatives.

A third dominant typology relates to disaster or emergency response, when temporal factors limit the reach and effectiveness of the state. Here, both local/national and international organizations utilize SMS communications systems such as FrontlineSMS to enhance access to public goods and services in a variety of ways. During the 2011 and 2012 drought in the Horn of Africa, the international NGO ActionAid, as part of the Infoasaid.org consortium, used FrontlineSMS—together with the Interactive Voice Response (IVR) tool, FreedomFone.org—to provide pastoralist communities with timely and regular information on issues such as food and livestock prices in local markets, as well as location and content of food aid distributions, and to receive feedback from community committees. The pilot project won the "Innovation" award at the United Kingdom's 2012 Technology4good Awards.

During the floods in Pakistan in 2010, the International Organization for Migration (IOM) used FrontlineSMS for mass-messaging of basic hygiene and sanitation advice to Pakistanis, including through human network nodes (FrontlineSMS 2010). First Response Radio (FRR), a network of radio broadcasters, NGOs, and government partners with the goal of delivering critical information via radio to affected communities in the immediate aftermath of disasters, deploy FrontlineSMS as standard equipment with their "radio in a box" to support audience feedback and information gathering. Besides sending bulk messages, FrontlineSMS is also used in disaster settings to gather vital information to support responsive action. For example, the Commission of Women Victims for Victims (KOFAVIV by its Creole acronym) is a local nonprofit organization founded by and for rape survivors to fight sexual abuse. It uses FrontlineSMS for an alert hotline in Haiti's displaced persons camps, where volunteers monitor sexual violence. They alert the authorities, and they notify volunteer psychologists and lawyers who work with the victims.

Conclusion

Areas of limited statehood are often characterized by complex co-governance ecologies populated by a diverse array of actors having governance effects. We should not create too sharp a distinction between state and stakeholder, between formal governance and self-governance, and between directed action and collective action. Here, ICT innovations are entering into this existing complex governance landscape and having some important effects. Some ICT innovations are changing the possibilities of governance in this "long tail" by recalibrating the information-dependent demand and supply logics of social action.

The application of ICT4D and M4D innovations often better involves, and might at times be driven by, the governance constituency (or stakeholders) in question. However those applications that sustain and institutionalize themselves sufficiently to approximate "governance" mostly rely upon a constellation of other organizational actors of different types, with diverse objectives and occupying a range of scales, who seek to substitute for, or render more responsive and accountable, governance provided by the state.

FrontlineSMS in its genesis is inspired by a belief that end-users (communities, citizens, stakeholders) can better own and direct self-governance outcomes using ICT. The user-choice ideal is thus a foundational commitment and core ethos for this M4D innovation that is embedded within the technology, but it is married from the outset with an (increasingly significant) "for development" directionality that looks towards more institutionalized, scalable, and financially sustainable users and uses. FrontlineSMS is less a tool in the hands of communities and citizens that enables "self-governance" than a communications platform deployed by a range of nonstate actors, many existing and active ones, to better pursue their particular objectives with distinct governance effects. That said, taking the long view, the extensive deployment of innovations such as FrontlineSMS are building stronger informational "connective tissue" within "last mile" contexts and within and between governance actors themselves that is a foundation for more responsive and accountable governance.

Notes

1. The author thanks Dr. Claudia Abreu Lopes from the University of Cambridge Centre of Governance and Human Rights for her helpful assistance with the statistical analysis in this chapter and for feedback on earlier versions. Thanks are also owed to Ken Banks, Laura Walker Hudson, and Sean MacDonald from FrontlineSMS for their willingness to support this research by making available FrontlineSMS download and survey data, and for feedback on the chapter. The author also notes that the University of Cambridge Centre of Governance and Human Rights, which he directs, has collaborated with FrontlineSMS in the development of FrontlineSMS:Radio and on its "Africa's Voices" interactive radio and deliberative public opinion applied research project. The Cairns Charitble Trust, the Isaac Newton Trust and the Cambride-Africa Alborada Research Fund support this research.
2. A quote from publicity for the award to FrontlineSMS of the Curry Stone Design Prize, for which Zuckerman was a judge (CurryStone 2013).
3. The team behind FrontlineSMS:Medic then went on to start Medic Mobile.
4. More information on FrontlineSMS sister projects is available from the FrontlineSMS website: http://www.frontlinesms.com/.
5. The 2009 Katherine M. Swanson Equality Award (see TechAward 2013).

6. The FrontlineSMS user survey dataset was obtained and analysed pursuant to a license agreement with FrontlineSMS. This dataset contains 57 variables and 304 valid cases (174 cases in survey 2010/11 and 130 cases in survey 2011/12). The MS Excel file was converted into a SPSSv20 file and missing values were assigned code 99. Countries were coded according to 3166-1 Alpha 2 system and recoded into six macrogeographical regions (Africa, Asia, Europe, North America, South America, and Oceania). String variables containing multiple answers were transformed into several variables and then grouped into variable sets.

7. The same core questionnaire was used in the two rounds, but two questions were added to the second round concerning the target audience of SMS communications and whether the tool was used with other ICT tools, such as Ushahidi. Additionally, the answer options to the question "Which field do you work in?" differ between rounds: "Community and social care," "Humanitarian work," and "International Development" were excluded from the second round and "Election monitoring," "Emergency and crisis response," "Marketing," and "Media" sectors were added to the second round.

8. The chi-square test for goodness of fit revealed that the six regions in the downloads data and in the survey sample occur with equal probabilities [χ^2 (5) = 7.45, p = .189].

9. Users surveyed were able to choose multiple targets audiences to reflect possible multiple uses of the software.

10. A different initiative, ReVoDa was designed and built for the local NGO coalition EnoughisEnough (EiE) Nigeria, but depended on a downloaded application to the mobile phone: http://eienigeria.org/rsvp/protect/revoda.

11. See http://harassmap.org/en/.

12. Cumulative area graph for downloads-growth per world region. The FrontlineSMS downloads dataset was obtained and analyzed pursuant to a license agreement with FrontlineSMS. The initial dataset contains 28,338 cases out of which 2661 (9.4 percent) were considered not valid because all the fields/variables were empty or duplicated from a primary case. The final dataset contains 25,677 cases. The MS Excel file was converted into a SPSSv20 file and strings variables (e.g., date and sector) were transformed into more appropriate formats. Missing values were assigned code 99. Country codes using 3166-1 Alpha 2 standards were recoded into macro-geographical regions (Africa, Asia, Europe, North America, Central and South America, Oceania). Year was extracted from the variable "date."

7

Natural Disasters and Alternative Modes of Governance: The Role of Social Networks and Crowdsourcing Platforms in Russia

GREGORY ASMOLOV

Introduction

Natural disasters have always posed a challenge for people and governments. Nature bursts into the world and, in a short time, undermines whatever social order exists. Obviously, in addition to the victims and the human tragedy, natural disaster usually causes a disruption of governance services. Put another way, natural disasters challenge the state's capacity "to implement and enforce the monopoly of force and political decisions" (see Chapter 1, p. 5) in the area affected by the disaster. Even prosperous and developed state may take a longtime to return to a point of equilibrium in the aftermath of a powerful disaster. As Risse (2011) points out, "New Orleans right after Hurricane Katrina in 2005 constituted an area of limited statehood in the sense that US authorities were unable to enforce decisions and to uphold the monopoly over the means of violence for a short period of time."

An evaluation of the degree of statehood in a disaster area should consider several factors, including the speed of recovery and the number of services provided. The analysis, however, should focus on the role of the state in management of the emergency response by asking whether it has the capacity to enforce decisions. It must also assess the extent to which the state in control in the area affected by a disaster. This does not mean that the state is the only source of order and assistance. But it does imply that the state plays the dominant role in the organization and coordination of help and disaster relief. While governance capacity is always limited by disaster, what is really tested by an emergency is the robustness of statehood. A disaster is a state's governance capacity stress test.

Statehood and governance at a time of emergency are interrelated. If a natural disaster creates a temporary regional vacuum in state presence, what are the implications for the provision of governance in emergency and post-emergency situations? The limited statehood concept suggests, "limited and even failing statehood does not necessarily translate into the absence of governance" (see Chapter 1, p. 5). According to Livingston and Walter-Drop, "rather than being absent, governance can take on different forms, involving a different set of actors and different modalities than in the standard" (10).

For instance, while the Japanese government was heavily criticized for the disorganization of relief efforts in response to the Kobe earthquake in January 1995, the Yamaguchi-gumi—a Japanese crime syndicate—provided food and water to the victims (Sterngold 1995). Members of the mafia used their own resources, including motorbikes, boats, and a helicopter, to distribute supplies. This is a colorful example of a nonstate entity providing governance in an emergency when the state failed.

At the same time, it is important to differentiate between the source of an emergency response and the structure of management of emergency relief. We can identify three potential sources of emergency response:

1. State institutional response—emergency response that relies on state organizational structures and resources.
2. Outsourcing of emergency response—nonstate institutional actors from within the state (businesses, NGOs) or outside (including foreign state actors).
3. Crowdsourcing—response that relies on the participation of individuals (volunteers).

We can see the involvement of all types of actors in almost every emergency situation, since no state has resources that are sufficient to respond to a significant disaster. But who mobilizes these resources and decides how and for whom are they allocated? The capacity to play a dominant role in orchestrating an emergency response is one of the key attributes of statehood. Once the state fails to manage the emergency response, alternative actors can emerge and fill this gap. The question of this chapter is: What is the role of ICT in the emergence of alternative actors in emergency situations? To address this question we look at two cases in Russia. The case studies argue that the capacity of ICT to increase the transparency around the scale of disaster can be associated with citizen self-mobilization that has been enabled by the same technologies that contributed to transparency. Mapping the functions of ICT in emergency response in situation of limited statehood is followed by critical assessment if the described can be approached as alternative mode of governance and to what extent it is able to challenge the state's power.

The Russia Wildfires of 2010

In summer 2010, more than sixty people died and more than seventy villages and towns were damaged by unprecedented wildfires in western Russia. Thousands of people were left homeless and destitute. An emergency situation was declared in seven regions by the Russian president, Dmitry Medvedev. Yet, despite the declaration, some sharply criticized the government for its insufficient and ineffective response to the disaster. The extent of the criticism varied according to the medium. Traditional mass media, primarily television, which is controlled by the Kremlin, framed the situation as a "crisis under control" and praised the Russian leaders' efficient response. On the other hand, the social media were full of citizens' reports of the immense scale of the disaster. Many reports on blogs and social networks showed the government's failings, raising questions about the ability of the Russian authorities to manage the crisis (Khokhlova 2010; 2012).

User-generated Internet content also contributed to the public awareness of the ensuing sudden increase in the death rate among residents of Moscow. The thick layer of smoke that covered the Russian capital was extremely dangerous for elderly people and those with heart disease and asthma. Initially, while government officials denied the increase in death rates, blog posts by people who had lost relatives, as well as some who worked in media centers, showed that the situation was far from what official sources were reporting through state-controlled media. Moscow morgues were filled beyond their capacity (Asmolov 2010a). In these ways, the state lost its monopoly on reporting statistics (Scott 1998). Consequently, it was more complicated for them to manipulate information to minimize the scale of the disaster.

One blogger, whose village was damaged by fire, posted a public appeal to Prime Minister Putin:

> I have a question. Where does our money go? Why every year do we slide further and further toward a primitive society? Why do we need a f. .. ing innovation center in Skolkovo if we don't even have fire trucks? Why did we previously have such people as forest rangers who would warn firefighters about fires and did not allow those fires to spread and affect villages. I don't want a telephone in a village. I want fire ponds and my rynda back. (translated by Davidov [2010])

Rynda is the name given to a bell that was once used to call for help in times of emergency. While *Rynda* became a meme symbolizing this failure of government, the people's desire for control over the tools of emergency response and distrust in government was a major leitmotif in online discourse about the wildfires. Another blogger published an appeal to the minister responsible for emergency situations:

I've lost the last childish illusions that someone up there is taking care of us and protecting us (no, I'm not talking about God, I'm talking about the leadership of the country, you included). Now I've become an adult and count on myself only. (translated by Asmolov 2010b).

ICT-ENABLED NONSTATE RESPONSE

The activities of Russian Internet users were not limited to sharing information about the disaster and undermining the rosy official accounts. One of the first initiatives was the launching of a special Livejournal (LJ) blog community, *Pozar_Ru* (pozar is the Russian word for fire) for those who were interested in helping. In just a few days, several thousand bloggers had become members of the community. Several groups dedicated to the provision of assistance started to work on social networking websites Facebook and Vkontakte (the largest Russian social network). Regional social networking groups and city forums were used to coordinate assistance at a local level. The members of these communities were interested not just in expressing their frustration about the situation, but also in mobilizing resources that were needed to help victims of the disaster and to fight the fires.

Some people posted specific calls for help, for evacuation of people from the affected areas and for other forms of humanitarian assistance. Those interested in helping were looking for different opportunities to contribute to emergency relief. The activities coordinated through these communities were not limited to helping wildfire victims. Bloggers created units of volunteer firefighters and went into the field with professional firefighting equipment that had been donated by Internet users. The volunteers units were created in cooperation with NGOs like Greenpeace, which also sent people to fight the forest fires. Internet users also actively shared instructions on how to fight various types of wildfires, and on what equipment volunteers should have. In this case, bits led to a distribution of atoms (firefighters and needed supplies).

A number of bloggers took leadership responsibilities and played a major role in the coordination of assistance. A medical doctor, Elizaveta Glinka (blog name *doctor-liza*), became a major leader of the collection and distribution of humanitarian assistance. Her apartment was turned into a headquarters for aid coordination and a storehouse. Similarly, journalist Igor Chersky (blog name *i_cherski*) played a major role in the coordination of volunteer firefighting units. Internet users expressed trust in the coordination activities of these bloggers and their decisions about priorities for allocation of resources. The activity of the leaders was viewed as being free of politics and focused on the practical aspects of emergency relief. Reputation and trust were key factors in the success of this coordination. The balance of trust shifted from relying on institutional actors and anonymous authorities to trusting in particular online individuals.

However, while the Internet provided a platform for the twenty-four-hour coordination and exchange of information on the emergency, it also created a

Figure 7.1 "The Help Map" website front page (Russian-fires.ru).

problem of information overload. A constant flow of requests for and offers of help made efficient coordination more and more difficult. Better coordination, allowing the precise allocation of resources according to need and providing easy access to total situational awareness for the online community, could make Internet-mediated emergency relief more efficient and sustainable.

At the beginning of August 2010 a crowdsourcing website, Help Map for Victims of Wildfires (Russian-fires.ru) was created.[1] This was based on the event-mapping platform Ushahidi and was the first time Ushahidi was used in Russia. The major purpose of the Help Map was not the collection of crowdsourced information about the wildfires, but primarily the facilitation of mutual aid and provision of a bridge between those who needed help and those who wanted to help (Brannon 2010). It was a tool for collective action. This was reflected in the categories of the map, such as "What Is Needed" (with subcategories: need home, need clothes, need food, need evacuation, etc.) and "I Want to Help" (subcategories: I have clothes; I have transport; I have food; etc.).

Unlike in some other emergency-related Ushahidi deployments, the major target audience of the platform was Internet users rather than institutions, reflecting the crowd-to-crowd nature of the emergency response. It also aggregated information from various sources, including blog communities and social networks. During the first ten days of its work, the Help Map site had more than 60,000 unique visitors (Machleder and Asmolov 2011). Visitors could choose a particular region on the map and receive all available information about this region. If the user was interested in providing help, he or she could see the closest location where help was needed. The website could also show those with particular needs where the closest source of potential help was located. A volunteer who wanted to send some help to a region, but didn't know how to do so, would be able to find a car owner who was willing to drive to the area of disaster. A group of citizen pilots offered their planes as a volunteer squadron to fight the wildfires. In the absence of effective state intervention, the digital environment was used to coordinate the provision of relief supplies and services.

The volunteer team moderating the site created an offline situation room that served as a coordination center. In addition to the moderation and verification of messages, the coordinators tried to create as many "matches" as possible between those who wanted to help and those asking for assistance, relying on information aggregated by the map. Blogger *ottenki-serogo*, who visited the Ushahidi-based coordination center in Moscow, described the role of the Help Map:

> For the first time (can anyone recall anything like this?), Internet volunteers not only united in their will to help, but launched a website, opened a call center, deployed a system of monitoring and information exchange. [. ..] They are not connected to any organizations or political parties, they are independent, and they will slowly dissolve when the trouble retreats and gather again to help if, God forbid, something else happens. (translated by Asmolov 2010b)

The Help Map case also showed that ICT can facilitate the coordination of complicated and multidimensional collective actions taking place over a wide geographical territory by reducing information costs. Because the Help Map launch relied on a worldwide network of volunteers and digital technology, it did not require substantial institutional financial support. This is in contrast to the expectations of the resource mobilization research literature that ascribes importance of well-resourced institutions when assessing the likely success of a mobilization (McCarthy and Zald 1977). Additionally, the simplicity of the launch allowed the system to be created in only two days.

While the role of blog communities and social networks was to collect and share information about various initiatives and resources that could be used in the emergency response, the crowdsourcing platform provided a mechanism for managing the response and minimizing the impact of information overload. The emergence of an online leadership, together with online tools for management, made the mobilization of crowd-based resources and collective action more systematic and efficient.

Floods in 2012

The case of wildfires can provide a model for how ICT can enable new modes of collective action in order to fulfill particular governance functions. However, does this type of networked response go beyond a single case? In summer 2012, another disaster struck in Russia, massive flooding in a regional city. At the beginning of July 2012, following a few days of heavy rain, a sudden flood brought immediate devastation to the city of Krymsk and few surrounding villages in southern Russia. According to official data, 172 people were killed and 640 buildings destroyed. The city of Krymsk, with a population of 60,000, was paralyzed by the disaster. Although floods are common in this region, local authorities were caught unprepared. Journalist A. Babchenko wrote in a blog post entitled "The state is totally absent in Russia":

> We should understand one simple thing—we don't have a state. In the case of an emergency situation you will face the tragedy alone. No one will come to help you. No one will warn you. No helicopters. No divers. No police. No paramedics. You will again be abandoned, my friend, as usual. It should be clearly understood. The future security of your family should be constructed on the basis of this tenet. (Babchenko 2012)

"The public's grief is now mixed with a deep distrust of the government," concluded a journalist Masha Lipman (2012). She suggested, however, that there was a mechanism of compensation: "As the government is losing credibility, civil society is building trust." The "diffusion of trust" from state to civil society leads to the emergence of the crowd as a major actor in emergency response.

Research conducted by sociologists from the Higher School of Economics in Krymsk found interesting patterns of trust in the areas affected by the disaster (Kostyushev 2012). According to the data collected by the Russian sociologists, the most trusted sources of information were, first, neighbors and relatives; second, volunteers; and, third, Internet sources. The emergency services, the actors affiliated with the state, were in fourth place. The federal government itself was in the ninth place, with the regional government (thirteenthth), political parties (fifteenthth), and the local administration (sixteenthth) at the bottom of the list. All other parameters of this research, including satisfaction with the role of emergency response, demonstrate that volunteers were "trust leaders" and were considered by the victims as the main source of help.[2]

As in the case of the wildfires, volunteers actively used various Internet applications to assist victims. One of the largest groups on Vkontakte had more than 15,000 members. It was used for sharing information about new groups of volunteers to go to the disaster area, transport, lists of things the victims needed,and so on. From the first hours, Twitter was used for the dissemination of information. Hashtags #krymsk and #pomozhem ("Let's help" in Russian) became trending topics on Twitter in Russia. Later, volunteers who were in the area of the floods, actively used Twitter to provide real-time, firsthand information, and as a tool for public communication between help centers in the big cities and volunteers on the ground.

In addition to social networks and blogs, the coordination was managed through special dedicated websites. The website pomozhem.org (named after the hashtag) provided a simple whiteboard with the major information about the emergency response coordination. A crowdsourcing platform called Virtual Bell—the Atlas of Emergency Aid created a special map focused on the area of the floods (Teplitsa 2012). The platform allowed a volunteer to create a personal profile where he or she could define what help they were ready to provide and where. Additionally, crowdsourcing Help Map (http://krymsk.crowdmap.com) was deployed, based on the Crowdmap website, which allows a map to be created within hours.

The work of crowdsourcing platforms and coordination could not have happened without a detailed map of the disaster area. Such maps were not available online at the moment of the disaster. The Russian Open Street Map activist community mobilized to create an updated and detailed online map of Krymsk and the surrounding villages. By the next day, volunteers and crowdsourcing platforms were already using the map.

As with the wildfires, the Internet was also used for to organize groups of volunteers to go to the disaster area. The organization of groups was linked to finding transport for the volunteers. While most efforts to obtain transport from the emergency services failed, private firms and individuals were able to provide alternatives. Additionally, crowdfunding was used to rent transport (Lenta 2012). In one case, volunteers organized a special coach in a train going to the disaster region. A Facebook event page entitled "Volunteer train" was used to invite volunteers to join the train.[3] The volunteers arriving in Krymsk organized a tent camp with an organized leadership structure and division of responsibilities.

Social media were also used to request assistance from big firms and corporations. In one case a coordinator from Help Map was looking for a way to send a psychologist to the disaster area. She tweeted a request for assistance to the official Twitter account of Russian air company, Transaero. A tweet from Transaero responded: "We are helping as much as possible and taking humanitarian assistance on board our flights, but we cannot totally replace the government." Despite the negative reply, this demonstrated that the Internet was providing new channels for direct interaction and coordination between individuals and companies.

The Internet made the volunteers into actors in the emergency response. For instance, a moderator of one of the Vkontakte groups was approached by DHL with an offer to provide a plane to send aid to Krymsk. In another case, the coordinator of the Moscow help center negotiated with one of Russian mobile phone companies and obtained free phone cards for hundreds of victims (Lenta 2012).

Compared with the case of the wildfires, the state also increased its online presence. Three days after the disaster, an official website for the emergency response operation krymsk2012.ru was launched by the regional authorities. The website creators argued that, unlike the rumors that fill the Internet, this official Internet site provided credible information about sources of help and news about the emergency response operation. What was also noticeable, however, was that the website emphasized the efficiency of the state emergency response, while almost ignoring online initiatives by volunteers.

ICT as an Alternative Governance Modality?

What do these cases tell us about ICT and governance in areas of limited statehood during a disaster? It first must be noted that governance has a constructed nature. It consists not only of particular actions, but also of the *perception of these actions*. Before determining appropriate solutions, it is first necessary to define the nature of the problems. The case studies demonstrate that ICT in areas of limited statehood begin to play a role in addressing the exigencies of a crisis even before the public is mobilized. The participation of individuals and the nature of collective action are associated with the perception of the situation. If people believe that the government provides an effective emergency response and keeps the situation under control, they will have less incentive to disrupt their daily lives and contribute their personal resources (time, money, physical work, etc.) to emergency relief. That is what states do.

Authoritarian regimes tend to replace an effective response with an informational blockade, or at least to conceal their limited capacity to address an emergency through media manipulation. In order to analyze the processes of definition of the problems of governance, these need to be approached as a part of the power relationship between institutions and individuals, state and nonstate actors. Peter Bachrach and Morton Baratz suggested that political power is found in the ability to "limit the scope of political process to public consideration of only those issues which are comparatively innocuous to (political actor) A" (Bachrach and Baratz 1962). Steven Lukes emphasizes that the meaning of the "second face of power" is control over an agenda such as when "potential issues are kept out of the political process" and the "scope of actual decision making is limited to 'safe' issues" (Lukes 2005).

Natural disaster suggests a number of unsafe issues for state actors. First, the limited capacity of the state to respond to a disaster can threaten the state's image and legitimacy and potentially lead to social or political unrest. Additionally, a potential topic of concern is the increase in citizens' activity as a response to the disaster. Any emerging activity of citizens, even if it is not political, may be approached as a potential threat to the status quo. A mobilized public is more unpredictable than a quiescent one. Therefore, the agenda is controlled in order to ensure the inaction of citizens or limit the scope of action. Consequently, the best emergency response strategy for an authoritarian state that lacks the capacity to address a crisis is to deny that it exists. We saw this pattern in both the wildfires and in the flood of Krymsk.

ICT as an enabler of "mass self-communication," as Manuel Castells calls the many-to-many communication capacity of the Internet, allows citizens a greater ability to challenge the power of the state to control the agenda (Castells 2007). With broadly distributed digital networked platforms that are autonomous of the state, citizens can push back when state authorities try to use communication power to manage perceptions. We saw this most clearly in the example of the state trying to deny the severity of the wildfires and their effects on the mortality rate in Moscow. Autonomous communication networks of citizens, including victims of disaster, volunteers who participate in an emergency response, and ordinary Internet users, use ICT to impose their own definition of a disaster and to change the balance of power between state and society. Event-mapping via a crowdsourcing platform like Ushahidi is an example of the mobilization of citizen power to present a different framing of an emergency and, as a consequence, a different set of governance priorities deriving from the situation. From this perspective, event-mapping, social networking, and blogging are all elements of counter-power.

The socially constructed nature of statehood in an era of robust digital technology means that hard-to-control and highly variable views on reality tends to expose the situational limits of statehood. Viewed in these terms, weak states are inclined to respond to emergencies by denying its existence. Yet it is now much more difficult to conceal the extent of a disaster and control the framing of problem definition in a world full of sensors and networks. Efforts to manipulate or control information often lead to greater distrust. This is not the only possible outcome. After all, as odd as it may at first seem, a disaster is an opportunity for the state to demonstrate its competence. Elena Evgrafova (2012) of the Russian edition of the *Harvard Business Review* points out that the unprecedented scale of US emergency preparation for Hurricane Irene in 2011 served as a demonstration of strong, effective statehood. According to Evgrafova, emergency response has a different nature in the information environment of the 21st century:

> Imitation and simulacra—those are attributes of the 20th century. The era has changed. It became extremely difficult to lie to people. Today, the winners of the propaganda struggle are going to be not those who know "tactics," but those who do important things and demonstrate honorable behavior, even if no one observes it.

The case studies of both the Russian wildfires and the Russian floods demonstrate the constructed nature of governance. The Ushahidi-based crowdsourcing platform Help Map as well as other online platforms limit the capacity of the state to set the agenda, define the problems, and argue that everything is under control. The constant flow of information from victims and volunteers exposes the limited degree of statehood.

A common argument concerning the role of Internet users in Russia suggests that they are active in expressing criticism and sharing information about a problem online, but that the ability of the Russian blogosphere to have any effect beyond the virtual space is more problematic. Some Russian columnists have argued that Russian society is a "like society," meaning people "like" things on Facebook, but do nothing beyond that (Allenova 2011).

Our cases seem to refute that claim. We can see that ICT played a meaningful role in the facilitation of offline action. While an increase in transparency and effort to hold the government accountable does not have an impact on state policy, it leads to the emergence of self-reflexivity and self-accountability as a substitute for the lack of state action and develops into a new, nonstate mode of governance. In this context, nonstate modes of governance have three layers requiring analysis:

1. *The scope of functions:* What are the functions and services that can be delivered through ICT-mediated collective action? (And can these functions be considered an alternative mode of governance?)
2. *The role of ICT:* To what extent is the role of ICT significant for enabling alternative modes of governance that rely on collective action? (And can the same functions be carried out without ICT?)
3. *Sustainability of ICT-mediated, crowd-based emergency response:* Why, in some situations, do we see ICT-mediated collective action, while in others we do not? (And can the crowd be a reliable actor in emergency response?)

The case studies demonstrate that crowdsourcing platforms, the blogosphere, and social networks supported a variety of functions, including, among others, mapping the needs of victims and providing situational awareness of the disasters; organization of firefighting units and provision of professional equipment; deploying groups of volunteers to participate in emergency relief; collection of humanitarian aid; organization of victim evacuation. In some cases, we can also see functions traditionally associated with the ultimate monopoly of the state in emergency situations, such as airlift capacity. One can identify some functions that cannot be fulfilled by collective action, but we can see that gradually the scope of governance functions that cannot be fulfilled through bottom-up collective action decreases.

The capacity for an alternative mode of governance has increased in these cases through the collaboration of the crowd, NGOs and businesses and the emergence of networked coalitions. For instance, Help Map was used to coordinate actions among volunteers, Greenpeace, and various charity organizations. In the case of the flood, we can see how *Vkontakte* and Twitter made the volunteers into legitimate actors and enabled their collaboration with companies (e.g., DHL, Transaero).

Crowdsourcing platforms and social networks transform volunteers into actors with an address and provide mechanism for the facilitation of collaboration between actors. Additionally, ICT make possible the expansion of the range of engagement in emergency response. If in the past, in case of the natural disaster, the major part of activities took a place on community level, now we can see that a significant number of responders come from other regions, in particular big cities.

ICT also provides new opportunities for a new type of representation of crisis that supports collective action. A discourse analysis of the Help Map demonstrates that the platform was primarily used for the exchange of data and instructions to support particular actions.[4] The information exchange on crowdsourcing platforms in emergency situations is reminiscent of emergency scanner-based communication in the military or the police. The majority of messages involved direct appeals for particular forms of assistance. Active use of metadata in crowdsourcing platforms, including geolocation and categories, also supports coordination and action. The map as a medium has specific features that make it an operation support tool. Mapping expert Eric Gundersen notes: "Whenever you need a common operating picture you need a map" (Scola 2011).

Additionally, ICT contributes to the capacity of volunteers to learn and to improve their functioning. Social networks and blogs are used for the distribution of instructions on how to participate in volunteer activities, what volunteers should have with them when they go to a disaster area, and so forth. The major contribution of ICT, however, is in the coordination of large-scale distributed, nonhierarchical, multi-functional collective actions with many participants, over a wide geographical territory, and in a situation of information overload. Crowdsourcing platforms like Help Map, as well as other Internet platforms and tools, including groups and events in social networks, communities in the blogosphere, hashtags on Twitter, Skype chats, Google groups, and so on, allow complicated modes of coordination to appear.

While in the past the coordination of large-scale collective action was expensive and available primarily to hierarchical institutions, event-mapping makes it accessible to individuals and non-institutional entities and empowers these. Gundersen concludes: "Mapping has always been expensive, and the dudes that had the maps [are the ones who] had the money. Now, almost anyone can make a map" (Scola 2011). And as Livingston and Walter-Drop note in this volume, "The central characteristic of ICT is its effect on information and transaction costs. These costs, however, are central to collective action" (see Chapter 1, p. 10). The case studies demonstrate how decrease of cost provides new opportunities for the management of complicated, large-scale actions. Consequently, volunteers not only participate in the emergency response, but also play a leading independent role in the organization of the emergency relief operation. This is what makes this type of action an alternative mode of governance.

The questions that remain are whether this type of response has a recurring nature and whether it can be sustained. For instance, one of the bloggers argued that the scale of crowd participation in response to the wildfires in 2010 was linked to the fact that the disaster had a direct impact on the Russian capital city. Otherwise, people usually do not care about disasters in remote villages and small cities.

Obviously, if a disaster takes place in a populated area with stable access to the Internet, the collection of information about the real scale of the disaster and the emergency response is made easier. Only then is the government's control of the framing weakened. In case of the flood in Krymsk, however, the disaster took place far from Moscow with relatively low Internet penetration. Still, the state was unable to control the framing of a disaster, and volunteers from big cities actively participated in emergency response.

The role of the Internet, however, should not be exaggerated. The tragedy in Krymsk happened just a few weeks after the post-election protests and the significant increase in political activism against the Russian government. In the case of an emergency, political activism was transformed into emergency activism. At the same time, when emergency response is associated with political activism, it can suggest a different type of responders' identity. Disaster studies demonstrate that in many cases, emergency response relies primarily on the members of affected community or people who live in the area that is relatively close to disaster (Barton 1969). In Russian case, one could witness that many responders came from regions that are relatively far from the disaster area. One may argue that ICT expanded the geographical range of participation in emergency response and lead to a shift from community-based to society-based disaster relief.

While there are significant factors that are not related to ICT, the Internet provided easier opportunities for participation and might change the structure of participation. It provided various tools and mechanisms for coordination, including the division of responsibilities and the planning and facilitation of collaboration between individuals and organizations. It upgraded the crowd of volunteers from a group of motivated individuals to a system that recognized itself as a powerful independent actor.

The case study of the floods in Krymsk may demonstrate the existence of a learning curve, where, from one emergency response to another, we can see more innovative tools for the coordination and expansion of the number of functions that can be fulfilled by ICT-enabled collective action, as well development of tool that require less technical knowledge. Additionally, more people learn how to use the existent tools.

Simplifying participation can also create new challenges. More people are trying to fulfill coordination functions and deploy crowdsourcing maps. For instance, in the case of the emergency response to the floods in 2012, a number of crowdsourcing platforms were created with similar functions, which made coordination more difficult. However, addressing this challenge is also part of a learning curve. Eventually, the success of the coordination depends on a mixture of technology and the reputation as well as professionalism of those using the technologies. In some other countries we can see that this challenge is being addressed by the development of networks of experienced volunteers, such as the international Standby Task Force of crisis mappers or the Virtual Operations Support Teams, who are always ready to provide an immediate and professional response.

The emergence of alternative modes of governance as a response to natural disasters has a situational, local, and temporal nature. The question is, however, to what extent the influence of bottom-up collective action that substitutes for government in situations of limited statehood can go beyond emergency situations. As was pointed by Livingston and Walter-Drop elsewhere in this volume, the same state can be strong in the sense that it has a monopoly over violence and capacity to marshal force, while also having a limited capacity to provide basic services to citizens. The emergency-related citizen mobilization, as it was described above, doesn't diminish the traditional forms of state power. The state still controls military, police, and security services and is able to use various means of repression. One may argue that the potential outcome is political polarization of the civic society and the state, while the traditional vertical political system and citizen-based egalitarian system exist in alternative realities.

Following the wildfires in 2010, a number of journalists and bloggers suggested that the crowd-based emergency response demonstrated a new alternative model for Russian society. A well-known columnist, Andrey Loshak, wrote about a new collective solidarity and a new social spirit that relied on mutual aid and suggested that people should be able to manage theirs life without the state (Loshak 2010). Following the tragedy in Krymsk, Sasha Senderovich (2012) described a transformation of political protest into responsibility towards society where "buoyed by social networks and new communities, they [young Russians—G.A.] are creating what could become a blueprint for a new form of civil society." Senderovich argued that "pervasive cynicism about communal action that took hold after the Soviet state and its professed collective ethos collapsed may be making way for a new sensibility—the idea that citizens can organize, be responsible for one another, and ultimately have an effect on how Russia governs itself."

This expansion indeed goes beyond natural disasters. In one project, Liza Alert, a network of volunteers is mobilized to look for children or old people who get lost in forests. It takes about an hour to activate a network and send the first volunteers into the field. The volunteers have their own professional equipment and conduct field trainings. The mobilization, however, would not work if the project had not put the issue of missing children on the agenda by creating an online platform. The official statistics on how many people get lost in Russian forests are not available, but according to activists the problem has the dimensions of a natural disaster (Asmolov 2011b).

In other cases, citizens use the Internet to conduct independent criminal investigations of murder cases where there is an apparent lack of sufficient police action, a phenomenon that Sidorenko (2010) calls "[i]nvestigative crowdsourcing." The crowdsourcing platform "Virtual Rynda," (named after the bell that was used to call people to help) suggests a crowd-to-crowd mechanism for the facilitation of mutual aid on a variety of social problems (Cleek 2011).

Even if the state is not missing, its role is increasingly questioned, criticized and contested on daily basis. As a consequence, situations of limited statehood lead to reconsideration of the relationship between states and citizens. This relationship is a major factor shaping the role of ICT-based collective action in areas of limited statehood. Nonstate actors, including the crowd, can be active participants in emergency relief whatever the degree of state participation and statehood. What differs is the form of participation and whether this emerges as an alternative mode of governance or is embedded within the state's response. A part of statehood is not only structural readiness to address a disaster, but also structural readiness to collaborate with nonstate informal actors, including the crowd, as a part of an emergency response. The approach of the state to volunteers shapes the role of bottom-up self-organization in emergency situations.

Following the earthquake in Kobe, the government of Japan declared a special national Disaster Prevention and Volunteerism Day. The purpose of these events was to promote the ideas of volunteerism and civic engagement as part of disaster preparedness and response. The Russian case studies, however, demonstrates that the reaction can be quite the opposite, especially in a case where the state considers citizens' collective action not as an opportunity to improve its governance, but as a threat to its statehood. As a response, state actors can focus not on the development of a capacity for collaboration, but on regulating and restricting volunteer activities.

For instance, in Russian case, a few days after the disaster in Krymsk, local authorities asked volunteers to move their camp from the city center to a remote area. In another case, the administration of one of Moscow's suburbs, Mytishi, claimed that the collection of humanitarian aid on the central square of the city was an illegal demonstration.

In July 2012, the Russian Civic Chamber and members of parliament from the Russian ruling party, United Russia, introduced a proposal for a new law regulating volunteerism. The draft included a requirement for volunteers to register and sign an official contract for volunteering. This means that volunteers would not be able to work without being "hired" by some official organization, which would also have legal responsibilities if the contract is violated. The law makes volunteering a complicated bureaucratic process. A strict, hierarchical framework would restrict volunteerism with a spontaneous, bottom-up nature. Russian newspaper *Vedomosti* suggested that the legislation reflects the fears of officials and aims to reduce the scale of volunteer activities. The newspaper concluded:

> The state should learn [from volunteers—G.A.]. But, apparently, in the perverted mind of the officials volunteers are competitors. And it looks like they are dangerous competitors. The inefficiency and impotency of the state become obvious against the background of what citizen activists do. (Vedomosti 2012)

While ICT provide new opportunities for state–networks synergy that can increase the degree of statehood and provide better governance, such opportunities are missed in some political environments. Lack of state capacity and will to be open for collaboration with independent volounters might lead to polarization between states and volunteers. As consequence, alternative, ICT-enabled modes of governance replace potential partnership.

Conclusion

A popular Russian proverb says: "A holy place never remains empty." The case studies above have demonstrated that for some, this proverb can also be applied to governance.

The paper suggests that the construction of government's role in emergency response and the participation of nonstate actors in disaster relief are interrelated. In the cases of the wildfires in western Russia in 2010 and floods in southern Russia in 2012, we can see that citizens' cooperation was empowered by "a shared understanding that the government had failed to get the situation under control and, moreover, did not want to be held accountable for it" (Asmolov 2010b).

ICT plays a role in both processes. Mass self-communication that relies on social networks, crowdsourcing, and mobile communication allows breaking of the state's monopoly on the representation of disaster and makes citizens the dominant actors in shaping the narrative of an emergency situation. Information technologies also provide mechanisms and tools for fulfilling a variety of governance functions, including complicated coordination that makes nonstate actors, and the crowd in particular, into independent, dominant actors in emergency relief.

The role of ICT should not be exaggerated. It is strongly associated with a social and political context in a particular society, as well as with the magnitude of the disaster and the degree of statehood. Accordingly, the form of crowd participation in emergency response can take different forms. If the state is able to take on leadership in creating a new model that allows synergy with citizens, the role of the state remains dominant. If the state chooses to ignore or regulate and restrict nonstate actors, this leads to the emergence of new models of alternative governance and social order that can have a long-term influence on political reality.

Notes

1. The author was one of the principle actors in the creation and implementation of this deployment.
2. Another Russian research team conducted a survey in rural areas of Russia that were affected by wildfires in 2010 and reached a different conclusion, finding that "natural disasters increased support for the government in rural areas" (Sobolev et al. 2012). Additional research is needed to say what effect natural disasters have on public trust in authorities. One of possible explanations is that the degree of trust can be associated with the degree of expectations from the government. Unlike cities, Russian rural areas are generally areas of limited statehood with low presence of state. A disaster creates an opportunity for state's engagement in these areas. Any type of state's engagement is very uncommon for those who live in rural areas, and therefore any type of state's affiliated response following a disaster might lead to increase of trust.
3. https://www.facebook.com/events/123078594500509/.
4. The analysis was conducted in Asmolov, G., Russian Wildfires 2010: Challenging Power Relationship Through Crowdsourcing Platforms, presented at IAMCR 2013 Conference Dublin, 25–29 June 2013. http://www.iamcr2013dublin.org/content/russian-wildfires-2010-challenging-power-relationship-through-crowdsourcing-platforms-emerge.

8

Mapping Kibera. Empowering Slum Residents by ICT

PRIMOŽ KOVAČIČ AND JAMIE LUNDINE

Introduction

Nairobi's informal settlements constitute areas of limited statehood situated in the heart of the national power centers of the state. A severe lack of basic services and state institutions create a governance vacuum that is readily filled by informal sector actors who address, in their own ways, the most pressing needs and issues within these communities. In part because the state is weak and sometimes missing, there is very little statistical information available on the quality and quantity of service delivery in these areas.[1] A recent rise in availability and accessibility of ICTs in Kenya allow these nonstate actors to fill in some of the information gaps left by the inability, incompetence, or lack of interest by the state.

In this chapter, we present insights gathered from over three years of digitally documenting Nairobi's informal settlements. From our perspective as on-the-ground practitioners employing technology in community development and mobilization, we present a critical evaluation of the role of new technology in filling the governance void found in these areas of limited statehood. The first section of the chapter will provide a brief description of the rise of digital mapping as an alternative form of documentation within the context of Kenya's information communication technology boom, filling in state functions of providing statistical information about citizens in informal settlements. We document our experience in facilitating digital mapping in Kibera and Mathare, two major slums in Nairobi. We will also offer a comparison of our urban experiences with digital mapping and community mobilization in a more rural area of Kenya.

We find that ICT-enabled projects can indeed provide an alternative governance modality in Nairobi's informal settlements and in remote rural areas. Small groups of citizens, with limited resources, can collect thousands of community-determined points of interest, gather statistical data on local populations, and create comprehensive databases of available amenities. Communities use these data in the context of various initiatives intended to improve the provision of collective goods, even when the state is absent. Finally, we ask if this model of nongovernmental approaches to documentation is sustainable. In reply, we offer a practical guide for sustainable collaboration between digitally mobilized citizens and state actors. We conclude that citizens, empowered with new tools, can fill in the information void found in the "areas of limited statehood."

Informal Settlements in Nairobi

Informal settlements—slums—are perhaps the most poignant physical representation of urban poverty. According to the UN-Habitat, Nairobi, Kenya has the highest per annum urban growth rate in Africa.[2] Nairobi's population skyrocketed between 1980 and 2009 from 862,000 to about 3,100,000—a growth accompanied by an expansion of informal settlements.[3] It is estimated that more than half of the population of Nairobi, approximately 1.5 million people, live in informal settlements; some estimates put the number of informal settlements in Nairobi as high as 200.[4] The population estimates for these areas vary. For example, estimates of the population of Kibera—referred to by many as the largest informal settlement in sub-Saharan Africa—vary between 170,000 and 1 million (Ekdale 2011). Whatever the exact number, one thing is clear: a large and growing population of people live in informal settlements.

According to the UN-Habitat's definition of an informal settlement, informal settlements across sub-Saharan African have the most deprived conditions, a conclusion easily confirmed by even the most casual observation. To varying degrees, all of them lack security, access to clean water and sanitation, sufficient living space, and durable housing. Built from mud, wood, plastic, and scrap metal, the simple shacks seem to have grown from the dirt itself.[5] In these areas, the state often fails to provide even the most basic of public goods and is experiencing "significant problems with regard to rule-making, implementation and enforcement" (Livingston and Walter-Drop, Chapter 1), classifying many informal settlements as "areas of limited statehood."

Where the state's rule implementation, service provision, and monopoly over force are challenged, weak, or even missing, the informal sector moves in. The informal sector in Nairobi employs two-thirds of the city's labor force as merchants, businessman, security guards, investors, manual laborers, teachers, and community health workers.[6] This is a complicated system through which most of the services normally associated with the state are provided, albeit limited in accessibility, quality, and coverage. With the rise of new technology, these non-state actors are now able to at least partially fill some of the information gaps left by the absence of the state. All of this takes place in the heart of the national power center of the state.

Availability of Geospatial Information and Statistics of Informal Settlements

This section will explore the relationship between the government of Kenya and informal settlements in Nairobi, as reflected by state, nongovernmental, and citizen-generated statistics, generally, and maps in particular. A map offers a model of reality by highlighting selected relationships between elements in space and time. Whether two-dimensional, three-dimensional, static, dynamic, paper, online, real-time, topographic, or thematic, maps convey information or the lack of information about a specific area. Sometimes what isn't found on a map is as analytically important as what is. The absence of geospatial information or information in general of a particular area can mean that the area is either inaccessible, remote, lacks interest (to at least the mapmaker), or is politically or militarily sensitive; it may also mean that the state in the area is "spatially challenged," in that the "projection of its governance is hardly enforceable in that particular geographic area and period of time" (Meier, Chapter 9). In the modern world of big data and popular web-based mapping platforms, people wrongly assume that, if it is not on the map, it does not exist. That is not the case.

The African continent in general remains poorly mapped, with much of the existing data unreliable, out-of-date, or held as proprietary information by commercial concerns. The lack of reliable mapping data can be illustrated with even a simple comparison of Google map data and imagery used in Google Maps. Figures 8.1a and 8.1b show the same location in Kibera. The first image is the available map data; the second is a DigitalGlobe satellite image of the same location at the same resolution.

The map is devoid of features, save a river and the Multi-Vision Biocenter, the large round building in the satellite image. Kibera as an informal settlement doesn't exist, according to the Google map data.

Rural areas are particularly poorly represented, which is understandable considering the size of the continent, the remoteness of some of the areas, and the costs that would be involved in mapping them. Kenya is no exception. While many parts of the country are still missing from the map, some parts of the capital, Nairobi, are fairly well documented. Most middle- and upper-class neighborhoods in Nairobi are reasonably well documented on paper and online maps. In contrast, maps of the city's most densely populated areas—the informal settlements—remain scarce and frequently not publicly available. Not only maps but also other information about these areas is scarce.

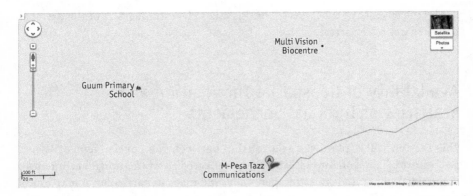

Figure 8.1a n/a

Figure 8.1b n/a

One of the most telling examples of the lack of accurate information about informal settlements is the numbers around the population of Kibera, Kenya's largest informal settlement. For years, the "official" number of the population of Kibera was between 500,000 to a million people. The number was widely used by international organizations, by countless NGOs working in the area, and by the Kenyan government.[7] The White House even reported the number as high as 1.5 million people.[8] Other organizations, doubting the "official" estimates, conducted more scientific approaches to determine the population density of the area. The Map Kibera Project began in 2008 by conducting a survey in one of thirteen "villages" in Kibera. A village in this context means a section of the slum. Then, based on the combination of population density and satellite imagery, researchers extrapolated the number to the entire informal settlement coming up with an estimated figure ranging from 235,000 to a maximum of 270,000 people.[9] Finally, in 2009 the Kenya Population and Housing Census reported Kibera's population as 170,070, which was much lower than previous estimates.

The conflicting numbers and years of continuous neglect by the government casts a doubt on the latest government figures. There are several dynamics worth thinking about when considering population figures in informal settlements: The population of informal settlements is dynamic and changes over different periods and over seasons; many people living in the areas do not have homes; many residents distrust the government.[10] It seems that it is only safe to say that the estimated population in Kibera in 2012 varies between 170,000 and 1 million people.[11]

The population figures are not the only information that is unavailable or unreliable. There are no accurate, reliable, and available data on public or private facilities or organizations that operate in these areas. Whatever the exact figure, a great number of people need health facilities, schools, businesses, religious institutions, water, sanitation, roads, street lights, police, and other services. Walking into an informal settlement, one sees many institutions and structures, but the data about these facilities and the quality and status of service are unavailable.

The availability of basic data such as these can be a telling indicator of the basic relationship between the state and the area. In the case of informal settlements in Nairobi, the lack of accurate maps and open information about the settlements clearly shows the inability or unwillingness of the state to collect accurate data about the area. A lack of data suggests Kibera and the other Nairobi slums, situated as they are in the capital of Kenya, are correctly understood as an "area of limited statehood" (Livingston and Walter-Drop, Chapter 1). Collecting comprehensive datasets and putting a place on the map points to its existence. It can support citizens in their efforts to assert their right to state services or assist states in planning how to provide basic public goods to some of their most marginalized communities. The next section discusses the rise of ICTs in Kenya and explores some of the practical effects of ICT on governance; practical uses of ICT-enabled collective action to fill in the governance void; and various usages of ICT by the communities to address the problems arising from the missing or unresponsive state institutions (Livingston and Walter-Drop, Chapter 1).

The Rise of the ICT sector in Kenya

In contrast to the lack of public information about informal settlements is the fact that Nairobi is a city in the thrall of information age. This section will explore the "ICT boom" in Kenya, with a specific focus on Nairobi as an ICT metropolis (often referred to as the "Silicon Valley of Africa" or the "Silicon Savanna").[12] We will also discuss the use of ICT in informal settlements as seemingly contradictory phenomena when compared to the lack of sanitation, adequate housing, and other basic services in the same areas. The point of this part of our argument is to establish that (1) technologies needed for basic collaborative undertakings are available in even the most deprived slums in Nairobi, and (2) the ICT innovations within the slums would not have begun to emerge in 2009 without broader Kenyan technology ecosystem.

The use of ICT in Kenya has increased rapidly over the past decade. The availability of mobile technology, access to Internet, provision of government services (referred as *e-government*), and open data initiative all contribute to a growing information ecosystem in the country. Perhaps the most ubiquitous tool within the ecosystem is the mobile phone. According to research conducted in May 2011, Kenya had a mobile penetration rate of 67.5 percent in 2011, translating into approximately 26.4 million mobile phone users. Ten years earlier, in 2002 the penetration rate was minimal 3.61 percent, translating into just over a million users.[13] The "mobile phone price wars" of 2010 saw the price of an SMS—by far the most popular and cheapest mode of mobile communication—drop from 3 Kenyan Shillings (3.75 USD cents) to 1 Kenyan shillings—(1.25 cents)—per message.[14] This has reduced the transaction costs and made mobile phones even more affordable at the individual and household level.

Internet usage has also seen a significant increase in Kenya. The arrival of broadband Internet cable, through undersea connection via the Indian Ocean in 2009, and government and private investment in Kenya's communication infrastructure has increased the availability and reduced the cost of Internet access.[15] Mobile Internet is the most common way Kenyans access the web, particularly in areas where computer and other Internet access options is limited. Young people in Nairobi's informal settlements no longer have to visit the few Internet cafés to check their e-mail, access chat and instant messaging services, and get updates on their Facebook and Twitter accounts. While low-cost mobile and Internet hardware and services are improving communication and access across Kenya, some still question whether the products and services are reaching the most marginal and vulnerable within Kenyan society.[16]

With the exponential growth in the ICT industry, particularly in mobile phone and Internet usage in Kenya, has come a rise in innovative phone- and web-based applications. Many of these applications are aimed at improving social and development trends within the country. For example, in response to the post-election violence of 2007/2008, Kenyan technologists put together a crowdsourcing platform called Ushahidi, introduced elsewhere in this volume in chapters by Asmolov and Meier respectively (Asmolov, Chapter 7; Meier, Chapter 9). The "legacy" version of Ushahidi allowed citizens to share information about violence and community responses through an online mapping platform, with SMS, e-mail, and web-form integration, all during a time when rumors and misinformation were spreading violence and the mainstream media was unable to dispel rumors due to media blackouts and politically motivated reporting.

Alongside citizen-driven innovation are a number of government-led ICT initiatives. For example, as part of the state's commitment to the Open Government Partnership,[17] the Kenyan government has launched an Internet-based Open Data

Portal, on which certain government datasets are published and downloadable in many different formats. Since its launch, many applications have been built or improved using open data. But while the government datasets have been open and available since 2011, many people remain skeptical about the potential of open data to transform Kenya and create real change in communities. Like many geographical and other datasets (as described above), much of the data on the site are outdated, representing the situation for example in primary and secondary schools in 2007 or local authority expenditure from the 2008 to 2009 fiscal year.[18] The accuracy of datasets is another major challenge; Geographic Information Systems (GIS) coordinates for schools and health centers are off by several kilometers in some rural areas. The format in which the datasets have been published allow for developers and technologists to work with the information, but many worry that the average Kenyan cannot interact with the information. Some people question the Kenya government's commitment to Open Government and Open Data and suggest rather that the Portal was set up to satisfy donor requirements (specifically the World Bank) but does not represent a real change in the way the government—whose elected members are caught up in daily corruption scandals—operates.

The growing technology ecosystem, including social capital, infrastructure, and policy, encourages growth and innovation in the ICT sector. As demonstrated here, Kenyan citizens, entrepreneurs, and the state are focusing on and leading with initiatives to generate and democratize information. While the Kenyan government is promoting and participating in open data activities and encouraging investment in ICT infrastructure that reaches throughout and across the country, there remains little information and state investment in ICTs in Kenya's informal settlements. Despite this gap, residents of the slums have not been completely excluded from the ICT revolution; they are also consumers of mobile phones, Internet sites, and web-based social networking, to name a few; they are also producers of data and content, as explored in the following sections.

Practical Examples of ICT and Governance in Nairobi's Slums

Within the context of the ICT boom in Kenya, this section describes the evolution of thought and approaches to introducing new applications of ICTs in Nairobi's areas of limited statehood—namely, using ICT to document statistics about the Nairobi slums. We look at Map Kibera—a project to make the first freely available and open map of Kibera and the projects that evolved from it: Map Mathare, an open data mapping project combined with participatory development; and an accountability project in Kwale aimed at supporting ongoing good governance initiatives in an area of limited statehood located in the geographic periphery of the state. Last we look at Spatial Collective, a social enterprise that aims to employ technology not only to present information but to produce concrete action, business and employment opportunities, and complement state actions in the areas of limited statehood.

KIBERA

Kibera is located approximately 4 kilometers southwest of the city center and is one of Africa's best-known and biggest slums. Map Kibera started as a response to the absence of openly accessible geographic information about Kibera. It was founded on a premise that with the rise of widely available and simple to use ICTs, citizens can themselves become producers and consumers of information that suits their needs. To this end, a group of youth from Kibera was trained in how to use basic Global Positioning System (GPS) devices and OpenStreetMap, an open data digital-mapping database, and then spent a number of months mapping points of interest, such as health, education, water and sanitation, and security issues and tracks or paths and roads in their villages.

Map Kibera started as a digital-mapping project but has since grown into an ongoing community information initiative that includes event mapping, a community news website (Voice of Kibera)[19], and a video journalism project (Kibera News Network).[20]

The concept behind Voice of Kibera (VoK) was to create an interactive form of data visualization—to tell the story behind the map. The VoK was an Ushahidi instance that aggregated SMS information, video content from Kibera News Network (KNN), and blog posts about Kibera from around the web. The SMS information was sent by a small team of SMS reporters and edited by an editorial board of Kibera residents representing several organizations, including Hot Sun Foundation, KCODA, and the Kibera Journal. KNN is an informal group of young people who came together to learn video journalism techniques. Using basic handheld cameras, the young people in the project learned how to shoot footage and narrate a story, as well as the components of a good news story and the ethics of journalism and reporting. During the first months of the initiative, a small group of approximately ten young people documented stories on train accidents along the railway line through Kibera, landslides affecting local residents, the electronic voter registration system in Kenya, and the 2010 Kenyan referendum. The information KNN gathered was shared online through a You-Tube channel the team established.[21] The stories provided context for the information gathered through the mapping exercises, with a different, at times more accessible (accessible in terms of understanding by a general audience) method of delivering the information.

Digital mapping of Kibera was successful in generating open geospatial data about Kibera. During approximately eight months of mapping, the participants uploaded to OpenStreetMap many kilometers of roads, and thousands of points of interest. At one point, Kibera was most densely mapped area in Nairobi in

OpenStreetMap. But there were also some shortcomings. Despite the tagline developed by the VoK team, *Bonga Story Yako* ("tell your story") in Sheng,[22] the SMS reports were never successfully crowdsourced, but relied on a team of volunteers who sent in events, activities, and news from around Kibera in return for airtime vouchers supplied by the funding from UNICEF (Hagen 2011). Furthermore, with the institutionalization of Map Kibera through the registration of a Kenya-based Trust, Map Kibera Trust in 2010, other local Kibera-based organizations who had originally partnered on the projects (now housed within the Trust) slowly ceased to actively contribute to the projects. The young people involved in the programming were producing large datasets, videos, and other information about their communities and their lives; but outside of the Trust and a small number of graduate students and researchers at international institutions, the data were not accessible to or consumable by local organizations.[23]

During a participatory research assessment of the projects conducted by the Institute of Development Studies (IDS) at the University of Sussex in November 2011, the entire Map Kibera team was consulted and asked to reflect on these experiences, individually and as a group.[24] Some of the findings from the research informed programming and the revision of the approach going forward. The research provided important lessons to the future of such projects, that

> technologists particularly those operating within the open source model of development, prefer to work quickly, publishing their results to a wide audience, to attract interest and engage others in the collective effort. Participatory development practitioners usually adopt slower rhythms of work that include crafting and implementing a strategy for engaging with communities which takes into account the particularities of context and power dynamics, and is continuously revised and adapted. (Berdou 2011, 18–19)

The Map Kibera team tried to address some of the shortcomings in the projects they undertook upon the expansion of their activities.

MATHARE

Building on the lessons learned in Kibera, the Map Kibera team in Kenya worked with experienced community development professionals to adapt and improve on the model of community mapping and information gathering and dissemination. Mathare is an urban slum situated about 5 kilometers east of the Nairobi city center. Mathare in many ways resembles Kibera, but is also in many ways distinct. It is notorious for drugs, gangs, a lack of services, jobs, and poor hygiene and sanitation conditions. It also has fewer NGOs working in the area than Kibera does. Mathare remains an extremely impoverished area, situated in a deserted rock quarry, on state-owned and private land. It was a major hotspot prior and during the post-election violence of 2007–2008. It remained volatile well after the post-election violence.

From early to mid-2010, the Map Kibera team was approached by several organizations and asked to replicate the OpenStreetMapping of Kibera in Mathare. With the experience in Kibera in mind and the evaluation to guide the development of an iterative model, the Map Kibera team worked together with Plan Kenya to develop a community engagement strategy. Plan Kenya, the local branch of an international child-centered organization with sixteen years of community development experience in Kenya, secured funding for the project from Plan International.

The work in Mathare began with a deliberate focus on community development, outreach, and networking, surveying the development environment and identifying the main state and nonstate actors in order to figure out how to make ICT relevant to their cause. The project in Mathare followed the model of open data and open source software, combined with participatory development techniques of consultative meetings, open participation, and ongoing dialogue. The participants' response to ICT (specifically GPS devices, hand-held cameras, and storytelling software) as a tool for community development became the main focus; the tools and software were introduced but left for the community to determine its application.

Freedom of expression and the ability to experiment and design ideas with the help of ICT became the driving force behind the program. OpenStreetMap, blogs, Facebook, and Twitter accounts were set up, and information started flowing. The participants of the program fully embraced the power of ICT to express themselves. They organized themselves in two groups, with the first group focusing on mapping and the second on social media. They realized that ICT can help them understand their lives better and started thinking that if they were to become advocates of Mathare, they had to turn the attention to themselves and use the technology and time to critically investiage how they lived their lives. They made a film about the environmental issues in the slum; conducted "mobility mapping" in order to answer the questions on how they negotiate the spaces in which they live; collected field measurements, such as the heights of structures (shacks, brick buildings, etc.) and the topography of the terrain to create a 3D map of Mathare for the purpose of highlighting the geographically challenged location of the settlement.

The goal was that Mathare residents, through mapping and social media tools, relate their stories to an audience outside of the slum and beyond the borders of the nation, but more importantly start the conversations within the community through constant small forums. The open door policy enabled involvement of a broader community, and everybody who was interested in learning about mapping or social media could join. Rotating venues of meeting places and trainings included different geographical areas of the community to participate, ask questions, and give feedback on a regular basis. This step made it possible to recalibrate the project according to the communities' needs and wishes. As a result, the

community came to feel more ownership of the project, and organizations immediately used the data for advocacy purposes because they tailored the outputs to
serve their immediate purpose. These initiatives grew from the basic mapping and
data collection into very detailed and high quality analysis of the conditions in the
area. ICT was used to enable citizens the freedom of expression and to become the
information holders.

KWALE COUNTY

In addition to the vast inequity within the capital city, there is also marked dis-
parity between the capital and the outlying counties. Kwale County is an administrative area of Kenya, located along the south Coast near Kenya's second largest
city, Mombasa. Despite being among the most popular tourist destinations in the
country, with Diani beach hosting national and international tourists year-round
in luxury hotel, Kwale County is one of the poorest performing counties in terms
of health, education and social indicators in Kenya. In other words, it is an area of
limited statehood located in the periphery of the state.

Like the digital mapping in Mathare, the facilitation of ICT-enabled programming was designed to support ongoing work that the young community members were undertaking within existing organizations. The theme of the existing
interventions in Kwale County fell within the broad area of "accountability"; in
this instance encompassing the themes of child rights, social accountability, and
eco-tourism. As part of the Youth Empowerment through Technology, Arts and
Media (YETAM) program, Plan Kenya invited youth and facilitators from Map
Kibera Trust to support three groups in Kwale County with digital mapping and
new media techniques and technologies. The training offered by the Map Kibera
team focused on documenting evidence to support on-going advocacy work by
these three groups.

To support their work on social accountability, one of the groups, Kwale Youth
and Governance Consortium, mapped over a hundred publicly and privately
funded community-based projects. As one channel of sharing this information,
the Consortium set up a blog called *Nuru ya Kwale* (Light of Kwale).[25] According
to the group, the blog "features and addresses issues concerning promotion of
demystified participatory community involvement in the governance processes
towards sustainable development." This involved sharing evidence about various projects, stories, and information on community experiences that are well
known in a localized context but were not documented and shared widely. During
the course of the YETAM project, the youth presented the findings of their mapping work, documented online through OpenStreetMap and the *Nuru ya Kwale*
blog, to government officials responsible for running publicly funded projects.
The government officers, once confronted with the information on the blog, were
concerned with the findings and questioned the methodology and outcome of

the work but were also responsive to the feedback and (despite turning the youth away from their offices the previous month) invited the youths to their offices to get the relevant files to supplement some of the unknown or missing information.

The impact of digital mapping and new media on social accountability and government processes is still an open question. Whether the social accountability work would have provoked similar feedback from duty bearers if presented in an offline platform instead of as a dynamic-online platform is unknown. In Kwale, the experience demonstrated that the government officers responsible for delivering services were rather alarmed that the data were already publicly accessible to a national and international audience; despite the lack of publicity and the few number of hits the blog would have received in only a short time, when presented with the tool and the locally generated information the officers were quick to respond with invitations to their local offices and to open up other government generated data (whereas previous requests for time and information went unanswered). There is a definite need to question the use of new technology in governance work and to develop innovative methods for teasing out impact of open, online information channels in decision-making processes.[26]

MONITORING SERVICE DELIVERY

Another example of ICT-based collective action is Spatial Collective, a social enterprise, founded in 2012. Its goal is to harness existing and new technologies to connect community stakeholders; to support various community initiatives in areas of limited statehood with concrete collective action; and to build a network of partner organizations who contribute to the collective by supporting local action on identified issues. Importantly, a major focus of the collective is on creating opportunities and employment for people from areas of limited statehood.

Spatial Collective started in Mathare with a premise that technology, especially ICT, is crucial to addressing the needs of the marginalized but in itself insufficient to deliver positive impact on socio-economic condition. By harnessing the power of widely available technology, such as mobile phones, the Internet, consumer-grade GPS units and digital cameras, open source technology combined with proprietary software, and social media, the organization seeks to address collective issues, problems, and views. By representing collective opinions on dynamic digital maps, static paper maps, online forums, at established community information points and government offices, and by disseminating this information through mobile networks, online platforms, and social media, Spatial Collective's projects employ technology not only to present information (e.g., a water supply shortage), but also to produce concrete action (e.g., to facilitate the delivery of water to remedy the shortage).

Spatial Collective does not aim to replace state functions but rather to complement the state's activities. The team understands the limitations of the government and other state or nonstate actors to initiate, implement, or enforce immediate change resulting from complicated bureaucratic procedures, unavailability of funding, and lack of specialized personal. Spatial Collective introduces an alternative governance modality that uses ICTs to express the shared awareness and to link these views with the ongoing or proposed governance initiatives, but it also facilitates collective action among the marginalized for the achievement of the common goals. From humble beginnings, with groups of volunteers creating basic community maps, to technologically advanced enterprises, which connect technology and ongoing governance initiatives and various social movements, the emergence of Spatial Collective is a clear indicator of the transformative power of technology and of the people's willingness to embrace these changes in the areas of limited statehood.

Conclusions

Nairobi's informal settlements remain on the periphery of Kenyan state's development initiatives. After many decades, they still lack the most basic services, such as access to clean water and sanitation. Open defecation is common. Continuous neglect has seen the rise of the informal sector that employs its own rules and regulations, as well as power dynamics separate from (but with interactions with) those of the state.

Kenya's "ICT boom," specifically Nairobi's rise as an ICT metropolis, made some of the technologies ubiquitous even among the most marginalized living in the "areas of limited statehood." ICT-enabled projects have started to provide an alternative governance modality in Nairobi's informal settlements, a seemingly contradictory phenomenon compared to the lack of sanitation, adequate housing, and other basic services in the same areas. The project to map Kibera highlights the effectiveness of citizen-driven data collection. Where the state constantly fails to gather data, a small group of citizens, with limited resources, collected thousands of points of interest, kilometers of roads and paths, and created a comprehensive database on health, education, water and sanitation, and security issues and relatively successfully used online platforms (Ushahidi, YouTube) to transmit the stories about Kibera into the world. Although the project had its shortcomings in making data useful to the ongoing governance initiatives, it sparked similar projects all over the world. The project showed that ICT-enabled collective action can fill in the information void found in the "areas of limited statehood."

Projects in Mathare and Kwale addressed some sustainability issues by involving the broader community of residents, leaders, politicians, and organizations working in the area in a decision-making forum, enabling them to decide what the communities' priorities are and how they will be addressed. The resulting initiatives were better tailored to the communities's needs and immediate usage of data for the purpose of fundraising and advocacy by some of the groups involved.

The emergence of Spatial Collective points to the transformative and influential power of technology and the collective's perception of ICT as the connecting factor among the citizens and between the citizens and the state.

Some questions still remain, mainly concerning the question how to measure the long-term impact of ICT initiatives in areas of limited statehood. ICT is becoming ubiquitous in our daily lives, even in areas of limited statehood, and the number of ICT-related projects grows daily. The ICT can have a significant role in governance and can be extremely impactful but only if it supports the ongoing governance initiatives.

Notes

1. Scott James, *Seeing Like a State*, (New Haven: Yale University Press, 1998).
2. UN-Habitat, Nairobi Urban Sector Profile, 2005, http://www.unhabitat.org/pmss/listItem-Details.aspx?publicationID=2791 where 71% of the urban population growth is absorbed by informal settlements, which have an annual population growth of 6% http://www.unhabitat.org/categories.asp?catid=206.
3. Ibid.; Kenya National Bureau of Statistics (2010). Population and Housing Census. Available at: http://www.knbs.or.ke/detailed_population_results.php.
4. SDI and Pamjoa Trust http://www.citiesalliance.org/sites/citiesalliance.org/files/CA_Docs/resources/Nairobi%20Inventory/NairobiInventory_fullversion.pdf.
5. UN-Habitat, Secretary General's visit to Kibera, Nairobi 30-31, Januay, 2007, Slums: Some Definitions, http://www.unhabitat.org/content.asp?cid=4316&catid=7&typeid=46.
6. Nairobi Urban Sector Profile, 2005, page 14, http://www.unhabitat.org/pmss/listItemDe-tails.aspx?publicationID=2791.
7. Un-Habitat: "An estimate of total population in the settlement ranges from 500,000 to 700,000 inhabitants," http://www.unhabitat.org/content.asp?cid=3220&catid=206&typeid=13; See Kibera Tours: "Kibera has a population estimated at one million.," http://kibera-tours.com/page/about-kibera; and see"It [Kibera] has an estimated population of 500 thousand," Speech by His Excellency Hon. Mwai Kibaki, C.G.H., M.P., President and Commander in Chief of the Armed Forces of the Republic of Kenya, http://www.unhabitat.org/content.asp?cid=383&catid=576&typeid=8&subMenuId=0.
8. It's [Kibera] one of the largest slums in the world at just about 1.5 million people...," Audio Slideshow: Dr. Biden Sees the Neighborhoods of Kenya, http://www.whitehouse.gov/blog/2010/06/08/audio-slideshow-dr-biden-sees-kibera-kenya.
9. Map Kibera Project—Maps and Statistics, http://mapkiberaproject.yolasite.com/maps-and-statistics.php.
10. Brian Ekdale, What's in a Name (and a Number)?, http://www.brianekdale.com/?p=107.
11. Carolina for Kibera, http://cfk.unc.edu/whatwedo/whykibera/.
12. See   http://www.impactiq.org/letter-from-nairobi-vanity-capital-and-vanity-companies/ and http://bit.ly/WiXeWm.
13. iHub Research. Mobile Technology in East Africa, subscribers and penetration. (April 2011) http://ihub.co.ke/downloads/ea_infographic.png.
14. See http://www.ictworks.org/news/2010/08/27/3-reasons-why-kenyan-mobile-tariff-price-war-matters-ict-companies and March 19, 2011 The Daily Nation Price wars drive calling rates to lowest in Africa http://www.nation.co.ke/business/news/Price+wars+drive+calling+rates+to+lowest+in+Africa+/-/1006/1129094/-/lo41gpz/-/.
15. All Africa, February 28, 2009 http://allafrica.com/stories/200903021720.html.
16. Mobile Phones Will Not Save the Poorest of the Poor http://slate.me/QpYS3H.

17. The Open Government movement is a multilateral initiative of governments from around the world that have committed to "promot[ing] transparency, empower[ing] citizens, fight[ing] corruption and harness[ing] new technologies to strengthen governance." Open component to open government is a greater openness of public institutions that allows citizens to engage with elected and appointed government officials more openly, often using ICT channels. Another component of the movement involves opening data collected by government, using public resources, to the general public. See www.opengovpartnership.org/.

18. See data here: https://opendata.go.ke/d/p452-xb7c for example.

19. Voice of Kibera, http://voiceofkibera.org/.

20. Kibera News Network, http://kiberanewsnetwork.org/.

21. See www.youtube.com/kiberanewsnetwork.

22. Sheng is local slang, spoken in Nairobi, primarily among youth. It is a combination of English, Swahili and local languages.

23. For a more in-depth discussion see Berdou, Evangelia (2011) "Mediating Voices and Communicating Realities: Using information crowdsourcing tools, open data initiatives and digital media to support and protect the vulnerable and marginalized." Institute of Development Studies, Brighton, UK. Available online at: http://www.dfid.gov.uk/R4D/PDF/Outputs/Misc_InfoComm/IDS_MediatingVoices_FinalReport.pdf Accessed July 3, 2012.

24. A version of this paragraph originally appeared in a blog post authored by Jamie Lundine on January 24th, 2011. See http://www.mapkibera.org/blog/2011/01/24/whose-map/.

25. See http://www.nuruyakwale.wordpress.com.

26. A version of this section originally appeared in a blog post authored by Jamie Lundine on February 14th, 2012. http://healthgeography.wordpress.com/2012/02/14/information-with-an-impact/.

9

Crisis-Mapping in Areas of Limited Statehood

Introduction

Crises often challenge or limit statehood and the delivery of government services. The concept of "limited statehood" thus allows for a more realistic description of the territorial and temporal variations of governance and service delivery. Total statehood, in any case, is mostly imagined—a cognitive frame or prestructured worldview. In a sense, all states are "spatially challenged" in that the projection of their governance is hardly enforceable beyond a certain geographic area and period of time. But "limited statehood" does not imply the absence of governance or services. Rather, these may simply take on alternate forms, involving procedures that are non-institutional (see Chapter 1). Therein lies the tension vis-à-vis crises, since "the utopian, immanent, and continually frustrated goal of the modern state is to reduce the chaotic, disorderly, constantly changing social reality beneath it to something more closely resembling the administrative grid of its observations" (Scott 1998, 83). Crises, by definition, publicly disrupt these orderly administrative constructs. They are brutal audits of governance structures, and the consequences can be lethal for state continuity. Recall the serious disaster response failures that occurred following the devastating cyclone of 1970 in East Pakistan. To this day, Cyclone Bhola still remains the most deadly cyclone on record, killing some 500,000 people. The lack of timely and coordinated government response was one of the triggers for the war of independence that resulted in the creation of Bangladesh (Kelman 2007, 6). While crises can challenge statehood, they also lead to collective, self-help behavior among disaster-affected communities—particularly in areas of limited statehood. Recently, this collective action—facilitated by new information and communication technologies—has swelled and resulted in the production of live crisis maps that identify the disaggregated, raw impact of a given crisis along with resulting needs for services typically provided by the government (see Chapter 7). These crisis maps are sub-national and are often crowdsourced in real time. They empirically reveal the limited contours of governance and reframe how power is both perceived and projected (see Chapter 8). Indeed, while these live maps outline the hollows of governance during times of upheaval, they also depict the full agency and public expression of citizens who self-organize online and offline to fill these troughs with alternative, parallel forms of services and thus governance. This self-organization and public expression also generate social capital between citizen volunteers—weak and strong ties that nurture social capital and facilitate future collective action both on and offline.

The purpose of this chapter is to analyze how the rise of citizen-generated crisis maps replaces governance in areas of limited statehood and to distill the conditions for their success. Unlike other chapters in this book, the analysis below focuses on a variable that has been completely ignored in the literature: *digital social capital*. The chapter is thus structured as follows. The first section provides a brief introduction to crisis mapping and frames this overview using James Scott's discourse from *Seeing Like a State* (1998). The next section briefly highlights examples of crisis maps in action—specifically those responding to natural disasters, political crises, and contested elections. The third section provides a broad comparative analysis of these case studies, while the fourth section draws on the findings of this analysis to produce a list of ingredients that are likely to render crowdsourced crisis-mapping more successful in areas of limited statehood. These ingredients turn out to be factors that nurture and thrive on digital social capital such as trust, social inclusion, and collective action. These drivers need to be studied and monitored as conditions for successful crisis maps *and* as measures of successful outcomes of online digital collaboration. In sum, digital crisis maps both reflect and change social capital.

Theorizing Crisis-Mapping

Crisis maps are not new. In 1668, Louis XIV of France commissioned three-dimensional scale models of eastern border towns so that his generals in Paris and Versailles could plan realistic maneuvers. As late as World War II, the French government guarded them as military secrets with the highest security classification. Crisis maps of the opening battle of the Sino-French War in the 1880s also exist, one drawn by the Chinese and one by the French. During World War I, the United Kingdom's Daily Mail produced war maps that projected and revealed the British government's select view of the war's global scope; the maps simply depicted the military and economic capabilities of each warring nation. This state-centric, top-down view and administration of the World War was published as the authoritative perspective of the crisis. To be sure, maps have traditionally represented "not just the perspective of the cartographer herself, but of much larger institutions—of corporations, organizations and governments" (Anderson 2013). The scale was thus fixed at one and only one scale, that of the state.

What about the "view from below"? What about the local view from the ground and the very real human consequences of war, such as food shortages, mass rape, and citizen casualties, and so on? Crowdsourced, citizen-generated maps did not exist during World War I or II, or during Cyclone Bhola. Like the books of old, the maps of yesteryear were produced and controlled by the few, typically the elite and victors. Today, however, mapmaking has been radically democratized, leading to the rise of a "mapping reflex" whereby live maps that depict a view from below are launched every day by ordinary individuals around the world. But this new type of geography is not only radically different from traditional approaches because it is user-generated and participatory; the fact that today's dynamic maps can also be updated and shared in near real-time opens up an entire new world of possibilities to facilitate independent agency and local responses—especially during times of crisis. To be sure, having a real-time map is almost as good as having your own low-flying helicopter. These live maps provide immediate situational awareness, a third dimension and thus a plurality of additional independent perspectives—a flock's-eye view—on local events unfolding in time and space.

One might refer to this type of counter-mapping as guerrilla geography—a clear assault and threat to the state-centric monopoly on perspective and thus perception of governance. Perhaps the most well-known technology for guerrilla geography and crisis-mapping is the free and open source Ushahidi platform, which has already been introduced and described earlier in this volume (see Chapter 7). The Ushahidi platform is best described as a multi-media inbox linked to a live map. The first Ushahidi map was launched in response to the 2007/2008 electoral violence in Kenya, hence the Swahili name. The platform was used to map local news reports on the violence and to crowdsource the reporting of human rights violations using e-mail and SMS. In this way, the "crowd" was able to document human rights violations across the country—evidence that would otherwise have gone completely undocumented. When used for crisis-mapping, Ushahidi is thus an example of information and communication technology that can disrupt the state's penchant for perceived uniformity. The technology can be used to contest state-centric cognitive frames and lay bare the realities of limited statehood across space and time—especially during a crisis.

Why is this important vis-à-vis governance? Because live, public maps can help synchronize shared awareness, an important catalyzing factor of social movements, according to Jürgen Habermas (1962). Recall Habermas's treatise that "those who take on the tools of open expression become a public, and the presence of a synchronized public increasingly constrains undemocratic rulers while expanding the right of that public" (Shirky 2011). Just as knowledge is power, maps too are power. "This transformative power resides not in the map," however, "but rather in the power possessed by those who deploy the perspective of that particular map" (Scott 1998, 87). Remember that "in many countries, place-names, let alone the alignment of boundaries, remain a powerful symbol of independence and national pride, and not merely indicators of location" (Valdéz 2013). To be sure, "maps are so closely associated with power that dictatorships regard information on geography as a state secret" (Osnos 2013). James Scott (2012) refers to these particular symbols of statehood as "landscapes of control and appropriation" and warns against "equating visual order with working order and visual complexity with disorder." As he explains: "A great deal of the symbolic work of official power is precisely to obscure the confusion, disorder, spontaneity, error, and improvisation of political power as it is in fact exercised, beneath a billiard-ball-smooth surface of order, deliberation, rationality, and control" (Scott 2012). But while history used to be written by the victors, today some argue that crowdsourced crisis maps are becoming the new first drafts of history; landscapes of resistance and self-determination. These maps depict nonstate perspectives from different scales and thus project the perception—and perhaps actuality—of non-state power. In sum, "we must keep in mind not only the capacity of state simplifications to transform the world but also the capacity of the society to modify, subvert, block, and even overturn the categories imposed upon it" (Scott 1998, 49).

The Ushahidi platform may enable a form of live-mapped "sousveillance," which refers to a bottom-up awareness created by recording of an activity using portable personal technologies. In many respects, however, the use of Ushahidi goes beyond sousveillance in that it generates the possibility of "dataveillance" and a possible reversal of Jeremy Bentham's Panopticon—a prison design that allows the prison authorities to observe all that happens around them without themselves being observed. "With postmodernity, the panopticon has been informationalized; what once was organized around hierarchical observation is now organized through decoding and recoding of information" (Lyon 2006, 153). In *Seeing Like a State*, Scott argues eloquently that this process of decoding and recoding was for centuries the sole privilege of the state: "Every act of measurement was an act marked by the play of powerful relations" (Scott 1998, 27). In contrast, the Ushahidi platform provides a participatory digital canvas for the public decoding, recoding of information, or measurement, and the synchronization of said measurement, which can facilitate alternative forms of governance. In other words, the platform serves to democratize dataveillance by crowdsourcing what was once the exclusive realm of the "security-informational complex," thus democratizing the act of measurement and hence governance.

In "Domination and the Arts of Resistance: Hidden Transcripts," published in 1990, Scott distinguishes between public and hidden transcripts. The former describes the open, public interactions that take place between dominators and oppressed, while hidden transcripts relate to the critique of power that "goes on offstage" and that the power elites cannot decode. This hidden transcript is comprised of the second step, social conversations, that Katz and Lazarsfeld (1955) argue ultimately change political behavior. Scott writes that when the oppressed classes publicize this "hidden transcript," they become conscious of its common status. Borrowing from Habermas, the oppressed thereby become a public and more importantly a synchronized public. In many ways, the Ushahidi platform is a vehicle by which the hidden transcript is collectively published and used to create shared awareness—thereby threatening to alter the balance of power between oppressors and oppressed. Crisis maps thus allow citizens to break free from the cognitive frames and prestructured worldview imposed by the state. There is also a clear link to governance since the reframing of this worldview also leads to the reframing of governance services along with the sources and provisions thereof.

In the fields of geography and cartography, some refer to this new wave of democratized mapmaking as "neo-geography." But this new type of geography is not only radically new for the reasons already stated. Crowdsourcing a live crisis map also catalyzes conversations between citizens, raises questions about geographic patterns or new incidents, and leads to more questions regarding the status quo, especially in areas of limited statehood that are repressive and struck by a crisis. To be sure, mass media alone do not change people's minds. Recall that political change is a two-step process, with the second—social step—being where political opinions are formed (Katz and Lazarsfeld 1955). In other words, "This is the step in which the Internet in general, and social media in particular, can make a difference" (Shirky 2011). Collaboration on live crisis-mapping efforts catalyzes this second, social step of conversations. In doing so, this collaboration creates weak and strong ties, both of which are important for collective action in social movements.

In sum, maps have been central to governance and state-formation for centuries: "They were designed, above all, to facilitate the central administration of production and the control of public life" (Scott 1998, 348). At minimum, they give the misleading impression of total statehood—an impression easily shattered during times of crisis: "If we imagine a state that has no reliable means of enumerating and locating its population, gauging its wealth, and mapping its land, resources, and settlements, we are imagining a state whose interventions in that society are necessarily crude" (Scott 1998, 77). Today, civil society groups can create shared awareness using crisis maps, which can facilitate more targeted and independent interventions from below. These crisis maps reveal that the imagined landscape of total statehood is in fact a very limited island of governance indeed. In effect, these maps trace the narrow contours of limited statehood across time and space. The use of new ICTs like the Ushahidi platform can thus facilitate and render more visible alternative procedures of governance and the agency behind them.

Crisis-Mapping in Action

The purpose of this section is to compare the above theoretical discourse to four real-world case studies from Haiti, the United States, Egypt, and Libya. These short case studies are necessarily brief, as they were deliberately selected to high-light specific insights that are analyzed in more detail in the following section.

Haiti. Two years after the Ushahidi platform was first launched and used to map Kenya's election violence, a live crisis map using Ushahidi was set up following the devastating Haiti earthquake that struck Port-au-Prince in January 2010 and killed over 200,000. According Craig Fugate, the Administrator of the US Federal Emergency Management Agency (FEMA), this crisis map provided the most comprehensive and up- to-date information available on Haiti. Both the US Marine Corps and Coast Guard used the map to save hundreds of lives in Port-au-Prince and neighboring towns. As one of poorest countries on the planet, Haiti had long been characterized as an area of limited statehood prior to the earthquake. This latest disaster further incapacitated the state, killing many government officials and civil servants.

So who created the invaluable crisis map that saved hundreds while at the same time revealing the serious limitations of Haitian state governance (and the humanitarian community)? Neither the Haitian government, nor FEMA, nor the United Nations had the means or skills to create this live map. Instead, it turns out that the crisis map was launched by student volunteers from The Fletcher School at Tufts University in Boston, some 1,500 miles away from Haiti. They self-organized into groups and monitored both social and traditional media to extract and map any relevant information related to the earthquake. Within days, a dedicated SMS short code was set up that allowed anyone in Haiti to text in their most urgent needs and location. These text messages were subsequently translated and geo-located by members of the Haitian Diaspora. None of the volunteers engaged in this initiative had done anything quite like this before—nor had anyone else for that matter. But their efforts resulted in greater situational awareness for a number of first responders.

Washington, DC. In early February 2010, just weeks after the earthquake struck Port-au-Prince, a major snowstorm paralyzed the US capital. Popularly called "Snowmaggedon," the snowstorm knocked out electricity in 20,000 homes and businesses, blanketing roads, railroads, and runways with snow, thus forcing the closure of all public transportation. A live crisis map using the Ushahidi platform was launched by *The Washington Post* and PICnet, a web-development consulting firm. What is notable about this crisis map is that it sought to crowdsource reports of needs from the disaster affected population as well as solutions. In other words, the project proposed to use the crisis map as a self-help map—a platform for self-organization and crowdsourced response. This Washington, DC, crisis map and the project in Haiti subsequently inspired Russian activists in Moscow to launch a self-help map of their own when massive fires ravaged Russia six months later (see Chapter 7).

While the United States is obviously not considered an area of limited statehood in the same way that Haiti is, the disaster resulting from Hurricane Katrina in 2005 clearly demonstrated the limited capacity of the federal government vis-à-vis governance services before and after a major disaster. The same was true of the Category 3 storm Snowmaggedon that paralyzed the city of Washington, DC. The resulting crisis map drove home an important, albeit obvious, point: government disaster responders cannot be everywhere at the same time, but the crowd is always present. And crises always catalyze collective behavior among crowds. The difference today is that ICTs make it easier to crowdsource both shared situational awareness and response regardless of whether the state is actively responding to a crisis or not.

Interestingly, however, the Washington, DC, crisis map was largely a failure. The total number of reports posted to the live map was very low. The number of reports offering help could be counted on just one hand, for example. This is particularly surprising given the high visibility of *The Washington Post* and the fact that residents of Washington, DC, have widespread access to smartphones and the Internet. Many of the right ingredients for success were present and yet the crisis map did not gain any traction.

Egypt. Hosni Mubarak barred international election observers from monitoring the country's parliamentary elections in November and December 2010. An Egyptian marketing company thus launched a project called U-Shahid using the Ushahidi platform. The purpose of this initiative was to crowdsource citizen-based election-monitoring efforts during the parliamentary elections. U-Shahid was launched well ahead of the elections with a dedicated trainer organizing a series of workshop in five key Egyptian cities. Customized workflows to collect, process, verify and map reports of election irregularities were drafted. The team also developed an "organigram" for the operation and set up contingency plans in the event that their project would be shut down by state security forces.

The U-Shahid project mapped some 2,700 reports during the two rounds of parliamentary elections, which included 211 supporting pictures and 323 videos. The team was also able to verify more than 90 percent of the content that ended up on the map by using basic journalistic techniques, such as triangulation and follow-up. In total, the web-based map received close to 60,000 hits, the vast majority of which came from within Egypt. (Interestingly, the next highest number originated from Saudi Arabia.) The group proactively disseminated this information, using both new and traditional media channels. Their efforts were featured on Egyptian television, on BBC Arabic programming, and in dozens of articles in ten different languages. The U-Shahid crisis map was considered by many as a success—not least because of the difficult political challenges of operating in a repressive state.

Libya. The political crisis in Libya began to escalate just weeks after Mubarak was deposed in Egypt. On March 1, 2011, a live crowdsourced, social media crisis map of Libya was launched at the request of the UN Office for the Coordination of Humanitarian Affairs (UN OCHA). OCHA did not have any Information Management Officers in Libya during the early onset of the humanitarian crisis. However, they realized that a rich amount of multi-media information had been shared on social media during the uprisings that had occurred in neighboring Tunisia and Egypt. The crisis map was therefore used to map social media content (and later mainstream media content as well) that was most relevant for the purposes of decision-making for humanitarian response. Information from the live crisis map was integrated within official UN information products used to support decision-making.

As in the case of the Haiti map, the Libya crisis map was not launched by any established organization or professional humanitarian network. Instead, OCHA activated the Standby Volunteer Task Force (SBTF), a global network of some 900 volunteers based in over 80 countries around the world. The purpose of the SBTF is to provide humanitarian, human rights, and development organizations with a dedicated volunteer base for live crisis-mapping. The SBTF was launched in October 2010 and has since been activated over twenty times by various organizations. Interestingly, the impetus for the SBTF was the Haiti crisis map. After the earthquake struck, Port-au-Prince, the volunteer effort that sprung to life was reactive and thus unprepared. Volunteers from the Haiti operation realized the life-saving power of creating crisis maps and thus decided to create a team of standby volunteers who were already trained in crisis-mapping to support future responses to humanitarian crises.

Comparative Analysis in Search of Success

Determining what constitutes success in crisis-mapping efforts is an ongoing challenge, not least in areas of limited statehood. Whether or not the efforts described above are in fact successful ultimately depends on what the goals of these maps were in the first place. These goals, however, are rarely articulated but often implied. One could take a "state-centric" approach and simply devise quantifiable, macro-level metrics such as the number of reports submitted per crisis map, the number of hits received on the website hosting the map, the extent of media coverage, and so on. Going by these metrics, one would judge the Haiti crisis map a success and the Washington, DC, crisis map a failure. In fact, most Ushahidi maps would be deemed a complete failure if these metrics were used to assess success. A recent empirical study of Ushahidi maps revealed that the vast majority of maps (93 percent) had fewer than ten reports (Bailard, Baker, Hindman, Livingston, and Meier 2012).

But is ten an appropriate threshold for this metric? Or should the number be of reports be greater than 100 for a map to be considered successful? These thresholds may have to depend on the local context or otherwise run the risk of being purely arbitrary and largely meaningless. Another approach might be to try to measure the impact of these crisis maps on the "external" social, political, and economic environment. This too is a challenge, since few independent and comprehensive impact evaluations have ever been carried out on these maps (primarily due to cost). This "environmental" approach, while important, is thus mainly limited to anecdotal evidence.

There is a third lens, however, through which to assess the impact of crisis maps and understand the conditions of their success. This might be called the "people-centered" lens. The focus here is more "internal" and argues that the added value and impact of crisis maps lies in the social capital that results from collaborating on these maps over the long term rather than in the immediate moment. The field of sociology defines the term "social capital" as the expected collective benefits from the preferential treatment and cooperation between individuals and groups, which can result in increased productivity. A people-centered approach thus places more emphasis on the development of both weak and strong ties over time than on the deliverable—the crisis map. There is increasing evidence that social capital is a potent force for development and humanitarian response. A report by the International Federation of the Red Cross (Levinger and Bloom 2011) found that National Societies that fostered strong and weak links across networks performed better irrespective of the political and economic realities in a given country than those that did not engage in purposeful networking. In other words, the former were more organizationally effective as a result of building social capital. This lens is often missing from the discourse on the role of ICTs in areas of limited statehood. Social capital is less tangible than a map and measuring this type of digital human capital is more challenging.

The notion of crisis mapping as a *process* that produces and accumulates social capital relates well to the concept of *metis* described by Scott in *Seeing Like a State*. Coming from Greek mythology, *metis* refers to wisdom and cunning—practical, local knowledge. *Metis* is based on experience and practice: "The skills of metis may well involve rules of thumb, but such rules are largely acquired through practice (often in formal apprenticeship) and a developed feel or knack for strategy. [...] In a sense, metis lies in that large space between the real genius, to which no formula can apply, and the realm of codified knowledge, which can be learned by rote" (Scott 1998, 315–16). Scott relates this directly to crisis situations: "Adapting quickly and well to unpredictable events—both natural events, such as the weather, and human events, such as the enemy's move—and making the best out of limited resources are the kinds of skills that are hard to teach as cut-and-dried disciplines" (315). As such, "the practice and experience reflected in metis is almost always local" (317).

The "local" in the context of digital social capital is grounded in the messaging and social-networking platforms that are used to coordinate crisis-mapping efforts. These include Skype, Ning, Google Docs, Google Groups, and e-mail. These technologies provide a "locality" for deliberation and coordination, for the sharing of "local" knowledge, practice, and experience. The vast majority of these efforts are carried out via text rather than voice calls. This is a matter of "practical efficacy," which as Scott notes, "is the key test of metis knowledge" (331). So while Skype is the most critical of the technologies used to self-organize and coordinate, it is the instant-messaging function that is used almost exclusively. Together with the Google Docs, which are used to share evolving knowledge, Skype lends a sense of "location" to the efforts; a locality where *metis* can be shared and reshaped according to the different needs.

This is how volunteers from the SBTF collaborate across multiple time zones and from dozens of different countries around the world—collaboration that catalyzes weak and strong ties, which in turn builds social capital and facilitates collective action. To be sure, recent studies have shown that "such interactions are not necessarily of inferior quality compared to simultaneous, face-to-face interactions" (Tibbitt 2011). What's more, "In addition to the preservation and possible improvement of existing ties, interaction through social media can foster the creation of new relations" (Dufty 2012, 43). In sum, social interactions facilitated via social media and networking platforms build trust, which improves collaboration and generates social capital.

Let's revisit the crisis map case studies highlighted above in the context of a people-centered approach that emphasizes the build-up of social capital and the accumulation of *metis*. In many ways, the Haiti crisis map launched the field of crisis-mapping. How did the map materialize when viewed through a people-centered lens? Volunteers from The Fletcher School at Tufts University created the map just hours after the tragic earthquake hit Haiti. Why? The initial impetus was due to the fact that several Fletcher students were in Port-au-Prince and missing at the time. So this pre-existing social network—latent social capital—was critical to the success of the Haiti crisis map. To be sure, the presence of an existing social network and community facilitated the collective action and collaboration that ensued. Recall that the hundreds of volunteers that joined the efforts were from Tufts University and also from the Haitian Diaspora (another pre-existing social network). These international and online multi-network efforts resulted in strong and long-term ties with a *local* Haitian software company called Solutions.ht, which subsequently built a local crisis mapping platform called *Noula* thanks to the direct support and engagement of volunteers from Tufts University.

Taking a "people-centered" lens also means evaluating the build-up of social capital over the long term. Doing so, vis-à-vis the Haiti map, reveals that it was volunteers from the Haiti efforts that ultimately launched the SBTF, which has since provided multiple humanitarian organizations with critical support in several key crises. Moreover, the initial members of the SBTF were not only those volunteers who had responded to Haiti, but also those who were engaged in the aftermath of the Chile earthquake and the Pakistan floods, and eventually the volunteers who spearheaded the Russia Help Map following the massive wildfires there (see Chapter 7). Indeed, it was the Haiti map that inspired Russian activists to launch their own crisis map in response to the fires, modeling their approach based on *The Washington Post*'s crisis map of Washington, DC. The following year, Japanese volunteers in Tokyo launched a live crisis map following the devastating earthquake and tsunami—again after having been inspired by the efforts in Haiti. They also reached out to the SBTF and Japanese students at The Fletcher School who had contributed to the Haiti efforts for support.

Note however that the Washington, DC, crisis map is largely considered a failure if "state-centric" metrics, such as number of reports, is used. Indeed, the map got very little traction even though it was featured and hosted on *The Washington Post*'s website. The project was launched by a major organization, so it was perhaps more top-down than the other case studies analyzed earlier. Does this imply a lack of pre-existing social capital, which in turn explains the relative failure of the crisis map? Either way, the map served to inspire others—like Russia's wildfires—that were considered highly successful.

One reason why the U-Shahid project in Egypt was so well prepared and designed was because one of the co-founders of the SBTF was U-Shahidi's principle trainer. She shared the lessons, or *metis*, she learned at U-Shahid with the SBTF, and her contacts in the country and region became important when UN OCHA requested a live crisis map of Libya only months later. The team at U-Shahid has subsequently launched a live map during the Egyptian revolution and several other maps since, learning and improving their approach with each iteration. Their latest map, which built on this *metis*, focused on Egypt's presidential elections held in July 2012. This time, more than fifteen trainers and seventy-five coordinators were trained to work in the "operation room" supporting 2,200 trained observers located all over Egypt. The observers sent more than 17,000 reports and up to 25,000 SMSs, most of which were mapped live. This is a far cry from 2,700 reports back in 2010.

In the midst of Egypt's revolution in January 2011, another major snowstorm hit the East Coast of the United States, impacting major cities such as Washington, DC, and Boston. As a result, members of the SBTF contacted PICnet to clone and spearhead the launch of several new self-help maps for each of these affected cities. By that time, in early 2011, members of the SBTF had already been engaged in a number of other deployments, recruiting hundreds of new volunteers, thus adding to their social capital. When the United Nations requested a live crisis map of Libya several weeks later, the SBTF had accumulated enough capital and strong ties to see them through their longest and most challenging deployment yet. This project, more than any other, had the most direct impact on the United Nations, going so far as changing the OCHA's own information management workflows as a result of collaborating with a more *metis*-based, informal network. UN professionals working side-by-side (on Skype) with digital volunteers from around the world also adopted some of this new "local expertise" on crisis-mapping. Since then, SBTF volunteers have also been engaged in supporting other crisis-mapping efforts as "side deployments," independently of the SBTF. These side deployments have included supporting pro-democracy and human rights projects in partnership with activists in Syria and the Sudan.

When seen through this "people-centered" lens of accumulated social capital, it is difficult to look at a crisis map quite the same way again. Crisis maps are facilitating the growth of social capital across international networks, such as in case of the SBTF, and at the local level, which was more strongly exhibited by the U-Shahid example. These maps, however, don't depict the *metis*, the weak and strong ties—the social bonds and social capital—that went into mapping hundreds or thousands of dots. Nor do the maps reveal the resulting strengthening of these bonds and the swelling of the social capital, or the learning and expanded *metis*. For example, it has been said that the DC snowstorm crisis map failed since it got very little traction. This is true for the initial deployment of 2010 but certainly not the case for subsequent deployments of the Snowmageddon platform in Washington, DC, New York, and Boston in early 2011. To be sure, one uncovers a different narrative when applying the lens of social capital; a narrative interwoven by threads of learning and *metis*. As the major snowstorm approached these cities, members of the SBTF reached out to the team behind the initial Snowmageddon platform to have it re-launched and re-customized for the other cities. Members of the Task Force based in Washington, DC, New York, and Boston subsequently took the lead in promoting and populating their own crisis maps. The accumulation of social capital through the task force is the glue that made these deployments possible even though the first Snowmageddon map was of limited value at the time.

In sum, crisis maps are likely to be more successful if this social capital is at least partially in place before the crisis and has room to grow—particularly within the framework of limited statehood. In other words, while live crisis maps delineate the contours of limited statehood and governance—thus breaking the myth of total statehood—they can also build the social capital to offer alternative offline services and possibly constrain bad governance. At minimum, the social capital and *metis* that are accumulated facilitate self-organization and collective action, which are critical for self-governance. These crisis maps thus provide far more than critical situational awareness from the bottom up. They are platforms for self-organization and engines of social capital. In sum, "it appears as if Ushahidi's potential was rather that of creating a space where people can come together, from the remoteness of their homes and without having ever met, to actually become active participants in crises that happened thousands of miles away from their homes. In fact, through Ushahidi maps, a new relationality emerges centered on the sharing of a concern for crisis" (Achi 2012).

Conclusion

Recall Cyclone Bhola, which devastated East Pakistan in 1970. A week after the hazard struck, the Pakistani president acknowledged that his government had made "mistakes in its handling of the relief efforts due to a lack of understanding of the magnitude of the disaster" (Wikipedia 2013). In other words, they did not have real-time situational awareness. They did not have a live crisis map, nor did the half-a-million people who were killed because of Pakistan's limited statehood, capacity, and situational awareness. The fury that resulted fueled the protests against the regime and spurred the war of independence that led to the birth of Bangladesh. Today, crowdsourced, self-help crisis maps enable citizens to improve their own situational awareness and coordinate their own disaster relief efforts independently of the state.

Take, for example, the case of citizen-based, self-organized humanitarian convoys in Libya, which were coordinated using the Twitter hashtag #LibyaConvoy and IntaFeen.com, a check-in and mapping platform developed in Egypt. The convoys were seen as largely successful, delivering important food and medical supplies to Tripoli and Benghazi. Now imagine that these #LibyaConvoy service-delivery efforts had been connected to the Libya crisis map launched by the United Nations. The result would have been a combined online and offline humanitarian response operation driven entirely by self-organized volunteers much like the Russia Help Map described in Chapter 7.

Scott rightly notes that "The quantitative technologies used to investigate social and economic life work best if the world they aim to describe can be remade in their image" (Scott 1998, 347). Today, however, the rise of citizen-based crowdsourced crisis maps means that the public sphere can describe the world as is rather than as seen or wished by the state. Scott writes: "Here, I believe, there is something to the classical anarchist claim—that the state, with its positive law and central institutions, undermines individuals' capacities for autonomous self-governance—that might apply to the planning grids of high modernism as well. Their own institutional legacy may be frail and evanescent, but they may impoverish the local wellsprings of economic, social, and cultural self-expression" (349). When backed by an authoritarian state, according to Scott, these maps of "legibility and control do partly succeed in shaping the natural and social environment after their image. To the degree that such thin maps do manage to impress themselves on social life, what kind of people do they foster?" (348). They foster passive, impoverished, and unengaged individuals who believe in the myth of statehood and obediently await government services during a crisis. State-centric maps are dead maps, cemeteries comprised of archaic forms of control, devoid of metis and social capital.

Live crowdsourced maps counter the prestructured worldview imposed by the state's planning grids. They reveal the limitations of governance, particularly during a crisis, and also offer a platform for self-expression and self-organization; for the provision of relief supplies and humanitarian aid—typically the state's responsibility. These crisis maps, Scott explains, not only fill the local wellsprings of human agency, they also crowdsource additional social capital that further facilitates collective action and self-governance: "An institution, social form, or enterprise that takes much of its shape from the evolving metis of the people engaged in it will thereby enhance their range of experience and skills" (356). This is precisely what the SBTF does and what many crowdsourced crisis-mapping efforts entail. The result? Alternative service delivery following a disaster *and* the accumulation of social capital that further increases the chances of successful crisis maps and the likelihood of offline action. These efforts not only build digital social capital across international networks online but can also nurture local and offline capacity building as evidenced in the case of Haiti and Noula.

Of course, social capital is not the only explanatory variable in the equation for successful crisis maps. Nor is social capital a sufficient condition. Several other factors are necessary to ensure success. Preparedness is critical—hence the launch of the SBTF. In addition, the U-Shahid case was successful in large part because the team began preparing for the election-monitoring efforts months in advance. In neighboring Sudan, a similar project was attempted to monitor the presidential elections of 2010. It failed for two reasons. First, the group in charge hardly spent any time on preparedness and contingency-planning. Second, because of funding issues, the group was only able to secure an SMS short code to crowdsource reports via text message *after* the elections had started. So there are more necessary conditions for success than social capital. But these have already been written about whereas the focus on social capital has largely been ignored (Bailard, Baker, Hindman, Livingston, and Meier 2012; Meier 2011a).

While developing a conceptual framework to measure digital social capital goes beyond the scope of this chapter, it is clear that studies that analyze "offline" social capital are relevant to this research. Networks, trust, collective action, social inclusion, and communication are recurring themes in the research and discourse on social capital. Networks, for example, can be measured by the density and variety of membership. In sum, for a theory of change that focuses on digital social capital, these are the variables that need to be studied and monitored as both conditions for successful crisis maps *and* as measures of successful outcomes.

10

From Crowdsourcing to Crowdseeding: The Cutting Edge of Empowerment?

PETER VAN DER WINDT

Introduction

In 2009 Columbia University launched a pilot project in the Kivus region of the Democratic Republic of Congo called *Voix des Kivus*.[1] The point of the project was to examine the potential for using SMS technology to gather conflict event data in real time.[2] Given previous experiences in Eastern Congo, the research team expected that collecting high-quality event data in Eastern Congo in the traditional way (sending out enumerator teams) would be challenging, while using traditional approaches to collect event information in real time would be impossible. As a result, the team launched an SMS-based pilot project called *Voix des Kivus*. Parts of the Kivus have cell phone coverage, and cell phones are relatively inexpensive. Moreover, while enumerator teams have problems crossing bad roads or washed-away bridges, phone signals do not. Finally, an SMS-message sent is received instantaneously.

The *Voix des Kivus* project used a crowdseeding approach that combines the innovations of crowdsourcing with standard principles of survey research and statistical analysis. It used a sampling frame, selected sites through systematic random sampling, and identified specific reporters in each site. Researchers then "seeded" mobile phones to select "phoneholders" and trained them to use the system and what to to report. Only these preselected reporters could contribute into the system, rather than anyone with a mobile phone or connection of some sort, as would be the case with standard crowdsourcing platforms.

This chapter draws on this experience to discuss how such ICT projects might empower populations by enabling the collection and distribution of information as an alternative mechanism of governance. A particularly popular system to marshal ICT's potential to collect and distribute information is crowdsourcing. *Voix des Kivus*, however, differed from this approach in that it made use of pre-identified message senders. This chapter will discuss that while this approach is particularly successful in collecting large amounts of high-quality information, in real time, from populations that otherwise would have been very isolated, the crowdseeding approach also leads to concerns for participant protection. In the case of *Voix des Kivus*, these safety concerns made it difficult to scale up the project, villages had to remain mutually anonymous making interaction between the phoneholders impossible, and the researchers were placed in the uncomfortable position of acting as data censors. This chapter turns first to a description of *Voix des Kivus*. After that the chapter turns to a discussion of these more ethical implications that arose while implementing the project. Finally, this chapter discusses whether or not *Voix des Kivus* was successful in empowering its Congolese participants.

ICT and Empowerment

ICT has major potential to empower people. First, new technologies provide ordinary individuals with the ability to *collect information*. Moreover, they can do so without relying on intermediaries, such as state institutions or NGOs that might distort such information. Furthermore, one of the defining features of an area of limited statehood is the absence of reliable data about basic conditions. Where consolidated states exist, bureaus and agencies collect health statistics, monitor the environment, and file police reports. Where the state is missing, no such system of data collection exists, except for where NGOs and civil society organizations can fill the void. Second, ICT enables ordinary people to create *new forms of organization*. Technologies such as mobile phones and the Internet can be used for collective action. Finally, ICT enables people to *distribute information*. Areas of limited statehood are often isolated, leaving events unnoticed—or noticed only after months of silence and delay. New technologies can address this by providing fast and cost-effective means to send (and receive) large amounts of information.

By facilitating the collection and distribution of information, ICT empowers people in two major ways.[3] First, ICT makes it more difficult for important issues to be left out of consideration in decision-making arenas. Second, ICT increases knowledge among ordinary people about their preferences and options. ICT in areas of limited statehood, in other words, is not just about service delivery, as important as that is. ICT also affects political processes. Political power is not simply a matter of winning contests in political institutions reflected in concrete decisions.[4] Power is also located in the capacity to create or reinforce barriers to the public airing of policy issues (Bachrach and Baratz 1962). That is, power is also found in the ability to shape the agenda of issues that are to be considered—this is known as the *second face of power*. Cohen (1963, 13) illustrated this appropriately by saying that the press "may not be successful much of the time in telling people what to think, but it is stunningly successful in telling its readers what to think about. The world will look different to different people," Cohen continues, "depending on the map that is drawn for them by writers, editors, and publishers of the paper they read." This fictional map might be purposely influenced by a decision-maker who tries to control the agenda, thereby trying to avoid the emergence of values and interests contrary to his interest. Because people can now obtain information directly, and from a possibly wide variety of sources, it is more difficult for such agenda-control. In addition, this map might also be biased because of more innocent reasons. Decision-makers might simply not be aware that certain issues are at play—this is particularly likely in areas of limited statehood where many events take place in isolation. ICT therefore empowers people by making it possible for hitherto unknown issues being raised.

Finally, one can also exercise power by influencing, shaping, or determining other people's wants and preferences. This is also known as the *third dimension of power* and follows from Lukes (1974).[5] Power is therefore also the ability to shape perceptions, cognitions, and preferences in such a way as to secure the acceptance of the status quo. This could be because no alternative appears to exist. Or this could be because it is seen as natural and unchangeable. People are simply resigned to their fate. Lukes (1974) introduces the importance of the concept of latent conflict in which those subject to power do not express or even remain unaware of their interests. By facilitating the collection of information ICT empowers these people by making it possible to learn about and recognize their interests. Furthermore, by making it cheap to distribute information, ICT make it possible for ordinary people to express these interests.

Voix des Kivus: Crowdseeding in Eastern Congo

To learn about the potential for ICT, and cell phones in particular, to empower people, this chapter looks at an SMS-based pilot project in the Democratic Republic of Congo. Columbia University implemented *Voix des Kivus* in 2009 in the Congolese province of South Kivu. In total the pilot project *was* implemented in eighteen villages spread over four territories.[6] The headquarters of *Voix des Kivus* was Bukavu, the capital city of South Kivu. Most of the province's NGOs are also located there. Each village had three phoneholders—individuals selected as recipients of a mobile phone—participating in *Voix des Kivus*: one representing the traditional leadership (often the chief of the village), one representing women's groups (often the head of the women's association), and one elected by the community. The chief is involved in most village affairs, from land conflict to marital disputes. The head of the women's association, on the other hand, is often the go-to person for issues such as domestic violence. Finally, a third person was elected to be a phoneholder.[7] Holders were trained extensively on the use of the phone and how to send messages to the system. They were provided with a phone, weekly credit, and a code-sheet that listed events of interest that might take place in the village.[8] Phoneholders automatically received weekly credit (around $1.50 or a one day's wage) that they could freely use. They were also reimbursed for the messages they sent. Sending messages to the *Voix des Kivus* was free to the phoneholders yet voluntary and self-directed. While users did not have to pay for each message, they were not given a financial reward for sending content to the system.

A standard cellphone linked to a laptop comprised the necessary equipment for receiving the messages. With other freely available software (FrontlineSMS, R, and LaTeX), messages received were automatically filtered, coded for content, cleaned to remove duplicates, and merged into a database. Graphs and tables were automatically generated and were then automatically mounted into bulletins spanning any period of interest and with different levels of sensitivity. Translations of noncoded text messages (often from Swahili or one of the local languages into French and English) were undertaken manually. To facilitate the sending of messages, code-books with pre-assigned codes to events were distributed. The codes were organized in ten categories: (1) presence of military forces, (2) attacks on the village, (3) deaths related to armed combat, (4) local violence and property loss, (5) displacement, (6) health events (7) natural disasters, (8) development and NGO activities, (9) social events and (10) special codes. The codes were distributed in French and Swahili to the phoneholders. If no event took place during the week the phoneholders would send the code "00." If an event took place that was not listed on the code-book or the reporter preferred to provide more detail, the code "98" followed by text could be send. Per SMS more than one event could be reported by separating codes with a semicolon.

Voix des Kivus was launched in August 2009 and during the first twelve months operated in only four villages. Then from August 2010 onwards the pilot project was expanded to eighteen villages. The project ended in 2011. In this short period *Voix des Kivus* received a total of 4,783 SMS messages with relevant content. The phoneholders sent messages about a total of 5,293 events of which 4,623 were unique—many village events were thus reported by more than one phoneholder. Of these SMS messages 1,244 were text-messages.[9] The uptake of the system was thus very enthusiastic, and the data that was generated was rich, including regular reports of conflict events: encroachments by various groups, abductions, looting, shootings, and sexual violence. Messages also contained accounts of crop failures and flooding, as well as of interventions by development organizations and other actors.

Did *Voix des Kivus* Empower Populations?

Voix des Kivus was successful in collecting large amounts of high-quality information, in real time, from populations that otherwise would have been very isolated

(Van der Windt and Humphreys 2012). The system was enthusiastically received by participating villages and compared to more traditional data-gathering system was cheap to implement. Given this seeming success of *Voix des Kivus*, did the project lead to empowerment of populations living in areas of limited statehood?

DID *VOIX DES KIVUS* LEAD TO NEW MODES OF ORGANIZATION?

The answer is "no." Because of the area in which *Voix des Kivus* operated it was common to receive highly sensitive information—a sort of 911 call from a jungle in Central Africa. For example, reports were sometimes about sexual abuse or other types of violence perpetrated by different actors (regularly including names of perpetrators). In contrast to a crowdsourcing system where information is received from an unidentified, anonymous public, crowdseeding systems such as *Voix des Kivus* make use of identifiable users, in this case the fifty-four phoneholders. As a result, a great concern throughout the period of operation was the security of the phoneholders, despite efforts to mitigate the threat.

Before implementation of the *Voix des Kivus* project the crowdseeding approach was discussed with a wide range of experienced NGOs workers and focus groups, and interviews were conducted in eleven villages in Eastern Congo. Out of a concern for the safety of the phoneholders, initial designs called for phoneholders to be "invisible." That is, the project would keep the fact that three villagers are *Voix des Kivus* phoneholders unknown to the other villagers. This proved impractical in small villages where secrets are hard to keep. Moreover, fellow villagers and actors external to the village might come to see these phoneholders as spies. Both NGO workers and villagers suggested taking the opposite approach. As a result, before entry in a village the crowdseeding approach would be discussed and presented to the village chief. Only after his approval did *Voix des Kivus* organize a village meeting in which at least 40 percent of the village had to be present. During the meeting a *Voix des Kivus* team would explain the pilot project in great detail—including the potential security risks. It was only after the approval by the village that *Voix des Kivus* could be implemented. The three phoneholders would function as representatives for the village, and the village as a whole would be a *Voix des Kivus* village. In addition to embedding the project inside the village, the researchers kept risks to the phoneholders to a minimum in several ways. Initially, *Voix des Kivus* operated in just four villages. Only after a year of close monitoring of these four villages, fourteen more villages were added. Finally, the project was particularly careful with whom to share the data and what data to share, as will be discuss more below.

In principle, collective participation in a system like *Voix des Kivus* can lead to a kind of networking effect in which disparate villages engage with each other more directly and coordinate actions. Doing so would create new modes of governance, even in the absence of a consolidated state. However, this kind of ICT-enabled collective action did not arise as part of the *Voix des Kivus* project for the simple reason that—out of concern for participant protection—the participating villages remained mutually anonymous. Villages were interested in the reports of other villages and wanted others to see their reports, but in practice the feedback they received was anonymous. Each village received only summary reports concerning their own messaging, plus aggregates of reports from elsewhere. Phoneholders were not able to get in contact with their peers from other villages owing to the security precautions imposed by the Columbia University team. The *Voix des Kivus* system was a hierarchical, vertical structure in which there was direct contact between the phoneholders and the system.

DID *VOIX DES KIVUS* ENABLE PEOPLE TO DISTRIBUTE INFORMATION?

The answer is "yes, but only to some extent." While *Voix des Kivus* started as an academic exercise to learn whether high-quality event data could be collected via SMS, the researcher team quickly learned the wider implications of the system. In a matter of weeks the project received hundreds of (often very sensitive) messages about events that had a negative impact on the lives of our phoneholders and their villages. As a result, the Columbia team found themselves ethically obliged to do more with the data than keep it in a database for future academic analysis. The researchers felt responsible for taking some sort of quick action in response to important events. Consequently, a system was set up with weekly bulletins. Each Monday a bulletin was produced and disseminated that presented information on events that took place in the preceding week. This emphasized the feeling among participants that *Voix de Kivus* gave them a "voice"—providing them with the ability to share their stories with the world. Indeed, after a year of operation, one of the phoneholders explained the volume of messages this way: "Many events take place here that nobody knows about. For the first time ever we are placed on a map." However, the level of community empowerment and ICT-enabled governance was limited for three reasons.

First, to ensure that subjects were not harmed, *Voix des Kivus* could not simply post unfiltered data as it entered the system. The researcher team therefore produced two different bulletins: a "non-sensitive bulletin" (without village identifiers), which could be distributed widely and was made available online each week, and a "sensitive bulletin" (with village identifiers but without holder identifiers). The question then arose: With whom can sensitive versions of the bulletin be shared? As a result, the researchers, dedicated to discovery and the scientific process, were placed in the uncomfortable position of acting as data censors. Should the bulletins be given to the Congolese army—who were themselves often the perpetrators of abuses reported through the system? Doing so might put the phoneholders and the entire village at risk of reprisal. Should the reports be given to the UN peacekeeping army (MONUSCO), the main actor in Eastern Congo that could respond to violent events? The concern here was the possibility that MONUSCO would share the information with the government. The instinct of researchers is toward open access. But in this case this laudable principle could bring considerable danger to phoneholders.

The problem was addressed by deferring the decision to affected populations: Allow the users to determine who should have access to different pieces of information. After consultation with the phoneholders, the Columbia team researcher created a system that allowed phoneholders to include an extra code (1–4) to a message to indicate the event's level of sensitivity, and thereby with whom the information was to be shared: "1" meant only with Voix des Kivus, "2" indicated Voix des Kivus plus close partners, "3" allowed for sharing with Voix des Kivus, close partners and MONUSCO, and indicated "4" everybody. It was hoped that such a system would create bulletins without putting researchers at Columbia University in the position of censoring data. Data received by the Voix des Kivus system would be gathered and collated without editing the content of the message (except to remove duplicate entries and deleting personal identifiers).[10]

While phoneholders made use of this system, in practice, many messages did not include such a dissemination-code, and phoneholders deferred the decision to researchers. They put their faith in the Voix des Kivus project to share information with those who could make good use of the data. Given the concerns over security, the data about violence were not shared without the specific dissemination-code allowing for distribution beyond Voix des Kivus and close partners. MONUSCO (the UN peacekeeping army) was therefore often excluded as a recipient of information about violent events. As a result, at many times the researcher team in New York were better informed about daily events in Eastern Congo than were local actors, such as humanitarian organizations or the peacekeeping army in Bukavu.[11] It is quite possible that populations would have been willing to take serious risks, exposing themselves to retribution for reporting events, in order to stand up against abuse. But as initiators of the project, the Columbia team felt that they would be responsible for adverse events. As a result, their ethical concern to do no harm resulted in a certain denial of agency to populations.

The concern for security thus limited the potential reach of ICT-enabled governance by those living in eighteen villages in the Eastern Congo. This points to potential weaknesses in the crowdseeding method. Crowdseeding limited empowerment in two more ways. First, in the face of ethical concerns, it was difficult to scale up. Second, the information was not put to use. As researchers it was important to expand quickly in order to obtain data from a large number of villages. The initial designs called for an expansion to 100 villages throughout the province. However, not only was Voix des Kivus expanded slowly, beginning with but four villages, the obligations to protect both phoneholders and villages created barriers to taking the project to scale, even though no incidents threatened the safety of the phoneholders and none of the phoneholders claimed that the project had somehow put them at risk. However, had the project been scaled up to its anticipated size, the attention of armed groups could have been drawn to in. As researchers on the other side of the planet, the Columbia team did not feel comfortable shouldering the responsibility for this possible outcome.

Second, during the implementation of *Voix des Kivus*, the researchers were careful not to make promises to those in the villages about any specific benefits associated with taking part in the program, beyond having access to a phone and receiving small credit payments. But, a system like *Voix des Kivus* inevitably creates expectations in participating villages. There was a palpable hope that if only the information about the situation of a village would get out to the world, then surely someone somewhere would provide relief. For example, phoneholders often said that while they did not expect direct material benefits from sending messages into to the *Voix des Kivus* system, they hoped that by doing so NGOs might intervene. Beyond reporting about events, the system was used in some cases simply to make requests, such as appeals for support with a health clinic or for support with schooling. In addition to the simple desire to express themselves—"We had a good Christmas"—the messages demonstrated the various instrumental uses to which communities wanted to put the system ("we need X medicine in village Y").[12] These are some of the weaknesses in the crowdseeding method used by *Voix des Kivus*. In the closing section we will consider a few of the benefits of the methods. But before we do that, we must next consider whether *Voix des Kivus* contributed to the creation of something like a new governance modality. We believe that given the limitations just considered, it did not.

The information collected by *Voix des Kivus* was shared with development organizations and international actors that received an approval from the phoneholders. These included several development organizations based in Bukavu who could use the data to evaluate the situation on the ground in the region. The program was also presented to the international community of development and protection agencies in South Kivu. The research team did so, among others, through a presentation at the weekly, UN OCHA–organized meeting of NGOs and international actors in Bukavu. For these actors, the system could in principle serve as an early warning mechanism; as a tool to prioritize interventions; or as a system to relay information to villages. In practice, many groups took interest in the project, including NGOs, philanthropists, and the US Department of State. Generally, the contacts came from people focused specifically on information technologies, as well as groups working on fundraising. The humanitarian organizations on the ground, including the various UN bodies and some of the organizations that received the data also voiced interest in the project, but with no concrete result. The potential was demonstrated and the data were collected. *But we know of no instances in which development or humanitarian agencies responded to incidents or issues raised by phoneholders.* The data never played a role in operational planning. As Livingston and Walter-Drop put it in this volume's concluding chapter, *Voix des*

Kivus enhanced the management of "bits," but it could do nothing about the redis-tribution of "atoms"—such as much needed food, clean water, security, and other public goods. Quite understandably, the researcher team was in the uncomfort-able position of knowing about events in the Democratic Republic of Congo, but without the ability to solve them. The reason for this, in part, involved a scaling dilemma. On the one hand, there was considerable hesitation among those lead-ing the project to scale up data collection without the needed confidence that the data would be put to proper use. Yet it would be clear how, exactly, the data could be used without scaling up.

DID *VOIX DES KIVUS* PROVIDE THE MEANS FOR PARTICIPANTS TO COLLECT INFORMATION THEMSELVES?

The answer is "maybe." The project was initially set up as a data-gathering exercise; via the system, we wanted to learn about conflict events taking place in Eastern Congo. However, cell phones can also be used to receive information. Moreover, in contrast to crowdsourcing, crowdseeding does not make use of an anonymous crowd and thus (tailored) information can be sent to the phoneholders. Indeed, when after a year of operation the research team visited the participating villages the phoneholders suggested for the system to disseminate information to them. In particular they suggested the dissemination of information related to food prices and markets, which could help them obtain better prices for their crops and thus augment their ability to maintain an adequate standard of living for themselves and their families. *Voix de Kivus*, as a result, set up a system whereby every second week an SMS-message was send to its phoneholders with price information about local staple in nearby markets—these products included rice, cassava, tomatoes, and butter, but also products like petrol. This is similar to other mobile-based information systems, such as Trade at Hand and the Grameen Foundation's Community Knowledge Workers (Grameen Foundation 2013; ITC 2008).

Another benefit specific to crowdseeding is that it provides to communities the means to participate in the system. In the case of *Voix des Kivus*, not only were phoneholders supplied with a phone and reimbursed for sent SMS-messages, but they also received a weekly phone credit of around $1.50 (more or less one day's wage) that they could freely use. One reason for this extra phone credit was to incentivize the participants for their continued support. Yet another reason was the hope that by providing the means, *Voix des Kivus* could help create more eco-nomic opportunities and enable people to participate more fully in civic society. For example, a farmer can get market prices for his goods, a job seeker can connect with a potential employer in a nearby village, and people in remote communities can participate in call-in radio shows about local issues. The Grameen Foundation (especially Grameenphone) is a good example of the use the mobile phone for such purposes. However, in *Voix des Kivus*'s period of operation we know of no instances in which people used their phones for anything other than simple contact with the system.

Is Crowdseeding the Cutting Edge of Empowerment?

Given the significant impediments created by the crowdseeding method used by *Voix des Kivus*, it is perhaps worthwhile to take a moment to consider the relative strengths and weaknesses of crowdseeding and crowdsourcing methods. This section discusses a set of benefits particular to crowdseeding that facilitate the empowerment of populations in ways that are described in this book.

Most mapping efforts are based on crowdsourcing; a particularly powerful system to marshal ICT's potential for the collection and distribution of information. In contrast to normal outsourcing, crowdsourcing outsources a task not to a specific body but to an undefined public (Howe 2009). Crowdsourcing is used for a wide variety of tasks—from solving problems to collecting information. There are two major benefits to crowdsourcing. First, it is possible to reach a large audience in a relatively inexpensive way. Based upon the idea that a group of people is often more intelligent than an individual, crowdsourcing has the potential to solve problems faster and improve data collection (Surowiecki 2005). A second benefit is that these large amounts of data can be obtained quickly—often in real-time. Many of these crowdsourcing systems make use of the Internet or cell phone technology. The Ushahidi platform, which is an open source project that allows users to crowdsource crisis information sent via mobile, is one example. People can send an SMS-message to a central platform, where the messages are gathered, stored, and visualized on a map and timeline. The platform has seen a wide application from humanitarian response in Liberia to monitoring radiation levels in Japan. Given the benefits of crowdsourcing, it is not surprising that researchers have used such systems. But it is worth considering the merits of each system.

The first benefit of a crowdseeding system is to increase the crowd. Under crowdsourcing people can only participate if they know about the project. Given the isolation of the villages in Eastern Congo, very few people would know about the *Voix des Kivus* project. As a result, the size of the crowd would decrease to only those people who are aware of the project. Worse, most people in the Congo do not have a phone. If they do have a phone, they often lack the money to pay for a text-message. As a result, a crowdsourcing system would make use of an even smaller part of the population: Only those who are aware of the project and those who are able to partake in it. As a result, especially in areas of limited statehood, we expect the crowd to be only a very small part of the population. A crowdseeding system that selects, visits, and trains the reporters, and provides a mobile phone with credit will make use of the whole population. Crowdseeding therefore makes it possible for people to participate that otherwise would have not.

Second, not only does crowdseeding increase the crowd, but it also selects a random subset to participate in the system. This increases the quality of the information provided in two ways. First, by selecting a representative sample, the system obtains a representative picture. The system receives messages from people who have a cell phone and are willing to pay the cost of an SMS. Indeed, not only are there few such people in the Congo, but they are probably from a relatively unrepresentative demographic group. Studies that have analyzed the demographics of Amazon Mechanical Turk, for example, find that the crowd-workers are not representative of the wider population (Berinsky, Huber, and Lenz 2012; Ross, Irani, Silberman, Zalvidar, and Tomlinson 2010). Second, people are strategic. We expected this to be a particular problem in the Democratic Republic of Congo because reporters hoping for humanitarian intervention might send incorrect information. A crowdseeding system builds a relationship with the phoneholders thereby increasing incentives to report truthfully. In assessing the strengths and weaknesses of crowdsourcing and crowdseeding, these positive outcomes must also be factored in.

Conclusion

ICT can empower people by creating new modes of governance and by enabling the collection and distribution of information. In some cases, crowdseeding holds greater potential than crowdsourcing to marshal these benefits of ICT because crowdseeding can increase the total number of participants (by making people aware of the system and by enabling them to participate), and it makes use of a representative part of this population of participants. The benefits are particularly clear in areas of limited statehood where people live in isolation and often do not have the means to participate in ICT-enabled systems. The experiences with *Voix des Kivus* in Eastern Congo show that it is possible to implement such a crowdseeding system. These experiences, however, also emphasize the limitations of a crowdseeding system: *Voix des Kivus* did not create new modes of governance; only a part of the data was distributed beyond the system; the usefulness of the information provided was limited because the project did not scale up; and external actors did not act on the voice provided to participants.

Nonetheless, we should not be overly pessimistic. A likely reason why no new modes of governance were created and why only a subset of the data was distributed was because the implementers of *Voix des Kivus* were protective of the systems' participants, perhaps overly protective. More important, *Voix des Kivus* collected sensitive data that some groups likely do not to want to see collected.

Things would be very different if the topic of investigation was bird species and not conflict events.

Voix des Kivus also shows the need for what one might call the "shadow of hierarchy"—the implicit need of participation by the state(s) or humanitarian actors. While *Voix des Kivus* made it possible to learn about problems facing participating communities (the bits), it could do nothing about the redistribution of things such as such as food, clean water, security, and other public goods (the atoms). Agencies external to *Voix des Kivus* did not act upon the provided information because the project was not brought to scale. Only then, one might say, would the data become useful. But Columbia University did not want to scale up the project for security reasons. When brought to scale, more people—among others the local violent groups—would be more likely to know about the project. Also, the research team felt—as academics on the other side of the Atlantic—that they were not the right people to bring it to scale. However, it might very well be possible that the scale–insecurity relationship is hump-shaped. That is, an initial expansion would bring more risk, but if the project is implemented throughout the region, known among many and supported by many, that the risks would be low again.

Notes

1. I would like to thank Macartan Humphreys, Junior Bulabula, Simon Collard-Wexler, Yair Ghitza, Patrick Meier, Stefan Lehmeier, and Neelanjan Sircar. Thanks also to Tracy Longacre, Desire Cimerhe, and Alain Kabeya for outstanding in-country work. Most importantly I thank our fifty-four phoneholders.
2. This project was led by the author and Macartan Humphreys and was funded by USAID.
3. We leave a discussion of ICT's importance for empowerment by creating new forms of organization to the discussion of the "Russia Help Map" in Chapter 7.
4. This view of power is also known as the *first dimension of power*. Dahl (1961) is a seminal read here.
5. See Gaventa (1982) for a seminal illustration of this third dimension of power.
6. The territory is the administrative unit below the province and above the chiefdom.
7. These reporters can also be selected randomly to obtain a representative sample *within* the village.
8. All documents can be found on the project's website: http://www.cu-csds.org/projects/event-mapping-in-congo/. This also includes the computer code to create bulletins and a "Voix des Kivus Implemention Guide" for organizations that want to set up a similar system.
9. This is based on the FrontlineSMS export of August 1, 2011. Identical messages received from the same reporter within thirty minutes of each other, and identical messages received from different representatives in the same village within twenty-four hours of each other, are treated as single events.
10. Although we engaged in various forms of data verification to assess whether the data could be used for statistical analysis, the system could not reasonably vouch for the reliability of individual reports; rather, the principle employed was that reports should be viewed and interpreted as statements made by village representatives and not as independent or expert assessments of conditions on the ground. In the bulletins, a simple metric was provided

that indicated how many of the three phoneholders in a given village reported the same incident.

11. For a discussion about the confluence of local and distant realities see, for example, James Rosenau (2003) and Manuel Castells (2009b).

12. Note that the type of information received might to some extent depend on the type of seeder. It could be that if the seeder was an NGO and not a research team, as was the case for *Voix des Kivus*, participating communities might send more information about population needs.

11

Conclusions

STEVEN LIVINGSTON AND GREGOR WALTER-DROP

Introduction

The contributions to this volume have considered the role of ICT in areas of limited statehood. Statehood is best thought of as a continuous variable, ranging from fully consolidated states (such as those found in Scandinavia) to those with extremely low levels of consolidation (such as Somalia or the Democratic Republic of Congo). Statehood varies according to the state's ability to maintain a monopoly on the use of force and to pass, implement, and enforce political decisions. Variations are found according to relative deficiencies in particular territorial regions, policy areas, or among segments of the population. This more nuanced conception of statehood allows us to distinguish between *governance*, on the one hand, and *statehood*, on the other. Governance is about collective rules and the provision of collective goods. Although states "do" governance, so, too, do other actors, including clans, nonstate actors (such as NGOs), or international institutions. Governance by the state, consolidated or limited as it may be, is but one mode of governance.

This framework, taken from international relations theory and governance research, has been paired with ideas drawn from new political communication literature concerning collective action and the revolution in digital information and communication technology. While it is accurate to think of the revolution in information and communication technology as a global process with distinct regional forms, it can also be characterized by a common general outcome: relatively greater information abundance. Socially and politically significant information, often specific to local conditions and needs, that is at the same time scalable to global dimensions, is available not only to economically advantaged persons living in modern metropolises, but also to those living in remote or underdeveloped areas. We would be mistaken to conclude that the technologies used by some in the Global North for streaming movies, playing games, and accessing YouTube and Facebook necessarily have greater political significance than do the less sophisticated technologies used by others living in less privileged circumstances. The ICT discussed in this volume sometimes have a profound political, economic, and sociological effect on the lives and well-being of people far from the ordered environs of the Global North.

Yet most academic research on politics and digital technology has focused, almost exclusively, on the effects of ICT in the developed world. By contrast, this volume brings contributors together with a sustained focus on ICT in areas of limited statehood, mostly in the Global South. While the most prominent of these new technologies has been mobile telephony, Internet access is also more common in all corners of the planet, either through broadband connectivity or Internet-enabled mobile telephony. These developments, combined with open source digital-mapping platforms such as Ushahidi and Open Street Map, text aggregation and dissemination platforms such as FrontlineSMS and RapidSMS, and innovation centers such as iHub in Nairobi, enable new forms of collective action in areas of limited statehood. Indeed, Primož Kovačič and Jamie Lundine's chapter illustrates how simple mobile phones and digital maps bring new opportunities for community engagement and awareness to people living in some of the more desperate places on the planet.

Where the state is weak, missing, or indifferent, ICT-enabled community and NGO initiatives seek to fill governance gaps, either directly with initiatives that leverage technology in ways that address deficiencies in a public good, or by seeking to oppose, criticize, or improve state institutions. In the latter case, state institutes may be strengthened by capacity-building initiatives or by the associated benefits of ICT-enabled accountability mechanisms. These are the principle ideas explored in this volume. Against this background, our introduction outlined three questions that have been addressed by the contributions to this volume:

1. Under which conditions can ICT improve statehood and the governance capacity of state institutions?
2. Under which conditions can ICT improve state legitimacy? A corollary to this question has also been considered: When open revolt has emerged in the face of a state's crisis in legitimacy, under what conditions do ICT favor the state and under what conditions do they favor the opposition?
3. Under which conditions do technologically enabled collective-action initiatives in areas of limited statehood rise to the level of governance?

In this final chapter we return to these questions, summarize the arguments made by the contributors, and offer conclusions on the role of ICT in areas of limited statehood.

ICT and Statehood

The first half of the book is dedicated to an examination of the relationship between ICT and state institutions. These are perhaps best thought of as mid-range states—not Denmark, but certainly not Somalia. The first question we've posed above asked about ICT's potential to improve governance capacity of state institutions. J. P. Singh and Joseph Siegle have addressed this question most directly in their respective chapters. First, as examined by Singh, the state can adopt ICT and use it to improve its governance capacity. Second, relying on a more indirect pathway, civil society can use ICT to hold the state more accountable, a possibility considered by Siegle.

J. P. Singh details how Indian state institutions have employed ICT in an attempt to improve the delivery of state services. The effort, he finds, has had an uneven outcome. As he notes, e-government initiatives in India are successful mostly at a basic level, such as providing access to information and records, downloading government forms, and paying utility bills. These initiatives have fallen short of higher aspirations, such as providing "a broader transformation in the relationship between government and the people" (see Chapter 4, p. 48). Put another way, e-government in India is most successful in delivering goods and services related directly to information. Accessing forms and records, paying bills, or purchasing services can be handled with greater ease. In this respect, Singh seems to point to a modest effect. State ICT use under the conditions of limited statehood does not fundamentally alter resource deficiency, most bureaucratic inefficiency, or elite corruption. It merely improves access to information-based services. State institutional governance capacities are thus improved but not fundamentally altered.

This conclusion implies a conceptual differentiation that is important to our discussion. When considering the full range of governance objectives, there is significant variation with regard to the information content of the respective collective goods or services. There is a fundamental difference between the maintenance of land records, for example, and the provision of physical infrastructure, such as vaccines, roads, bridges, and disciplined and well-trained security forces. Yet this does not mean that bits as collective goods are necessarily trivial. In Africa, up to 90 percent of land in Africa is untitled, leaving farmer vulnerable to eviction and leading to land disputes (Wily 2011). A similar story is told in India. One study reported that according to one estimate over 90 percent of the land titles in India are "unclear" (Zasloff 2011). Land tenure is also a problem in urban areas, as anyone who has driven around Lagos, Nairobi, or many other African cities and observed the crudely spray painted "not for sale" notices on the sides of buildings can testify. Such notices are intended to thwart would-be scam artists from taking advantage of weak land title systems to sell property that does not belong to them.

Other governance initiatives require the reorientation of physical infrastructure and materials. Building and maintaining a road network, for example, involves information management and processing. Yet, ultimately, it is about moving physically constituted material. We have referred to this as the required movement of atoms. Information technology can improve the efficiency of this process, but it cannot fill the entire governance void created by limited statehood. At some point, a state or other hierarchical organization must step in.

A more indirect effect of ICT on the state runs through civil society. Along these lines, Joseph Siegle identifies possible positive effects of ICT on statehood. He starts from the observation that the accountability of state structures in areas of limited statehood is often deficient. Under these conditions, ICT can facilitate the development and strengthening of civil society. This, in turn, improves state accountability. If we assume that greater accountability will—all things being equal—create incentives for state actors to provide governance services that are suited to society's needs, then we can also conclude that ICT can contribute indirectly to the improvement of governance service delivery by strengthening accountability. The logic of this argument tracks with Nobel Laureate Amartya Sen's well-known observation about democracy and famine. "It is not surprising that no famine has ever taken place in the world in a functioning democracy—be it economically rich (as in contemporary Western Europe or North America) or relatively poor (as in post-independence India, or Botswana, or Zimbabwe)" (Sen 1999, 16). This is because democratic governments "have to win elections and face public criticism, and have strong incentives to undertake measures to avert famines and other catastrophes" (16). Famine occurs principally from the lack of accountability mechanisms built into distributing food. To the degree that ICT contributes to new forms of accountability, one should expect an improvement in the provision of basic public goods.

Although Sen limits his considered of "accountability mechanisms" to elections, ICT also serves as a source of greater accountability. For example, the use of mobile telephony, digital-mapping, and crowdsourcing in elections monitoring and the use of remote sensing satellite imagery in human rights and security-monitoring led to greater transparency and accountability. The ReclaimNaija election-monitoring deployment in Nigeria for both the state-level and federal-level elections mobilized tens of thousands of Nigerians to monitor elections procedures and report suspicious activities and shortfalls to oversight bodies (Bailard and Livingston 2012). "If the INEC (Independent National Elections Commission) hadn't seen these reports they would not have known about the level of problems being experienced by Nigerians; there would not have been this kind of proof," said Linda Kamau, an Ushahidi developer (Scialom 2011).

Another example of ICT-enabled accountability can be found in remote-sensing satellites, the same satellites that provide the geospatial data used to create detailed digital maps used by Ushahidi and other mapping platforms in crowdsourcing initiatives. From about 600 kilometers in space, these privately owned satellites capture images of objects on the earth's surface as small as 32 centimeters in diameter (O'Connell et al. 2001). Using satellite images, NGOs monitor possible security and human rights violations, track environmental concerns, and investigate the spread of nuclear weapons facilities and other weapons (Butler 2009). The Satellite Sentinel Project (http://www.satsentinel.org/)—an initiative of the Enough Project—uses high-resolution satellite imagery to track attacks on villages and compounds and look for mass graves in both the Sudan and the Southern Sudan. In doing so, the governments in Khartoum and the new state of the Southern Sudan are held to higher account for their treatment of civilian populations. Similarly, the Institute for Science and International Security (ISIS), a Washington, DC–based NGO, uses remote-sensing imagery to monitor the development of nuclear weapons and missile developments around the world. In fact, it was ISIS that revealed the existence of an Iranian fuels processing facility in 2002 (Aday and Livingston 2009).

ICT-enabled initiatives such as these support Siegle's argument about accountability and governance capacity. We can conclude that ICT enables various forms of collective action in civil society that allow for more and new forms of oversight of the state and state activity. This, in turn, can result in enhanced accountability structures and changes in the incentive structures as state actors make use of existing resources for the provision of collective goods. In other words, states can be held accountable for the way they utilize available resources. Yet, if the necessary resources, such as physical infrastructure, disciplined security forces, or trained doctors and well-stocked dispensaries are missing, information-based accountability structures *alone* will not provide for basic collective goods. Sen's logic is predicated on the claim that sufficient food stocks are available but malappropriated. Accountability rectifies the malappropriation. Let unlike food, some collective goods are altogether missing. The logic of accountability might work to the extent that state actors are *unwilling* to provide collective goods, but it will not work to the extent that the state is physically *unable* to provide it.

Second, the logic of Siegle's analysis assumes that civil society has a means of control or sanctioning power over state institutions. Accountability structures work via incentives that, in turn, depend on the possibility of sanctioning. If, however, the elites are firmly entrenched in state institution using the monopoly of force to control and suppress civil society, as if often the case in areas of limited statehood, attempts to improve accountability might result only in state backlash and repression. The result may be an escalation of political tension and the formation of an oppositional movement. This brings us to the issue of legitimacy and ICTs.

ICT and Legitimacy

The second question we asked in this book concerns ICT and its effects on state legitimacy. How does ICT affect the legitimacy of the state? We are, of course, not the first to consider this question. Manuel Castells, for instance, has written extensively about information technology's challenge to the state (Castells 2000a, 2000b, 2004, 2009a; see also Price 2002; Rosenau 2003). State-dominated communication media are challenged now by bottom-up digital communication, which he calls "mass self-communication." Castells maintain that users "have built their own systems of communication, via SMS, blogs, vlogs, podcasts, wikis, and the like" (Castells 2009, 65). We would add digital maps and crowdsourcing to this list. The inability of the state to meet and contain global economic, social, cultural, and political processes undermines public confidence in state institutions (Stadler 2006). These trends factor into what he sees as a worldwide crisis of the state.

In this context, the effects of ICT may be all the more significant. On the one hand, states facing crises of legitimacy can be expected to attempt to assimilate the advantages of ICT in efforts to strength their position and stabilize their institutional operations. On the other hand (and along the lines of Joseph Siegle's argument in this volume) ICT in the hands of civil society can expose state deficiencies. ICT also enables the formation and operation of opposition political groups and even facilitates open revolt (Karpf and Livingston 2013). Muzammil Hussain and Philip Howard provide insight into this question in their consideration of ICT's role in the Arab Spring, as does Gregory Asmolov in his consideration of the role of ICT in the hands of the Russian state.

Asmolov illustrates the Russian state's attempt to use ICT to strengthen its legitimacy. It does so by *simulating* transparency and accountability with the deployment of user-accessible but state-controlled sensors. In this manner, the Russian state seeks to construct symbolic rather than functional statehood in a modern-day digital Potemkin village. However, citizens using Web 2.0 technologies and deploying their own cameras and sensors—thereby exposing state manipulation—undermine the state's efforts. To switch metaphors, mass self-communication pulls back the curtain to reveal an insecure and simple man pulling the levers of a mechanical apparatus intended to create the impression of power and legitimacy. The Wizard of Oz goes to the Kremlin. Here, state-dominated ICT stand in contrast to "mass self-communication" in Castell's sense of that term. As a result, the intended positive feedback loop created by state's adoption of ICT is undermined by citizen-based ICT that not only exposes social and political problems in general but also the state's attempt to manipulate the public. The state effort is thus turned on its head, creating a stream of negative feedback.

Hussain and Howard speak to the multifaceted role played by digital technology in protest movements. ICT raises activists' awareness of one another and of other forms of statehood, and provides a virtual space for discussion and discourse. It can also be used for organizing protests or other forms of collective action. Mobile phones as much as social media present a significant challenge to states in legitimacy crises.

Both contributions suggest that the state's efforts at improving its image using ICT can be offset by the "crowd's" "self-communication," not least because the potential users are the same people most likely to use ICT themselves, often in a more creative fashion.

Substitution: ICT and Nonstate Governance

While the first part of the book considers ICT's effects on states under the conditions of limited statehood and mixed governance records, the second half of the book takes a deeper look into the question by addressing more extreme circumstances. If statehood is limited, the state's governance performance is usually poor. This, however, does not simply imply the absence of governance. Rather, it implies that governance takes different forms in the attempts of various actors to offset and substitute the lack of state governance performance (Risse 2011). Which role can ICT play under these circumstances? More specifically, our third guiding question asks: Under what conditions, if any, can ICT-enabled forms of collective actions in areas of limited statehood rise to the level of governance?

It may be helpful at this juncture to recall the basis for the claim that such a thing is conceptually feasible. The political significance of information and communication technologies is found in their ability to lower information cost, a key component of collaborative undertakings. For example, the traditional standard answer to problems involving any broadly distributed behavior or phenomenon— a crime, elections violence, illegal logging, and so on—would be the creation of an elaborate organization with thousands of well-disciplined and -trained employees, all of whom are compensated professionals. These professional monitors would then be sent to observe the behavior or phenomenon in question and armed with a robust means of reporting to a centralized administrative office that would, in turn, make proper use of the findings. In short, it would involve the creation of a capable and functional bureaucracy, exactly what an area of limited statehood lacks. Violence directed against communities in the Kivus in the eastern Democratic Republic of Congo where Van der Windt and his collaborators organized *Voix des Kivus* (see Chapter 10) is far beyond the effective reach of any administrative structure based in Kinshasa, a thousand miles away. On the other hand, Mathare and Kibera are located in the capital city of Kenya, yet they are literally off the governance map, as Kovačič and Lundine point out in their chapter. They are state no-go areas lacking even the most modest provision of public goods. Both, the Kivus region and the slums of Nairobi are examples for areas of limited statehood where the very idea of creating a capable and functional bureaucracy seems out of reach in the near term. Yet, mobile connectivity is found in both places. Can the latent organizing capacity built into the ICT system be put to use by the people to fill the governance void? The answer seems to be *sometimes*.

The theoretical argument in favor of such a claim runs like this: Where digital networks exist, "it is possible to achieve large-scale coordination at low cost" (Shirky 2008, 47).[1] This opens up the possibility of "serious, complex work, taken on without institutional direction. *Loosely coordinated groups can now achieve things that were previously out of reach for any other organizational structure*," owing to the costs of organizing (Shirky 2008, 47, emphasis added). In short, where it is built into an information system, collaboration has been freed of its dependence on hierarchy. Digital collaboration can reach where traditional governance structures could not because of cost-based scaling limitations. In an earlier era, bureaucratic organizational structures were necessary for coordination where only the state could meet the challenges poised by high collaboration costs. But digital technologies alter the calculation. This is what Bruce Bimber has in mind when he speaks of "information abundance" in the 21st century. The nature of political mediation has moved from formal hierarchical institutions to digital networks. It involves,

> information that is easily produced by virtually anyone, widely distributed, and cheap or free. This radical development in the political economy of information and communication associated with the Internet is again changing the information ecology, creating new opportunities for adaption by political organizations. (Bimber 2011, 750)

"Politics," Bimber continues, "is possible with or without formal organization, which means that an important feature of democracy in the emerging (information) regime is post-bureaucratic pluralism: *collective action in conditions of information abundance does not necessarily require substantial staff, money, or formalized organization*" (Bimber 2011, 750, emphasis added). Networks now fill many, if not all, of the burdens once carried by bureaucratic structures. By leveraging the reduced collaboration costs present in digitally networked environments, the state—like other hierarchical organizations—becomes a non-essential governance modality. It is rendered nearly obsolete by digital governance, so the logic goes, just as digital books and music are now obsolete (Anderson 2006b). This logic seems to point to a wholly positive affirmation of ICT-enabled collective action by nonstate actors as an alternative governance modality. When extended to areas of limited statehood, the argument would suggest that nonstate actors might use ICT to substitute for deficiencies in state governance delivery. And rather than trying to wrestle control of governance from a corrupt and inefficient state apparatus, as Singh and Asmolov described, community-based initiatives are free to fill the governance space with less friction. That is the theoretical argument for ICT-enabled collective action as an alternative governance modality. What have we found?

Once again, the results are mixed. While the contributions to this volume suggest significant potential in this regard, they also suggest caution. Sharath Srinivasan introduces FrontlineSMS, an open source softwareused to collect and distribute mobile phone text-messages. As Srinivasan notes, innovations in this sector emulate core "Web 2.0" ideas and inspirations—based on significantly less-advanced technology. This includes,

> enabling "user-generated content"; facilitating crowdsourcing and harnessing the "wisdom of crowds"; user-based tailoring of content and tool

development based around an "architecture of participation"; network effects; the Internet's "key affordances" for social activism and...how it opens up "long tail" economies. (see Chapter 6, p. 81.)

Text-management platforms replicate at another level the same sort of effects that have been so thoroughly explored in analyses of the Internet in the Global North. The distribution of FrontlineSMS use, however, is not uniform. Since its launch in 2005, the FrontlineSMS software had been downloaded over 25,000 times in over 70 countries (as of mid-2012). This is impressive. Yet according to Srinivasan, Africa and Asia account for almost 65 percent of total downloads. Within Africa, almost half of the users came from just four countries: about a quarter of users in Africa are found in Kenya; just short of another 10 percent are in Nigeria; another 8 percent are in Uganda; and Ghana accounts for another 6 percent. Within Asia, India, Philippines, Indonesia, and Pakistan, in this order, accounted for about 65 percent of the region's users. There are distinct concentrations in the use of FrontlineSMS, which Srinivasan attributes to certain structural features of these high-end user countries. Telecommunication liberalization and strong civil society are chief among them. Furthermore, according to his analysis of user survey data, dominant sectors of FrontlineSMS use are health and education, followed by activism, campaigning and elections, emergency and crisis response, and agriculture. As he summarizes these data on FrontlineSMS use patterns.

> FrontlineSMS governance-related use is thus local or national non-profit organizations working in a focused number of African and Asian countries in sectors where better informational flows are: (a) intrinsic to a governance activity; or (b) help these organizations to facilitate more optimal delivery of public goods or services.(see Chapter 6, p. 92.)

This is already pointing to a central feature of ICT-enabled governance that we have referred to in our analysis of state ICT use: The "bits" versus "atoms" problem. ICT-enabled governance is best suited to those aspects of governance relating to information. As Srinivasan puts it,

> There are key differences between deployments in which information is the public good, such as agricultural market prices, and those in which information flows enhance delivery of material public goods and services, such as coordinating more rapid and effective health services through community health volunteer networks. These are not, of course, binary conditions, but rather arrayed along a continuum. The ability of governance actors—whether state or nonstate, local, national, or international—to deliver many essential governance outcomes still relies on material factors that new digital communication tools alone cannot surmount. (See Chapter 6, p. 79)

The three subsequent chapters examined the role of crowdsourcing and event-mapping in areas of limited statehood. Gregory Asmolov illustrates the use of Ushahidi for monitoring wildfires and coordinating nonstate relief efforts in Russia in 2010. These efforts, he says, filled in deficiencies found in state disaster relief. What is most noteworthy about the case Asmolov presents is the demonstration of ICT-enabled collective action (see Chapter 7).

Something similar happened with the flooding of the city of Krymsk and surrounding villages in southern Russia in 2012.

Asmolov is the most sanguine of our contributors on the question of ICT-based collective action as an alternative mode of governance. What is most striking about his analysis is its emphasis on the role of ICT in overcoming logistical issues relating to the distribution of tangible resources. It seems to be in alignment with a part of what Srinivasan noted. ICT is most effective as an alternative governance modality where "effective informational flows also amplify the voice of constituents in shaping the meaning and prioritization of public goods and thus strengthen the accountability of governance actors" (see Chapter 6, p. 80).

Yet Asmolov, like Castells, sees greater promise in these developments. Mass self-communication that relies on social networks, crowdsourcing, and mobile communication allows breaking of the state's monopoly on the representation of disaster and makes citizens the dominant actors in shaping the narrative of an emergency situation. Information technologies also provide mechanisms and tools for fulfilling a variety of governance functions, including complicated coordination that makes nonstate actors, and the crowd in particular, into independent, dominant actors in emergency relief (see Chapter 7).

Primož Kovačič and Jamie Lundine analyze the role of mapping platforms for the empowerment of residents in urban slums in Africa. They describe user-based geographical information-gathering initiatives concerning basic infrastructure, healthcare issues, education, and security, information—and the public goods they involve. Kovačič and Lundine bring a technical expertise and practical experience to our analysis. They reach conclusions that are, in general, in alignment with Asmolov's.

> ICT-enabled project have started to provide an alternative governance modality in Nairobi's informal settlements, a seemingly contradictory phenomenon when compared to the lack of sanitation, adequate housing and other basic services in the same areas. The project to map Kibera highlights the effectiveness of citizen-driven data collection. Where the state constantly fails to gather data, a small group of citizens, with limited resources, collected thousands of points of interest, kilometers of roads and paths, and created a comprehensive database on health, education, water and sanitation, and security issues and relatively successfully used online platformss (Ushahidi, YouTube) to transmit the stories about Kibera into the world. (see Chapter 8, p. 127)

Note that the outcome of these efforts is a database. In itself, the project described by Kovačič and Lundine has not, as of this writing, delivered tangible public goods. It has, however, allowed the residents of the slums to tell their story to the world. And by providing essential information, it has facilitated governance capacity building efforts by other nonstate actors.

In his chapter, Patrick Meier compares various deployments of Ushahidi (ranging from post-earthquake Haiti via Egypt to Libya) in search of the (online and offline) conditions for its success. He also underscores a point made by Kovačič and Lundine, and by Asmolov: Crowdsourcing is politically transformative and liberating.

> Live crowdsourced maps counter the pre-structured worldview imposed by the planning grids of the state. They reveal the limitations of governance, particularly in a crisis and also offer a platform for self-expression and self-organization; for the provision of relief supplies and humanitarian aid—typically the responsibility of the state. (see Chapter 9, p. 142)

In mapping and crowdsourcing, local populations are given agency that bolsters social capital. This additional social capital facilitates more collective action and self-governance. A positive recursive spiral of positive social change is the potential result. For this spiral to be triggered, however, a certain amount of social capital has to be present. This reminds us of Srinivasan's finding that the use of FrontlineSMS was concentrated in areas with relatively strong civil societies.

Peter van der Windt takes the idea of ICT-based empowerment one step further, and in the process raises important questions about its limitations. Most mapping efforts are based on crowdsourcing, which assumes a technologically enabled "crowd." *Crowdseeding* by contrast involves the active development of nodes in areas otherwise off the global digital grid. *Voix des Kivus* operated in some of the harshest, remotest regions on the planet, in a place that has experienced more war, famine, and disease than any other region since the Second World War (IRC 2013). From the start, Van der Windt and his colleagues recognized that *Voix des Kivus* both empowered and endangered the communities where phones were seeded. Individual phoneholders, as the eyes and ears of communities often preyed upon by ruthless militias and marauding bands of thugs were at great risk. Fortunately, none of the phoneholders were harmed. The efforts to mitigate the risk to phoneholders and the communities they resided in, such as controlling access to reports and not enabling connectivity between villages and phoneholders, also limited the potential ICT-enabled collaboration.

In sum, ICT-enabled collective action as an alternative governance modality in areas of limited statehood holds great potential but also faces serious limitations. First, it is necessary to distinguish between the objectives of collective action in consolidated states and the objectives of collective action in areas of limited statehood. The objectives of collective action in consolidated state are chiefly the articulation and organization of demands on states (or corporations) where states are highly potent actors that dominate the governance landscape. In areas of limited statehood, the central objective of collective action is the pursuit of basic public goods that are absent due to the deficiencies and inabilities of the state.

Second, almost all chapters in Part 2 of this volume suggest fundamental differences in the potential of ICT resulting from the nature of the public goods or services at hand. Most important in this regard is the question where these public goods or services fall on a scale between "purely information based" ("bits") and "purely based on material objects" ("atoms"). Consider the use of FrontlineSMS to distribute information about agricultural pricing. Or, consider "M-Pesa" (a money transfer system widely in use in Kenya and Tanzania). Here the public good at hand (establishing the prerequisites for a functioning market) is immaterial in that prices, credits, and accounts themselves are information. Crime statistics, agricultural services, mapping of roads and typological attributes, and a variety of other public goods and services can be accomplished with ICT-enabled initiatives. In these cases, ICT directly enables elements of governance.

By contrast, food relief or vaccination programs are quite different. They are not about information alone for, ultimately, they require not only the movement of "bits," but also the movement of "atoms"—the vaccines. Here ICT can still play an important role on the "bit-side"—that is, by creating a (nonstate) governance institution, facilitating its actions, supporting self-organization, and so on. Thus, the actual distribution of tangible objects—atoms—is facilitated by information shared over digital platforms. Consider the case of the Ushahidi deployment to address the needs of stricken populations in the 2010 Russian wildfires. Citizens on their own responded to the needs of other citizens according to what they learned from postings on the Ushahidi deployment. But when public goods are about more than information, ICT-enabled collaboration may also reach its limits. Crowdsourcing can tell us about famine, diseased crops, shortages of medical supplies, and a need for better roads, clean water, and better sanitation. But in the end, trained doctors must be put on the scene, crop diseases must be treated, medicines must be delivered, and roads, water systems, and sewers must be built. Depending of the scope of the action, not all of this can be easily achieved by nonstate actors. Most problematic in this regard is security. Information about security threats is now more readily available by way of crowdsourcing or crowd-seeding information to a digital map. But as the *Voix des Kivus* project indicates, disciplined security forces must still be deployed to address the threat. This requires the material resources, organizational capabilities, and political will that can only be marshaled—if at all—by state actors or international institutions. New York–based researches can hardly be "911" for villages in Eastern Congo. Or to be more precise: They can take the call, but for the information to have any effect, state actors, or international institutions have to step in. In these cases, bits can do only so much.

A second problem of ICT-enabled collective action as governance is sustainability. As we look at the state governance modality we see enduring, institutionalized systems. Srinivasan made this point about the most common applications of FrontlineSMS:

> there is either no clear path for them to sustain activities and institutionalize the modes of coordination or public goods and service provision, or, in the case of activism based initiatives, it is not clear that they aim to do so. Initiatives, individuals, organizations and networks come and go, as is common in the broad space of civil society. Governance outcomes occur at an aggregate level only amidst somewhat ad hoc and unpredictable developments at a lower scale. (see Chapter 6, p. 94)

We thus conclude that the answer to the question under what conditions ICT-enabled forms of collective actions in areas of limited statehood could rise to the level of governance lies chiefly in the nature of the public goods or services at hand: In the case of information-based goods and services, ICT can directly enable governance. If the goods and services are not only about "bits," but about "atoms," ICT can greatly facilitate (1) the provision of distribution of these goods and services by pre-existing nonstate actors (such as national or international NGOs) and (2) the formation of civil society organizations that step into the governance void. Particularly in the latter case, however, there are problems of sustainability. In addition, the greater the scope of the service delivery, the stronger the "atoms" component, the more limited the role of ICT becomes. In particular, in the security field, state actors of international institutions with control over means of force are indispensible.

The Potential and Limits of ICT in Areas of Limited Statehood

In summarizing the findings of the contributions to this volume we arrive at two main conclusions about the potential and limits of ICT in areas of limited statehood:

1. Vis-à-vis the state, ICT enables various forms of collective action that allows civil society to hold state institutions and their protagonists accountable for their actions. This may improve otherwise deficient state governance performance by changing the incentive structure for the relevant actors. It may also lead to a rising conflict between state and civil society. In this conflict, ICT can be used by both sides, but ICT favors the side of civil society because its use is difficult to control and "self-communication" can reverse the effects of state ICT use.

2. With regard to governance, we find that for both, state, and nonstate actors, the potential for ICT to enable a new governance modality is strongly influenced by the nature of the respective public good or service at hand. This holds for state information services as well as for nonstate governance provision. The more these goods or services are about "bits," the greater the potential of ICT. The more they are on the "atoms" side on the scale, the more ICT advances are dependent on another condition to take effect: in essence, the existence of political actors able and willing to deliver "atoms." The greater the scope of the governance void, the more likely that the respective deficits cannot be compensated without the state and/or international institutions.

Based on these conclusions, we return once more to the theoretical debate that has inspired our work. Almost all of the new political communication research literature focuses on digital politics and collective action in the Global North. Though with variation, much of that literature coalesces around a central conclusion regarding the effects of lower collaboration costs and the enabling of new forms of collective action. What do our conclusions this tell us about the new political communication literature that, we think, correctly understands the general effects of digital networks on collective action? They point to the importance of thinking through the nature of what is at stake. We do not mean to be critical of the first generation of scholars who recognized and then tried to account for the effects of digital networks on politics. This pioneering work has inspired us to examine ICT effects in substantially different circumstances. What this book has done is draw attention to a wider array of collective action objectives in a very different geographical and political setting. Almost all of the scholarship about digital networks and politics in the Global North has centered on social movements, contentious politics, and deliberative debate. The presumed—and often realized—benefit is located in the lowered collaboration costs that open up either fast and bigger protest actions (what Jennifer Earl and Katrina Kimport have called "supersizing") or forms of protests that take place in digital space alone (what Earl and Kimport call "Theory 2.0 protest actions") (Earl and Kimport 2011). This book has placed boundaries around the theoretical expectations of digitally enabled collective action. In the end, collective action must accommodate the exigencies of material reality. Much can be accomplished short of that of course, including saving lives by coordinating much needed immediate relief in the aftermath of a natural or manmade disaster. This should not be dismissed. But this alone does not provide all that is needed to live full and free lives in a well-ordered society. At the end of the day, governance that is sustainable and deeply meaningful to the lives and well-being of human beings almost certainly involves, in the end, governance structures that look a lot more like Finland or Denmark or one of the other fully consolidated states than it does the latest deployment of an ICT platform intended to address a governance shortfall somewhere in the world.

However, there are still important contributions of digital networks in areas of limited statehood. Perhaps the greatest impact of technology is the freeing of human potential. Van der Windt called to mind the political power found in the ability to silence people who should be speaking out about the violence done to them by others (see Chapter 10). Steven Lukes and John Gaventa called this the *third dimension of power* (Lukes 1974; Gaventa 1982). People in dire conditions are unheard and without much hope of improvement in their conditions. ICT opens a door to positive change. Kovačič and Lundine demonstrate the empowerment of people living in abject poverty through a simple process of recognition: "We are here." Mapping puts their voices and concerns, literally, on the map. Meier makes the same point when he writes that live crowdsourced maps "reveal the limitations of governance, particularly in a crisis and also offer a platform for self-expression and self-organization" (see Chapter 9, p. 142). In crime-mapping or in other community-based initiatives, aided by and sometimes made feasible by information and communication technologies, plus the guidance and inspiration of people volunteering their time and talents to make it all work, people are given voice. They are empowered. ICT cannot move mountains, but it can move hearts and inspire change.

Notes

1. Following Ronald Coase, transaction costs are the cost of doing business. They are analogous to collaboration costs, the term most often used in this volume (see Coase 1937).

References

Abbott, Jason. 2001. "Democracy@internet.asia? The Challenges to the Emancipatory Potential of the Net: Lessons from China and Malaysia." *Third World Quarterly 22* (1): 99–114.

Abdulla, Rasha A. 2005. "Taking the E-train: The Development of the Internet in Egypt." *Global Media and Communication 1* (2): 149–65.

———. 2007. *The Internet in the Arab World: Egypt and Beyond*. New York: Peter Lang.

Acemoglu, Daron, and James Robinson. 2012. *Why Nations Fail: The Origins of Power, Prosperity, and Poverty*. New York: Crown Puplishers.

Achi, Fiona. 2012. "Behind the Map: Crises and Crisis Collectives in High-Tech Actions." Blog Ushahidi. August 3. http://blog.ushahidi.com/index.php/2012/08/03/behind-the-map-crises-and-crisis-collectives-in-high-tech-actions.

Aday, Sean, and Steven Livingston. 2009. "NGOs as Intelligence Agencies: The empowerment of Transnational Advocacy Networks and the Media by Commercial Remote Sensing in the Case of the Iranian Nuclear Program." *GeoForum 40* (4): 514–22.

Aiyar, Mani Shankar. 2008. "State of Panchayats: The Journey Thus Far." In *Infrastructure and Governance*, edited by Sameer Kochhar, Deepak B. Phatak, H. Krishnamurthy, Gursharan Dhanjal, 81–6. New Delhi: Academic Foundation.

Akintayo, Akin. 2011. "A Year of Goodluck Jonathan on Facebook." Nigerians Talk. June 28. http://nigerianstalk.org/2011/06/28/nigeria-a-year-of-goodluck-jonathan-on-facebook/.

Alavi, Nasrin. 2005. *We Are Iran: The Persian Blogs*. Vancouver: Soft Skull Press.

Allenova, Olga. 2011. "Ostrov Like." *Kommersant Vlast 40* (944) (October 10). http://www.kommersant.ru/doc/1788783.

al-Saggaf, Yeslam. 2004. "The Effect of Online Community on Offline Community in Saudi Arabia." *Electronic Journal of Information Systems in Developing Countries 16* (2). http://www.ejisdc.org/ojs2/index.php/ejisdc/article/view/97.

Anderson, Brian. 2013. "It's Map or Be Mapped in Brazil's Favelas." *Motherboard Online Magazine*, January 30. http://motherboard.vice.com/blog/its-map-or-be-mapped-in-brazils-favelas.

Anderson, Chris. 2006a. *The Long Tail: How Endless Choice Is Creating Unlimited Demand*. London: Business Books.

———. 2006b. *The Long Tail: Why the Future of Business Is Selling Less of More*. New York: Hyperion Book.

Arthur, W. Brian. 2009. *The Nature of Technology: What It Is and How It Evolves*. New York: Free Press.

Asmolov, Gregory. 2010a. "Russia: Bloggers Expose Death Rate Increase." Global Voices Online. August 20. http://globalvoicesonline.org/2010/08/20/russia-bloggers-expose-death-rate-increase/.

———. 2010b. "Russia: Online Cooperation as an Alternative for Government?" Global Voices Online. August 30. http://globalvoicesonline.org/2010/08/30/russia-online-cooperation-as-an-alternative-for-government/.

————. 2011a. "Russia: Election and the 'Other Side of the Panopticon.'" Global Voices Online. December 7. http://globalvoicesonline.org/2011/12/07/russia-election-and-the-other-side-of-panopticon/.

————. 2011b. "Russia: Networked Volunteers Save Lives of Missing Children." Global Voices Online. October 17. http://globalvoicesonline.org/2011/10/17/russia-networked-volunteers-save-lives-of-missing-children/.

Asuni, Judith B., and Jacqueline Farris. 2011. "Tracking Social Media: The Social Media Tracking Centre and the 2011 Nigerian Elections." Shehu Musa Yar'Adua Foundation. http://www.cfr.org/content/publications/attachments/Tracking-Social-Media-COMPLETE-final.pdf.

Attwell, Graham, and Raymond Elferink. 2007. "Developing an Architecture of Participation." Paper read at International Conference of Interactive Computer Aided Learning, at Villach, Austria, September 26–28.

Babchenko, Arcadia. 2012. "Gosudarstvo v Rossii polnostyu otsutstvuet." Starhinazapasa Live Journal. July 8. http://starshinazapasa.livejournal.com/424964.html.

Bachrach, Peter, and Morton S. Baratz. 1962. "Two Faces of Power." *The American Political Science Review* 56 (4): 947–52.

Bailard, Catie, Rob Baker, Matt Hindman, Steven Livingston, and Patrick Meier. 2012. "*CrowdGlobe: Mapping the Maps—A Meta-Level Analysis of Ushahidi and Crowdmap.*" Washington, DC: Internews Center for Innovation and Learning, July. http://irevolution.files.wordpress.com/2013/01/internewswpcrowdglobe_web-1.pdf.

Bailard, Catie Snow, and Steven Livingston. 2012. "Crowdmapping and Collective Action: Ushahidi as a Case of Technologically Enabled Mobilization." Paper prepared for the 2012 meetings of the American Political Science Association, New Orleans, August 30–September 3.

Baldwin, Katherine. 2010. "How One Newspaper Wants to Change Mozambique." *Time*, December 28. http://www.time.com/time/world/article/0,8599,2039433,00.html.

Banks, Ken. 2008. "Social Mobile and the Long Tail." Kiwanja Blog. January. http://www.kiwanja.net/blog/2008/01/social-mobile-and-the-long-tail/.

————. 2009a. "A Glimpse into Social Mobile's Long Tail." Kiwanja Blog. January. http://www.kiwanja.net/blog/2009/01/a-glimpse-into-social-mobiles-long-tail/.

————. 2009b. The "Long Tail" Revisited." Kiwanja Blog. January http://www.kiwanja.net/blog/2009/01/the-long-tail-revisited/.

————. 2009c. "Mobiles Help Put a Stop to Drug Stock-Outs." PC World. July 31. http://www.pcworld.com/businesscenter/article/169416/mobiles_help_put_a_stop_to_drug_stockouts.html.

————. 2009d. "Social Mobile: Empowering the Many or the Few?" In *SMS Uprising: Mobile Activism in Africa*, edited by Sokari Ekine. Oxford: Fahamu.

————. 2012. "Ken Banks: Genius Happens When You Plan Something Else." *Wired*, June. http://www.wired.co.uk/magazine/archive/2012/06/ideas-bank/genius-happens-when-you-plan-something-else.

Banks, Ken, Sean Martin McDonald, and Florence Scialom. 2011. "Mobile Technology and the Last Mile: 'Reluctant Innovation' and FrontlineSMS." *Innovations* 6 (1): 7–12.

Bansal, Manju. 2012. "Fingerprinting a Billion." *Forbes*, March 27. http://www.forbes.com/sites/sap/2012/03/27/fingerprinting-a-billion.

Barendregt, Bart. 2008. "Sex, Cannibals, and the Language of Cool: Indonesian Tales of the Phone and Modernity." *The Information Society* 24 (3): 160–70.

Barkan, Joel, Robert Mattes, Shaheen Mozaffar, and Kimberly Smiddy. 2010. "The African Legislatures Project: First Findings." Center for Social Science Research Working Paper, no. 277.

Barton, Allen. 1969. *Communities in disaster: a sociological analysis of collective stress situations.* Garden City, NY: Doubleday.

Basharova, Svetlana. 2013. "Prefektury otkrivayut operativye otdely po borbe s photoshop." *Izvestia*, February 12. http://izvestia.ru/news/544720.

BBC. 2007. "Texts Monitor Nigerian Elections." BBC News. April 20. news.bbc.co.uk/1/hi/technology/6570919.stm.

Beissinger, Mark R. 2007. "Structure and Example in Modular Political Phenomena: The Diffusion of Bulldozer/Rose/Orange/Tulip Revolutions." *Perspectives on Politics* 5 (2): 259–76.

Benkler, Yochai. 2006. *The Wealth of Networks: How Social Production Transforms Markets and Freedom*. New Haven: Yale University Press.

Berdou, Evangelia (2011) "Mediating Voices and Communicating Realities: Using Information Crowdsourcing Tools, Open Data Initiatives and Digital Media to Support and Protect the Vulnerable and Marginalized." Institute of Development Studies, Brighton, UK. Accessed July 3, 2012. http://www.dfid.gov.uk/R4D/PDF/Outputs/Misc_InfoComm/IDS_MediatingVoices_FinalReport.pdf.

Berinsky, Adam J., Gregory A. Huber, and Gabriel S. Lenz. 2012. "Evaluating Online Labor Markets for Experimental Research: Amazon.com's Mechanical Turk." *Political Analysis 20* (3): 351–68.

Bimber, Bruce. 2003. *Information and American Democracy*. New York: Cambridge University Press.

——. 2011. "Abstract of Information and American Democracy." *Revista Internacional de Sociologia 69* (3): 747–81.

Bimber, Bruce, Andrew J Flanagin, and Cythia Stohl. 2005. "Reconceptualizing Collective Action in the Contemporary Media Environment." *Communication Theory 15* (4): 365–88.

Brannon, Cullum. 2010. "Help Map Russia." Movements Case Study. August 12. http://www.movements.org/case-study/entry/helpmap-russia/.

Brock, Lothar, Hans-Henrik Holm, Georg Sørenson, and Michael Stohl, eds. 2012. *Fragile States: violence and the failure of intervention*. Cambridge: Polity Press.

Buckminster Fuller. 2013. "2011 Finalist: FrontlineSMS." The Buckminster Fuller Challenge. Accessed March 28. http://challenge.bfi.org/2011Finalist_FrontlineSMS.

Bunt, Gary R. 2000. *Virtually Islamic: Computer-Mediated Communication and Cyber Islamic Environments*. Cardiff, UK: University of Wales Press.

——. 2003. *Islam in the Digital Age: E-Jihad, Online Fatwas and Cyber Islamic Environments*. London: Pluto Press.

——. 2009. *iMuslims: Rewiring the House of Islam*. Chapel Hill, NC: University of North Carolina Press.

Business Pravo. 2009. "O vnesenie izmeneniya v federalnuyu tzelevuyu programmu 'Elektronnaya Rossiya' (2002–2010 gody)." Business Pravo. Accessed March 20. http://www.businesspravo.ru/Docum/DocumShow.asp?DocumID=156876&DocumType=31.

Butler, Rhett. 2009. "Satellites and Google Earth Provide Potent Conservation Tool." Yale Environment 360 Yale School of Forestry and Environmental Studies. March 26. http://e360.yale.edu/content/feature.msp?id=2134.

Castells, Manuel. 1996. *The Rise of the Network Society*. Vol. 1 of Information Age: Economy, Society and Culture. Oxford: Blackwell.

——. 1997. *The Power of Identity*. Vol. 2 of Information Age: Economy, Society and Culture. Oxford: Blackwell.

——. 1998. *End of Millennium*. Vol. 3 of Information Age: Economy, Society and Culture. Malden, Mass.: Blackwell.

——. 2000a. *The Rise of Network Society*. Vol. 1 of the Information Age: Economy, Society, and Culture Oxford: Blackwell Publishers.

——. 2000b. *End of Millennium*. Vol. 3 of The Information Age: Economy, Society and Culture. Malden, MA: Blackwell.

——. 2004. *The Power of Identity*. Vol. 2 of The Information Age: Economy, Society and Culture. Malden, MA: Blackwell.

——.2007. "Communication, Power and Counter-power in the Network Society." *International Journal of Communication 1*: 238–66.

——. 2009a. *Communication Power*. Oxford: Oxford University Press.

——. 2009b. *The Rise of the Network Society*. Vol. 1 of The Information Age: Economy, Society, and Culture. 2nd ed. New York: Wiley-Blackwell.

——. 2012. *Networks of Outrage and Hope: Social Movements in the Internet Age*. Cambridge: Polity Press.

Chawla, Rajeev. 2009. "BHOOMI: Online Delivery of Record of Rights, Tenancy and Crops to Farmers in Karnataka, India." In *e-Governance Case Studies*, edited by Ashok Agarwal, 76–99. Hyderabad, India: Universities Press.

CheckMySchool. 2012. "CMS Presents Social Accountability Lessons and Experiences at the Kaya Natin." *Check My School News*. May 6. http://www.checkmyschool.org/news/2012/05/06/cms-presents-social-accountability-lessons-and-experiences-kaya-natin-youth-leaders.

Chen, Thomas M. 2011. "How Networks Changed the World." *IEEE Network* 25 (6) (November): 2–3. doi:10.1109/MNET.2011.6085635.

Cleek, Ashley. 2011 "Russia: Connecting Neighbors, Saving Lives." Global Voices Online. September 12. http://globalvoicesonline.org/2011/09/12/russia-connecting-neighbors-saving-lives/.

Coase, Ronald. 1937. "The Nature of the Firm." *Economica 4* (16): 386–405.

Cohen, Bernard. 1963. *The Press and Foreign Policy*. New York: Harcourt.

Cooke, Bill, and Uma Kothari, eds. 2001. *Participation: the New Tyranny?* London: Zed Books.

CPJ (Committee to Protect Journalists). 2012. "914 Journalists Killed since 1992." CPJ. Accessed 26 May. http://cpj.org/killed/.

CRIS (Centre for Railway Information Systems). 2012. "PRS-Reservation System." CRIS an Organisation Under Ministry of Railways. Accessed August 21. http://cris.org.in/CRIS/Projects/PRS.

Cuny, Frederick. 1983. *Disasters and Development*. Edited by Susan Abrams. New York: Oxford University Press.

Current Affairs and Analysis. 2011. "E-Panchayats." Current Affairs and Analysis Blogspot. August 12. http://currentaffairsappsc.blogspot.com/2011/08/e-panchayats.html.

CurryStone. 2013. "Curry Stone Design Prize Festival at Harvard." CurryStone Designer Prize. Accessed March 29. http://currystonedesignprize.com/node/70.

Dahl, Robert A. 1961. *Who Governs? Democracy and Power in an American City*. New Haven: Yale University Press.

Davidov, Dmitry. 2010. "Russia: Fires, Rynda and Putin Create Internet Meme." Global Voices Online. August 6. http://globalvoicesonline.org/2010/08/06/russia-fires-rynda-and-putin-create-internet-meme/.

Davis, Mike. 2006. *Planet of Slums*. New York: Verso.

Deibert, Ronald, John G. Palfrey, Rafal Rohozinski, and Jonathan Zittrain, eds. 2010. *Access Controlled: The Shaping of Power, Rights, and Rule in Cyberspace*. Cambridge, MA: MIT Press.

Deibert, Ronald, John Palfrey, Rafal Rohozinski, and Jonathan Zittrain, eds. 2008. *Access Denied: The Practice and Policy of Global Internet Filtering*. Cambridge, MA: MIT Press.

Deibert, Ronald. 2008. "The Geopolitics of Internet Control." In *Routledge Handbook of Internet Politics*, edited by Andrew Chadwick and Philip N. Howard. London: Routledge.

DeitY (Department of Electronics and Information Technology). 2012. "National e-Governance Plan." DeitY Ministry of Communication and Information Technology Government of India. Accessed August 2. http://deity.gov.in/content/national-e-governance-plan.

DeSanctis, Geraldine, and Marshall Scott Poole. 1994. "Capturing the Complexity in Advanced Technology Use: Adaptive Structuration Theory." *Organization Science 5* (2): 121–47.

Dmitriev Mikhail, and Sergei Belanovsky. 2012. "Vlast Prohodit period poluraspada." *Vedomosti*, July 4. http://www.vedomosti.ru/opinion/news/2245274/vlast_prohodit_period_poluraspada.

Dni.ru. 2010. "Zhile'e pogreltzam postroyat v pryamom efire." *Dni*, August 3. http://www.dni.ru/society/2010/8/3/196526.html.

Donner, Jonathan. 2010. Framing M4D: "The Utility of Continuity and the Dual Heritage of 'Mobiles and Development'." *The Electronic Journal on Information Systems in Developing Countries 44* (3): 1–16.

Dufty, Neil. 2012. "Using Social Media to Build Community Disaster Resilience." *The Australian Journal of Emergency Management. Building a Disaster Resilient Australia* 27 (1). http://www.em.gov.au/Publications/Australianjournalofemergencymanagement/Currentissue/Documents/AJEM%2027-1/Volume_27_issue_one.PDF.

Earl, Jennifer, and Katrina Kimport. 2011. *Digitally Enabled Social Change: Activism in the Internet Era*. Cambridge, MA: MIT Press.

Economist. 2012. "India's UID Scheme: Reform by Numbers." *Economist*, January 14. http://www.economist.com/node/21542814.

Edelman, Murray. 1988. *Constructing the Political Spectacle.* Chicago: University of Chicago Press.

Edgerton, David. 2006. *The Shock of the Old: Technology and Global History since 1900.* London: Profile Books.

Ekdale, Brian (2011) "A History of Kibera," blog post published on Brian Ekdale's blog, May 4, 2011. Accessed July 5, 2012. http://www.brianekdale.com/?p=230.

Etling, Bruce, Karina Alexanyan, John Kelly, Rob Faris, John Palfrey, and Urs Gasser. 2010. "Public Discourse in the Russian Blogosphere: Mapping RuNet Politics and Mobilization." Berkman Center for Internet and Society Publications. October 18. http://cyber.law.harvard.edu/publications/2010/Public_Discourse_Russian_Blogosphere.

Etling, Bruce, John Kelly, Robert Faris, and John Palfrey. 2010. "Mapping the Arabic Blogosphere: Politics and Dissent Online." In *New Media and Society* 12(8): 1225–43.

Evgrafova, Elena. 2012. "Krymsk. Konetz piaru." Forbes Column. July 11. http://www.forbes.ru/sobytiya-column/vlast/84137-krymsk-konets-piaru.

Foucault, Michel. (1975) 1995. *Discipline and Punish: The Birth of the Prison.* New York: Vintage Books.

FrontlineSMS. 2010. "Texting for Life in Pakistan: The International Organisation of Migration." FrontlineSMS. October 15. http://www.frontlinesms.com/2010/10/15/texting-for-life-in-pakistan-the-international-organisation-of-migration/.

FrontlineSMS. 2012. "About Us." FrontlineSMS About US. Accessed September 1. http://www.frontlinesms.com/about-us/.

Fung, Archon, Hollie Gilman, and Jennifer Shkabatur. 2013. "Six Models for the Internet and Politics." *International Studies Review* 15 (1): 30–47.

Garrido, Maria. 2003. "Mapping Networks of Support for the Zapatista Movement: Applying Social-Networks Analysis to Study Contemporary Social Movements." In *Cyberactivism: Online Activism in Theory and Practice,* edited by Martha McCaughey and Michael D. Ayers, 165–84. New York: Routledge.

Gartner. 2011. "Gartner Says Worldwide Mobile Connections Will Reach 5.6 Billion in 2011 as Mobile Data Services Revenue Totals $314.7 Billion." Gartner Newsroom. August 4. http://www.gartner.com/newsroom/id/1759714.

Gautam, Vivek. 1996. "N. Seshagiri: Lifetime Contribution to IT." *DataQuest*, December 15. http://news.tn.nic.in/dr_n_seshagiri.htm.

Gaventa, John. 1982. *Power and Powerlessness: Quiescence and Rebellion in an Appalachian Valley.* Urbana, IL: University of Illinois Press.

George, Cherian. 2006. *Contentious Journalism and the Internet: Towards Democratic Discourse in Malaysia and Singapore.* Singapore: Singapore University Press in association with University of Washington Press.

Grameen Foundation. 2012. "Grameen Foundation Expands Technology Program for Poor Farmers in Uganda." Grameen Foundation. Accessed March 15. http://www.grameenfoundation.org/grameen-foundation-expands-technology-program-poor-farmers-uganda.

———. 2013. "Agriculture." Grameen Foundation What We Do. Accessed March 6. http://www.grameenfoundation.org/what-we-do/mobile-phone-solutions/agriculture.

Guida, James, and Martin Crow. 2009. "E-Government and e-Governance." In *ICT4D: Information and Communication Technology for Development,* edited by Tim Unwin, 283–320. Cambridge: Cambridge University Press.

Gupta, M. P., Jaijit Bhattacharya, and Ashok Agarwal. 2009. "Evaluating e-Government." In *e-Governance Case Studies,* edited by Ashok Agarwal, 1–56. Hyderabad, India: Universities Press.

Habermas, Jürgen. 1962. *The Structural Transformation of the Public Sphere: an Inquiry into a Category of Bourgeois Society.* Cambridge: MIT Press.

Hagen, Erica (2010) "Mapping Change: Community Information Empowerment in Kibera." *Innovations. MIT Press Journals* 6 (1): 69–100. Accessed July 5, 2012 http://mapkibera.org/wiki/images/4/42/INNOVATIONS-6-1_Hagen.pdf.

Halperin, Morton H., Joseph Siegle, and Michael M. Weinstein. 2010. *The Democracy Advantage: How Democracies Promote Prosperity and Peace.* Rev. ed. New York: Routledge.

Haque, Shamsul M. 2002. "E-governance in India: Its Impacts on Relations among Citizens, Politicians and Public Servants." *International Review of Administrative Sciences 68* (2): 231–50.

Harsch, Ernest. 2000. "Privatization Shifts Gears in Africa." *Africa Recovery 14* (1): 8–17.

Harwood, Asch. 2012. "Defining Mobile Phone Usage in Africa." The Future Forum. February 16. http://thefutureforum.org/technology/defining-mobile-phone-usage-in-africa/.

Hasan, Sadik. 2003. "Introducing E-government in Bangladesh: Problems and Prospects." *International Social Science Review 78* (3–4): 111–25.

Heeks, Richard B. 2002. "Information Systems and Developing Countries: Failure, Success and Local Improvisations." *The Information Society 18* (2): 101–12.

———. 2008. "ICT4D 2.0: The Next Phase of Applying ICT for International Development." *Computer 41* (6): 26–33.

———. 2010. "Development 2.0: The IT-Enabled Transformation of International Development." *Communications of the ACM 53* (4): 22–24.

Heller, Patrick, K. N. Harilal, and Shubam Chaudhuri. 2007. "Building Local Democracy: Evaluating the Impact of Decentralization in Kerala, India." *World Development 35* (4): 626–48.

Héritier, Adrienne, and Dirk Lehmkuhl. 2008. "The Shadow of Hierarchy and New Modes of Governance." *Journal of Public Policy 28* (1): 1–17.

Hill, David T. 2003. "Communication for a New Democracy: Indonesia's First Online Elections." *The Pacific Review 16* (4): 525–48.

Hill, David T., and Krishna Sen. 2005. *The Internet in Indonesia's New Democracy.* London: Routledge.

The Hindu. 2012. "Figures Bust Myth India's Bureaucracy is 'Bloated.'" *The Hindu*, January 30. http://www.thehindu.com/news/national/article2843014.ece.

Hogan, Sarah. 1999. "To Net or Not to Net: Singapore's Regulation of the Internet." *Federal Communications Law Journal 51* (2): 429–46.

Howard, Philip N., Aiden Duffy, Deen Freelon, Muzammil Hussain, Will Mari, and Marwa Mazaid. 2011. "Opening Closed Regimes: What Was the Role of Social Media During the Arab Spring?" Project on Information Technology and Political Islam Working Paper 2011.1. http://pitpi.org/wp-content/uploads/2013/02/2011_Howard-Duffy-Freelon-Hussain-Mari-Mazaid_pITPI.pdf.

Howard, Philip N., and Muzammil Hussain. 2012. *Democracy's Fourth Wave? Digital Media and the Arab Spring.* New York: Oxford University Press.

Howard, Philip N., and Nimah Mazaheri. 2009. "Telecommunications Reform, Internet Use and Mobile Phone Adoption in the Developing World." *World Development 37* (7): 1159–69. doi:10.1016/j.worlddev.2008.12.005.

Howard, Philip N. 2010a. *The Digital Origins of Dictatorship and Democracy: Information Technology and Political Islam.* New York: Oxford University Press.

———. 2010b. *The Digital Origins of Dictatorship and Democracy: Information Technology and Political Islam.* Oxford: Oxford University Press.

Howe, Jeff. 2009. *Crowdsourcing: Why the Power of the Crowd is Driving the Future of Business.* New York: Random House.

HRW (Human Rights Watch). 2004. *Some Transparency, No Accountability: The Use of Oil Revenue in Angola and its Impact on Human Rights.* Vol. 16, no. 1, Human Rights Watch Report. New York: Human Rights Watch.

Husnoyarov, F. 2010. "About Monitoring and Analysis of Media and Blogosphere in Real Time [RUS]." eGov 2.0 conference. http://www.gov2russia.ru/templates/program/presentations/egov-2-husnoyarov.ppt.

IRC (International Rescue Committee). 2013. "Conflict in Congo Deadliest Since World War II." IRC News. Accessed March 25. http://www.rescue.org/news/conflict-congo-deadliest-world-war-ii-says-irc-3730.

ITC (International Trade Centre). 2008. "Mobile Business Solutions" International Trade Centre Trade at Hand. http://legacy.intracen.org/trade-at-hand/.

ITU (International Telecommunication Union). 2010. *Measuring the Information Society.* Geneva: ITU.

James, Jeffrey, and Mila Versteeg. 2007. "Mobile Phones in Africa: How Much Do We Really Know?" *Social Indicators Research 84* (1): 117–26.

Kalathil, Shanthi, and Taylor C. Boas. 2003a. *Open Networks, Closed Regimes: The Impact of the Internet on Authoritarian Rule.* Washington, DC: Carnegie Endowment for International Peace.

———. 2003b. *Open Networks, Closed Regimes: The Impact of the Internet on Authoritarian Rule.* First Printing. Carnegie Endowment for International Peace.

Karatnycky, Adrian, and Peter Ackerman. 2005. *How Freedom Is Won: From Civic Resistance to Durable Democracy.* New York: Freedom House.

Karatzogianni, Athina. 2006. *The Politics of Cyberconflict.* London: Routledge.

Karpf, David and Steven Livingston. 2013. "Leveraged Affordances and the Specter of Structural Violence." In *State Power 2.0. Authoritarian Entrenchment and Political Engagement Worldwide*, edited by Muzammil M. Hussain and Philip N. Howard, London: Ashgate Publishing.

Karwal, Anita. 2009. "Effective Public Service Delivery and e-Governance: Who Drives Whom." In *e-Governance Case Studies*, edited by Ashok Agarwal, 57–69. Hyderabad, India: Universities Press.

Katz, Elihu, and Paul Lazarsfeld. 1955. *Personal Influence: The Part Played by People in the Flow of Mass Communications.* New Brunswick, NJ: Transaction Publishers.

Katz-Lavigne, Sarah. 2011. "Interactive Radio for Justice: Impact Assessment Report." Soul Beat Africa Community Radio. May 1. http://www.comminit.com/community-radio-africa/content/interactive-radio-justice-impact-assessment-report.

Kaufmann, Daniel, Aart Kraay, and Massimo Mastruzzi. 2006. *Governance Matters V: Governance Indicators for 1996–2005.* World Bank Policy Research Working Paper no. 4012, Washington, DC: World Bank.

Kelly, Sanja, and Sarah Cook. 2011. "Freedom on the Net 2011: A Global Assessment of Internet and Digital Media." Freedom House Report. Accessed October 10. http://www.freedomhouse.org/report/freedom-net/freedom-net-2011.

Kelman, Ilan. 2007. "Disaster Diplomacy: Can tragedy help build bridges among countries?" *UCAR Quarterly*, Fall: 6.

Kenya National Bureau of Statistics. 2010. Accessed October 10, 2012. http://www.knbs.or.ke/.

Khokhlova, Veronica. 2010. "Russia: Towns and Villages on Fire." Global Voices Online. August 10. http://globalvoicesonline.org/2010/08/01/russia-towns-and-villages-on-fire-5/.

———. 2012. Russia: "Netizens Respond Online and Offline to Devastating Krymsk Floods." Global Voices Online. July 9. http://globalvoicesonline.org/2012/07/09/russia-netizens-trying-to-explain-the-devastating-flooding-in-krymsk-helping-the-victims/.

King, Ritchie. 2011. "Building a Subversive Grassroots Network." *IEEE Spectrum.* http://spectrum.ieee.org/telecom/internet/building-a-subversive-grassroots-network.

Kirsh, David. 2001. "The Context of Work." *Human-Computer Interaction 16* (2): 305–22.

Klimek, Peter, Yuri Yegorov, Rudolf Hanel, and Stefan Thurner. 2012. "Statistical Detection of Systematic Election Irregularities." Proceedings of the National Academy of Sciences of the United States of America. June 27. http://www.pnas.org/content/early/2012/09/20/1210722109.abstract

Kostyushev, Vladimir. 2012. "Sociologiya bedstviya." *Novaya Gazeta 93*, August 20. http://www.novayagazeta.ru/politics/54030.html.

Krasner, Steven.1999. *Sovereignty: Organized Hypocrisy.* Princeton: Princeton University Press.

Latour, Bruno. 1987. *Science in Action: How to Follow Scientists and Engineers Through Society.* Cambridge, MA: Harvard University Press.

Lee, Melissa, Gregor Walter-Drop, and John Wiesel. 2013. "Taking the State (Back) Out? Statehood and the Delivery of Collective Goods." Paper Prepared for the 54th Annual Convention of the International Studies Association (ISA), San Francisco, April 3–6.

Lenta. 2012. "Gummanitarnaya mosh." *Lenta*, July 11. http://lenta.ru/articles/2012/07/10/volunteer/.

Levada Center. 2010. "Rossiyane o lesnykh pozharakh letom." Yuri Levada Analytical Center. August 26. http://www.levada.ru/26-08-2010/rossiyane-o-lesnykh-pozharakh-letom-2 010-goda.

Levinger, Beryl, and Evan Bloom. 2011. *Fulfilling the Promise: How National Societies Achieve Sustainable Organizational Development: A Multi-Country Study.* Geneva: International Federation of the Red Cross.

Lim, Merlyna. 2012. "Clicks, Cabs, and Coffee Houses: Social Media and Oppositional Movements in Egypt, 2004–2011." *Journal of Communication 62* (2): 231–48.

Lipman, Masha. 2012. "Floods and Suspicion in Russia." *The New Yorker*, July 12. http://www.newyorker.com/online/blogs/newsdesk/2012/07/floods-and-suspicion-in-russia.html.

Livingston, Steven. 2011. "Africa's Evolving Infosystems: A Pathway to Security and Stability." The Africa Center for Strategic Studies Research Paper No. 2. Washington, DC: National Defense University Press.

Livingston, Steven, and Gregor Walter-Drop. 2012. "Information and Communication Technologies in Areas of Limited Statehood." SFB-Governance Working Paper Series no. 38 September, Berlin, Research Center (SFB) 700, September.

Loshak, Andrej. 2010. "Prozhivem bez gosudarstva." OpenSpace. November 2. http://os.colta.ru/society/projects/201/details/18512/?attempt=1.

Lukes, Steven. 1974. *Power: A Radical View.* Basingstoke: Palgrave Macmillan.

———. 2005. *Power-A Radial View: Studies in Sociology.* London: Macmillan.

Lyon, David, ed. 2006. *Theorizing Surveillance: The Panopticon and Beyond.* Cullompton, UK: Willan Publishing.

Machleder, Josh, and Gregory Asmolov. 2011. "Social Change and the Russian Network Society: Redefining Development Priorities in New Information Environments." Internews Network. http://www.internews.org/research-publications/social-change-and-russian-network-society.

Mahmud, Nadim, Joce Rodriguez, and Josh Nesbit. 2010. "A Text Message-Based Intervention to Bridge the Healthcare Communication Gap in the Rural Developing World." *Technology and Health Care 18* (2): 137–44.

Margolis, Michael, David Resnick, and Chin-chang Tu. 1997. "Campaigning on the Internet." *The Harvard International Journal of Press/Politics 2* (1) (January 1): 59–78. doi:10.1177/10811 80X97002001006.

Marques, Rafael de Morais. 2010. "The Angolan Presidency: The Epicentre of Corruption." Maka Angola. August 8. http://makaangola.org/wp-content/uploads/2012/04/PresidencyCorruption.pdf.

Mazarella, William. 2006. "Internet X-Ray: E-Governance, Transparency, and the Politics of Immediation in India." *Public Culture 18* (3): 473–505.

McCarthy, John D., and Mayer N. Zald. 1977. "Resource Mobilization and Social Movements: A Partial Theory." *The American Journal of Sociology 82* (6) (May): 1212–41.

Medvedev, Dmitry. 2012. "Interview to The Times [Russian transcript]." Government of the Russian Federation. July 30. http://government.ru/docs/19842/.

Meier, Patrick. 2011a. "Do New Information and Communication Technologies Change the Balance of Power Between Repressive States and Civil Society?" PhD diss., The Fletcher School at Tufts University.

———. 2011b. "Information and Communication Technology in Areas of Limited Statehood: A New Form of Governance?" iRevolution. March 4. http://irevolution.net/2011/04/03/icts-limited-statehood/.

Meikle, Graham. 2002. *Future Active: Media Activism and the Internet.* Annandale: Pluto Press.

Mijatovic, Dunja. 2012. "Protection of Journalists from Violence." In *Human rights and Changing Media Landscape*, edited by Council of Europe Commissioner for Human Rights, 21–45. Strasbourg Cedex: Council of Europe Publications.

Milner, Helen. 2006. "The Digital Divide: The Role of Political Institutions in Technology Diffusion." *Comparative Political Studies 39* (2): 176–99.

NBCNews. 2010. "Texas Using Web Cameras on Mexican Border." NBC Us News Life. October 15. http://www.msnbc.msn.com/id/15546009/ns/us_news-life/t/texas-using-web-cameras-mexican-border/.

Nichol, Jim. 2012. "Russia's March 2012 Presidential Election: Outcome and Implications." Congressional Research Service Report prepared for Members and Committees of Congress. https://www.fas.org/sgp/crs/row/R42407.pdf.

Nisbet, Erik C., Elizabeth Stoycheff, and Katy E. Pearce. 2012. "Internet Use and Democratic Demands: A Multinational, Multilevel Model of Internet Use and Citizen Attitudes About Democracy." *Journal of Communication* 62 (2) (March 16): 249–65. doi:10.1111/j.1460-2466.2012.01627.x.

Norris, Pippa. 2001. *Digital Divide: Civic Engagement, Information Poverty, and the Internet Worldwide.* Cambridge: Cambridge University Press.

O'Connell, Kevin M., John C. Baker, Beth E. Lachman, Steven Berner, David Frelinger, and Kim E. Gavin. 2001. *U.S. Commercial Remote Sensing Satellite Industry: An Analysis of the Risks.* Washington, DC: Rand National Security Research Division.

Olson, Mancur. 1965. *The Logic of Collective Action: Public Goods and the Theory of Groups.* Cambridge, MA: Harvard University Press.

O'Reilly, Tim. 2005. "What is Web 2.0: Blogging and the Wisdom of Crowds." O'Reilly Spreading the Knowledge of Innovators. September 30. http://oreilly.com/pub/a/web2/archive/what-is-web-20.html?page=3.

——. 2003. "The Architecture of Participation." O'Reilly OnLamp the Open Source Web Platform. April 6. http://www.oreillynet.com/pub/wlg/3017.

Osnos, Evan. 2013. "Beyond the Google Map of North Korea." *The New Yorker*, January 29. http://www.newyorker.com/online/blogs/evanosnos/2013/01/beyond-the-google-map-of-north-korea.html.

PAC (Partnership Africa Canada). 2007. *Diamond Industry Annual Review: Angola.* Ottawa: PAC.

Pedersen, Karina, and Jo Saglie. 2005. "New Technology in Ageing Parties." *Party Politics* 11 (3) (May 1): 359–77. doi:10.1177/1354068805051782.

Petrazzini, Ben A. 1995. *The Political Economy of Telecommunications Reform in Developing Countries: Privatization and Liberalization in Comparative Perspective.* Westport, CN: Praeger.

Prakash, Amit, and Rahul De. 2007. "Importance of Context in ICT4D Projects: A Study of Computerization of Land Records in India." *Information, Technology and People* 23 (3): 262–81.

Price, Monroe E. 2002. *Media and Sovereignty: The Global Information Revolution and Its Challenges to State Power.* Cambridge, MA: MIT Press.

Protzenko Lyobov. 2013. "Inspektor—kazhdiy moskvich." *Rossiyaskaya Gazeta*, February 11. http://www.rg.ru/2013/02/09/moskva-site.html.

Ragin, Charles C. 2000. *Fuzzy-Set Social Science.* 1st ed. Chicago: University of Chicago Press.

Rao, Madanmohan. 2011. "Mobile Africa Report 2011: Regional Hubs of Excellence and Innovation." Mobile Monday Reports. http://www.mobilemonday.net/reports/MobileAfrica_2011.pdf.

RapidSMS. 2013. "Overview." RapidSMS Overview. Accessed February 20. http://www.rapidsms.org/en/v0.12.0/topics/architecture.html

Rebello, Ragdish. 2010. "India Cell Phone Penetration to Reach 97 Percent in 2014." IHS iSuppli Research. September 22. http://www.isuppli.com/Mobile-and-Wireless-Communications/News/Pages/India-Cell-Phone-Penetration-to-Reach-97-Percent-in-2014.aspx.

ReclaimNaija. 2013. "Who We Are." ReclaimNaija Incident Reporting System. Accessed March 28. http://www.reclaimnaija.net/cms/about-us/who-we-are.

RIA Novosti. 2012a. "Videostena dlya nablyudeniya za hodom golosovaniya otkryta v TZIKe." *RIA Novosti*, March 4. http://ria.ru/vybor2012_hod_vyborov/20120304/584256086.html.

——. 2012b. "Minkomsvyaz soobshila ob okonchanii web-translyatsii s izbirkomov." *RIA Novosti*, March 5. http://ria.ru/vybor2012_webcam/20120305/584867031.html.

———. 2012c. "Putin schitaet effektivnoy rabotu web-kamer na vyborah." *RIA Novosti*, March 5. http://ria.ru/vybor2012_webcam/20120305/585042480.html.

———. 2012d. "Systema Web-Translyatziy vyborov stala 'socialnoy videosetyu'—Schegolev." *RIA Novosti*, March 4. http://ria.ru/vybor2012_webcam/20120304/584389286.html.

Risse, Thomas. 2011. "Governance in Areas of Limited Statehood. Introduction and Overview." In *Governance without a State. Policies and Politics in Areas of Limited Statehood*, edited by Thomas Risse, 1–35. New York: Columbia University Press.

Rosenau, James, ed. 1992. *Governance without Government: Order and Change in World Politics*. Cambridge: Cambridge University Press.

———. 2003. *Distant Proximities: Dynamics beyond Globalization*. Princeton: Princeton University Press.

Ross, Joel, Lilly Irani, M. Six Silberman, Andrew Zaldivar, and Bill Tomlinson. 2010. "Who are the Crowdworkers? Shifting Demographics in Amazon Mechanical Turk." In *CHI '10 Extended Abstracts on Human Factors in Computing Systems*, edited by Keith Edwards and Tom Rodden, 2863–72. New York: Association for Computing Machinery.

Rugh, William. 2004. *Arab Mass Media: Newspapers, Radio, and Television in Arab Politics*. Westport, CT: Praeger Publisher.

Russell, Adrienne. 2001. "The Zapatistas Online." *International Communication Gazette 63* (5) (October 1): 399–413. doi:10.1177/0016549201063005003.

———. 2005. "Myth and the Zapatista Movement: Exploring a Network Identity." *New Media & Society 7* (4): 559–77. doi:10.1177/1461444805054119.

Salz, Peggy A. 2011. "Praekelt's Jonathan McKay: Africa Leads In 'Participation' Mobile Marketin." Mobile Groove. June 30. http://www.mobilegroove.com/praekelts-jonathan-mckay-africa-leads-in-participation-mobile-marketing-9700.

Samigullina, Alia, and Badanin Roman. 2010. "Strana na Ladoni." *Gazeta*, October 28. http://www.gazeta.ru/politics/2010/10/28_a_3432218.shtml.

Satyanarayana, J. 2011. *E-Government: The Science of the Possible*. New Delhi: PHI Learning Private Limited.

Schattschneider, Elmer E. 1960. *The Semi-Sovereign People: A Realist's View of Democracy in America*. Chicago: Holt, Rinehart and Winston.

Schumacher, Ernst Friedrich. 1973. *Small Is Beautiful: a Study of Economics as if People Mattered*. London: Blond and Briggs.

Scialom, Florence. 2011. "Nigerians Mobilize for Free and Fair Elections." *National Geographic*, April 12. http://newswatch.nationalgeographic.com/2011/04/12/nigerians-mobilize-for-free-and-fair-elections/.

Scola, Nancy. 2011. "Digital Mappers Plot the Future of Maptivism." Techpresident Blog Entry. June 3. http://techpresident.com/blog-entry/digital-mappers-plot-future-maptivism-0.

Scott, James C. 1990. *Domination and the Arts of Resistance: Hidden Transcripts*. New Haven: Yale University Press.

———. 1998. *Seeing Like a State: How Certain Schemes to Improve the Human Condition Have Failed*. New Haven: Yale University Press.

———. 2012. *Two Cheers for Anarchism: Six Easy Pieces on Autonomy, Dignity, and Meaningful Work and Play*. Princeton: Princeton University Press. E-book.

Sen, Amartya Kumar. 1999. *Development as Freedom*. Oxford: Oxford University Press.

Senderovich, Sasha. 2012. "Russia's Summer of Idealism." *The New York Times*, July 17. http://www.nytimes.com/2012/07/18/opinion/russias-summer-of-idealism.html.

Shapiro, Samantha M. 2009. "Revolution, Facebook-Style." *New York Times Magazine*, January 22. http://www.nytimes.com/2009/01/25/magazine/25bloggers-t.html.

Shevtzova, Lilia. 2010. "Degradatziya." *Novaya Gazeta*, December 1. http://www.novayagazeta.ru/data/2010/135/15.html.

Shirky, Clay. 2008. *Here Comes Everybody: The Power of Organizing Without Organizations*. New York: Penguin Books.

———. 2011. "The Political Power of Social Media: Technology, the Public Sphere, and Political Change." *Foreign Affairs 90* (1) January/February: 28–41.

Sidorenko, Alexey. 2010. "Russia: Online Activism Success Stories." Global Voices Online. October 25. http://globalvoicesonline.org/2010/10/25/russia-online-activism-success-stories/.

Siegle, Joseph. 2001. "Democratization and Economic Growth: The Contribution of Accountability Institutions." PhD diss., School of Public Policy, University of Maryland.

———. 2007. "Explaining the Variation in Economic Performance of Developing Country Democratizers." Paper prepared for the Community of Democracies' seminar on Democracy and Development: Poverty as a Challenge to Democratic Governance, Bamako, Mali, March 29–30.

———. 2012a. "Building Democratic Accountability in Areas of Limited Statehood." Paper presented at the International Studies Association Annual Meeting, San Diego, CA, April 1–4.

———. 2012b. "Overcoming Dilemmas of Democratization: Protecting Civil Liberties And the Right to Democracy." *Nordic Journal of International Law 81* (3): 471–506.

Singh, J. P. 1999. *Leapfrogging Development? The Political Economy of Telecommunications Restructuring.* Albany, NY: SUNY Press.

———. 2013. "Information Technologies, Meta-power and Preferences, and Transformations in Global Politics." *International Studies Review 15* (1): 5–29.

Singh, L. C. 2009. "Message." In *E-Governance Case Studies*, edited by Ashok Agarwal. Hyderabad, India: Universities Press.

Sinha, Varesh. 2008. "E-Gram." In *Infrastructure and Governance*, edited by Sameer Kochhar, Deepak B. Phatak, H. Krishnamurthy, and Gursharan Dhanjal, 101–3. New Delhi: Academic Foundation.

Sjoberg, Fredrik M. 2012. "Autocratic Adaptation: The Strategic Use of Transparency and the Persistence of Election Fraud." Social Science Research Network Papers. June 29. http://ssrn.com/abstract=2133565.

Sobolev, Anton, Yegor Lazarev, Irina Soboleva, and Boris Sokolov. 2012. "Trial by Fire: A Natural Disaster's Impact on Support for the Authorities in Rural Russia." Higher School of Economics Research Paper no. BRP 04/PS/2012. http://papers.ssrn.com/sol3/papers.cfm?abstract_id=2011975.

Solan. 2012. "Hardware Infrastructure." Solan. Accessed August 15. http://hpsolan.gov.in/it.html.

Sreberny, Annabelle, and Gholam Khiabany. 2010. *Blogistan: The Internet and Politics in Iran.* London: I. B. Tauris.

Sreekumar. T. T. 2007. "Decrypting eGovernance: Narratives, Powerplays, and Participation in the Gyandoot Intranet." *The Electronic Journal on Information Systems in Developing Countries 32* (4): 1–24. http://www.ejisdc.org/ojs2/index.php/ejisdc/issue/view/92.

SSP (Satellite Sentinel Project). 2012. "George Clooney." Satellite Sentinel Project Our Story. Accessed August 30. http://www.satsentinel.org/our-story/george-clooney.

Stadler, Felix. 2006. *Manuel Castells: The Theory of the Network Society.* Cambridge UK: Polity Press.

Sterngold, James. 1995. "Gang in Kobe Organized Aid for People in Quake." *The New York Times*, January 22. http://www.nytimes.com/1995/01/22/world/quake-in-japan-gangsters-gang-in-kobe-organizes-aid-for-people-in-quake.html.

Stohl, Cynthia, and Michael Stohl. 2007. "Networks of Terror: Theoretical Assumptions and Pragmatic Consequences." *Communication Theory 17* (2) (May 1): 93–124. doi:10.1111/j.1468-2885.2007.00289.x.

Stop Stock-Outs. 2013. "Partners." Stop Stock-Outs! Accessed March 28. http://stopstockouts.org/partners/.

Surowiecki, James. 2004. *The Wisdom of Crowds: Why the Many Are Smarter than the Few and How Collective Wisdom Shapes Business, Economies, Societies and Nations.* London: Little, Brown.

———. 2005. *The Wisdom of the Crowds.* New York: Anchor.

Tarrow, Sidney. 2010. *The New Transnational Activism.* Cambridge: Cambridge University Press.

Tibbitt, John. 2011. "Social Media, Social Capital and Learning Communities." Pascal International Observatory Blog Entry. http://pascalobservatory.org/pascalnow/blogentry/nordic-horizons.

Tech Awards. 2013. "The Tech Awards Laureate 2009." The Tech Awards Laureate Archive. Accessed March 28. http://thetechawards.thetech.org/laureate/archive/2009.

Teplitsa. 2012. "Russia: Online Platforms Coordinating Aid for Flood Victims." Translated by Sian Sinnott. Global Voices Online. July 11. http://globalvoicesonline.org/2012/07/11/russia-overview-of-online-platforms-coordinating-aid-for-flood-victims/.

Thompson, Mark. 2008. "ICT and Development Studies: Towards Development 2.0." *Journal of International Development 20*: 821–35.

Tides. 2013. "Previous Winners." Tides What's Possible Impact. Accessed March 28. http://www.tides.org/impact/awards-prizes/pizzigati-prize/winners/.

Tilly, Charles. 1978. *From Mobilization to Revolution*. Reading, MA: Addison-Wesley.

Tolbert, Caroline, and Karen Mossberger. 2006. "The Effects of E-Government on Trust and Confidence in Government." *Public Administration Review 66* (3): 354–69.

Tripathi, Vishwas. 2007. *e-Governance in India*. New Delhi: Anmol Publications.

Tufekci, Zeynep, and Christopher Wilson. 2012. "Social Media and the Decision to Participate in Political Protest: Observations From Tahrir Square." *Journal of Communication 62* (2) (March 6): 363–379. doi:10.1111/j.1460-2466.2012.01629.x.

Ursu, Yuri. 2013. "Vlasti Moskvi oobirayot snyegu fotoshopom." YuriUrsu Live Journal. February 2. http://yuriursu.livejournal.com/7301.html.

Valdéz, Juan José. 2013. "Sizing Up Google's New North Korea Map." *National Geographic Daily News*, January 31. http://news.nationalgeographic.com/news/2013/13/130131-world-google-maps-north-korea-cartography/#.

Vedomosti. 2012. "Ot redaktzii: A teper dobrovoltzi." *Vedomosti*, July 16. http://www.vedomosti.ru/opinion/news/2284886/a_teper_dobrovolcy.

Wagner, Caroline. 2008. *The New Invisible College: Science for Development*. Washington, DC: Brookings Institution Press.

Warner, J. R. 2013. "Africa's Great Shell Game." Africa Center for Strategic Studies Special Report.

Warschauer, Mark, Ghada R. El Said, and Ayman Zohry. 2002. "Language Choice Online: Globalization and Identity in Egypt." *Journal of Computer-Mediated Communication 7* (4). http://jcmc.indiana.edu/vol7/issue4/warschauer.html.

Weimann, Gabriel. 2006. *Terror On the Internet: The New Arena, The New Challenges*. Washington, DC: United States Institute of Peace.

Welch, Eric W., Charles C. Hinnant, and M. Jae Moon. 2005. "Linking Citizen Satisfaction with E-Government with Trust in Government." *Journal of Public Administration Research and Theory 15* (3): 371–91.

Wheeler, Deborah L. 2006. *The Internet and the Middle East: Global Expectations and Local Imaginations in Kuwait*. Albany, NY: SUNY Press.

White, Gregory, and Rob Barry. 2011. "Russia's Dubious Vote." *Wall Street Journal*, December 28.

Wikipedia. 2013. "1970 Bhola Cyclone." Wikipedia Bhola Cyclone. Accessed March 20. https://en.wikipedia.org/wiki/1970_Bhola_cyclone.

Wily, Liz Alden. 2011. "Rights to Resources in Crisis: Reviewing the Fate of Customary Tenure in Africa." Commercial Pressure on Land International Land Coalition Research Papers. December 2011. http://www.commercialpressuresonland.org/research-papers/rights-resources-crisis-reviewing-fate-customary-tenure-africa.

Windt, Peter van der, and Macartan Humphreys. 2012. "Crowdseeding Conflict Data: An Application of Decentralized Data Collection Methods to Estimate the Conflict Effects of Aid in Congo." Columbia Center for the Study of Development Strategies Working Paper. http://cu-csds.org/wp-content/uploads/2009/10/pwmh_crowdseedingconflictdata.pdf.

Wolcott, Peter, and Seymour Goodman. 2000. *The Internet in Turkey and Pakistan: A Comparative Analysis*. Palo Alto, CA: Center for International Security and Cooperation, Stanford University.

The World Bank. 2011. *World Development Report 2011: Conflict, Security, and Development*. Washington, DC: The World Bank.

The World Bank. 2012. *World Development Indicators 2012*. Washington, DC: The World Bank.

Wright, Robin. 2011. "The Pink Hijab." *The Wilson Quarterly*. http://www.wilsonquarterly.com/article.cfm?aid=1969.

York, Jillian. 2011. "How Are Protestors in Egypt Using Social Media?" Jilliancyork. January 27. http://jilliancyork.com/2011/01/27/how-are-protestors-in-egypt-using-social-media/.

Zald, Mayer N., and John D. McCarthy. 1997. *Social Movements in an Organizational Society: Collected Essays*. New Brunswick: Transaction Publisher.

Zasloff, Jonathan. 2011. "India's Land Title Crisis: The Unanswered Questions." *Jindal Global Law Review* 3, UCLA School of Law Research Paper no. 11-29. September 7. http://ssrn.com/abstract=1923903.

Index